Grade Aid with Practice Tests

for

Kosslyn and Rosenberg

Fundamentals of Psychology
The Brain, The Person, The World

Second Edition

prepared by

Marcia J. McKinley
Mount St. Mary's College

PEARSON

Boston   New York   San Francisco
Mexico City   Montreal   Toronto   London   Madrid   Munich   Paris
Hong Kong   Singapore   Tokyo   Cape Town   Sydney

ISBN 0-205-42098-2

Printed in the United States of America

10 9 8 7 6 5 4 3 2 1   09 08 07 06 05 04

Acknowledgments

This Grade Aid was not a lone venture. Rather, I am grateful to many people for its completion. Specifically, I thank:

♦   The authors of this text, Stephen M. Kosslyn and Robin S. Rosenberg, for writing a textbook that my students and I find educational and entertaining. I am honored to have had a small part in creating such a wonderful resource.

♦   The authors of previous editions of the Grade Aid (Marjorie S. Hardy and Wendy Domjan) for providing a firm foundation on which I could build.

♦   My editor extraordinaire, Erin K. Liedel, who provided patience and support beyond the call of duty and made the publication process much more enjoyable than it otherwise would have been.

♦   My research assistants and students, who pilot-tested these materials.

♦   My son, Nathan D. McKinley-Pace, for enduring my long hours during the writing process, although I suspect that I missed him far more than he missed me.

♦   The support team which ensured Nathan's care while I wrote, especially Jeff Pace and Judy McKinley.

Preface

This Grade Aid is designed to help you find your way in the new world you just entered: psychology. Through studying psychology, you will learn about yourself and others. How do people think? How can you learn to remember people's names better? Why do some people develop psychological disorders and others don't? The Grade Aid will help you to better understand, conceptualize, and integrate the material in the text.

In the Grade Aid, you will find:

♦ **Before You Read sections**, which contain a short summary of each chapter to help you understand its overall organization.

♦ **Chapter Objectives**, or what you should learn from the chapter.

♦ **As You Read sections**, including
  - A list of key terms, which you are encouraged to put on note cards for studying.
  - A collection of exercises designed to engage you in the active learning process, including tables to be completed, essay questions, and web activities. These activities will allow you to understand the material in different ways. No answer keys have been provided for these exercises, and that's no mistake! The idea is for you to complete these exercises as you are reading the text – the answers are clear-cut, and can either be found directly in the textbook or require you to apply course content to your own life. Make sure you take a break wherever you see "TRY A PRACTICE TEST NOW!" There is one practice test for each of the sections of the text chapter.

♦ **After You Read sections**, including
  - "Thinking Back" questions, which ask you to integrate material from the chapter with material from previous chapters.
  - A collection of practice tests designed to be taken after reading and reviewing particular sections of the chapter. The final practice test for each chapter is comprehensive and will allow you to see how well you remember the material from the entire chapter.

♦ **When You Are Finished sections** containing crossword puzzles that test your knowledge of the chapter material in a fun way!

Enjoy this new world of psychology!
Marcia McKinley
Mount St. Mary's College, Emmitsburg, MD

Table of Contents

Acknowledgements..1
Preface..2
Chapter 1: Psychology
     Before You Read...6
     Chapter Objectives...6
     As You Read...Term Identification..7
     As You Read...Questions and Exercises...8
     After You Read...Practice Tests...37
     When You Are Finished...Puzzle It Out...63
Chapter 2: The Biology of Mind and Behavior
     Before You Read..64
     Chapter Objectives...64
     As You Read...Term Identification...65
     As You Read...Questions and Exercises...66
     After You Read...Thinking Back...84
     After You Read...Practice Tests...86
     When You Are Finished...Puzzle It Out...103
Chapter 3: Sensation and Perception
     Before You Read...104
     Chapter Objectives...104
     As You Read...Term Identification..105
     As You Read...Questions and Exercises...106
     After You Read...Thinking Back...125
     After You Read...Practice Tests...127
     When You Are Finished...Puzzle It Out...142
Chapter 4: Learning
     Before You Read...143
     Chapter Objectives...143
     As You Read...Term Identification..144
     As You Read...Questions and Exercises...145
     After You Read...Thinking Back...169
     After You Read...Practice Tests...170
     When You Are Finished...Puzzle It Out...186
Chapter 5: Memory
     Before You Read...187
     Chapter Objectives...187
     As You Read...Term Identification..188
     As You Read...Questions and Exercises...189
     After You Read...Thinking Back...200
     After You Read...Practice Tests...201
     When You Are Finished...Puzzle It Out...217

Chapter 6: Language, Thinking, and Intelligence
    Before You Read..218
    Chapter Objectives...218
    As You Read...Term Identification..219
    As You Read...Questions and Exercises..220
    After You Read...Thinking Back...242
      After You Read...Practice Tests..244
    When You Are Finished...Puzzle It Out...266

Chapter 7: Emotion and Motivation
    Before You Read..267
    Chapter Objectives...267
    As You Read...Term Identification..268
    As You Read...Questions and Exercises..268
    After You Read...Thinking Back...285
    After You Read...Practice Tests...286
    When You Are Finished...Puzzle It Out...303

Chapter 8: Personality
    Before You Read..304
    Chapter Objectives...304
    As You Read...Term Identification..305
    As You Read...Questions and Exercises..305
    After You Read...Thinking Back...320
    After You Read...Practice Tests...321
    When You Are Finished...Puzzle It Out...339

Chapter 9: Psychology Over the Lifespan
    Before You Read..340
    Chapter Objectives...340
    As You Read...Term Identification..341
    As You Read...Questions and Exercises..341
    After You Read...Thinking Back...361
    After You Read...Practice Tests...362
    When You Are Finished...Puzzle It Out...378

Chapter 10: Stress, Health, and Coping
    Before You Read..379
    Chapter Objectives...379
    As You Read...Term Identification..380
    As You Read...Questions and Exercises..381
    After You Read...Thinking Back...403
    After You Read...Practice Tests...404
    When You Are Finished...Puzzle It Out...423

Chapter 11: Psychological Disorders

Before You Read..424
Chapter Objectives..424
As You Read...Term Identification..425
As You Read...Questions and Exercises...425
After You Read...Thinking Back..442
After You Read...Practice Tests...443
When You Are Finished...Puzzle It Out...461

Chapter 12: Treatment

Before You Read..462
Chapter Objectives..462
As You Read...Term Identification..463
As You Read...Questions and Exercises...463
After You Read...Thinking Back..479
After You Read...Practice Tests...480
When You Are Finished...Puzzle It Out...495

Chapter 13: Social Psychology

Before You Read..496
Chapter Objectives..496
As You Read...Term Identification..497
As You Read...Questions and Exercises...498
After You Read...Thinking Back..512
After You Read...Practice Tests...513
When You Are Finished...Puzzle It Out...524

Answer Keys

Chapter 1: Psychology...525
Chapter 2: The Biology of Mind and Behavior...530
Chapter 3: Sensation and Perception...534
Chapter 4: Learning...537
Chapter 5: Memory..540
Chapter 6: Language, Thinking, and Intelligence...543
Chapter 7: Emotion and Motivation..547
Chapter 8: Personality...550
Chapter 9: Psychology Over the Life Span...553
Chapter 10: Stress, Health, and Coping..556
Chapter 11: Psychological Disorders..560
Chapter 12: Treatment...564
Chapter 13: Social Psychology...567

Chapter 1
Psychology: Yesterday and Today

Before You Read . . .

In this chapter, you will learn what psychology is and what psychologists do. The chapter also presents a theme that runs throughout the book: levels of analysis. Basically, this means that we can understand most psychological concepts at the levels of the brain, person, and group.

In addition, you will learn how psychology has evolved and how it is practiced now. Be sure you learn the various schools of thought in psychology and the famous people in these schools, because you will be seeing these names again and again throughout the book!

The chapter also discusses how psychologists gain knowledge. Different academic disciplines gain knowledge in different ways. For example, English professors and students gain knowledge by reading and considering what others have written. Philosophers gain knowledge by thinking logically about different issues. Psychologists are like other scientists (including sociologists, chemists, biologists, and many others) in that they gain knowledge through the scientific method. In this chapter, you will learn about the six steps of the scientific method. You will also learn how the scientific method is applied to psychology and what the advantages of using the scientific method are.

Chapter Objectives

After reading this chapter, you should be able to:

♦ Define *psychology*.

♦ Describe the concept of "levels of analysis," and explain how it can be used to better understand psychology.

♦ Describe how psychology has evolved over time.

♦ Define the different fields of psychology.

♦ Discuss what the different types of psychologists do.

♦ Describe what the advantages of using the scientific method to gain knowledge are.

♦ Discuss each of the six steps of the scientific method, including how to perform the step and its significance.

- Describe the differences between experimental, correlational, and descriptive research, and explain when you would want to use each kind.

- Be able to evaluate psychological research.

- Discuss proper ethics in research, with humans and animals, and in clinical practice.

As You Read . . . Term Identification

Make flashcards using the following terms as you go. Use the definitions in the margins of this chapter for help. If you write the definitions in your own words, though, you will remember them better!

Academic psychologist
Applied psychologist
Behavior
Behaviorism
Bias
Case study
Clinical psychologist
Cognitive neuroscience
Cognitive psychology
Confound
Control condition
Control group
Correlation coefficient
Counseling psychologist
Data
Debriefing
Dependent variable
Double-blind design
Effect
Evolutionary psychology
Experimenter expectancy effects
Functionalism
Gestalt psychology
Humanistic psychology
Hypothesis
Independent variable
Informed consent
Introspection

Level of the brain
Level of the group
Level of the person
Mental processes
Meta-analysis
Operational definition
Population
Prediction
Pseudopsychology
Psychiatric nurse
Psychiatrist
Psychodynamic theory
Psychology
Psychotherapy
Random assignment
Reliability
Replication
Response bias
Sample
Sampling bias
Scientific method
Social worker
Structuralism
Survey
Theory
Unconscious
Validity
Variable

As You Read . . . Questions and Exercises

The Science of Psychology: Getting to Know You

What Is psychology?

Kosslyn and Rosenberg define **psychology** as the _____ of _____ and _____. Look at each part of this definition:

Part #1: Science

Which of your classes this semester are **sciences**? _____

_____

Which of your classes this semester are nonsciences? _____

_____

How do your science and nonscience classes differ? _____

_____

Because it is a **science**, psychology requires ideas to be tested by collecting facts. Some questions can be answered through science; others can't be. In the table below, decide whether or not you could answer each question with scientific methods. Explain why or why not.

Question	Answer with Science?		Why or Why Not?
Is there a God?	YES	NO	
Should marijuana be legalized?	YES	NO	
What makes people angry?	YES	NO	
How does stress affect health?	YES	NO	
What happens after we die?	YES	NO	

Part #2: Mental Processes

Name some **mental processes** that you are using as you answer these questions. _____

_____

Part #3: Behaviors

Name some **behaviors** that you are performing as you answer these questions. _____

_____

Which usually come first: **mental processes** or **behaviors**? Why? _____

_____

Kosslyn and Rosenberg describe the four **goals** of psychologists as:

Goal #1: To DESCRIBE mental processes and behavior.
How could you use research that *describes* mental processes and/or behavior in your own life?

_____

_____

Goal #2: To EXPLAIN mental processes and behavior.
How could you use research that *explains* mental processes and/or behavior in your own life?

_____

_____

Goal #3: To PREDICT mental processes and behavior.
How could you use research that *predicts* mental processes and/or behavior in your own life?

_____

_____

Goal #4: To CONTROL mental processes and behavior.
How could you use research about *how to control* mental processes and/or behavior in your own life?

_____

_____

Hopefully, you are taking this class because you really want to, not *just* because it fits into your schedule, you like the professor (although, hopefully you do!), or your friends are taking it. But, in any case, take a moment to see how much you can really learn from the field of psychology.

Look at both the *skills* you can learn in a psychology course, as well as the *material*. On the next page, list some of the things you hope to learn. To get some ideas, you may want to flip through your textbook (to look at all the different topics that you will be covering) or

GO SURFING ...

... at one of the many school websites that list the benefits of studying psychology.

Skills I will learn in psychology:

1. _____

2. _____

3. _____

4. _____

5. _____

Material I hope to learn in psychology:

1. _____

2. _____

3. _____

4. _____

5. _____

Levels of Analysis

We can study phenomena at various **levels of analysis**: the **brain**, the **person**, and the **group**. Identify a question that can be asked at each level in the following situations:

Phenomenon	Brain	Person	Group
Fighting with your roommate			
Falling in love			
Drinking too much			
Acing a test			
Wrecking your car			

Looking at Levels

Throughout this Grade Aid, you will be asked to consider the events that occur at the levels of the brain, the person, and the group to influence various psychological phenomena. You should list the factors in the charts provided and indicate how they may interact by drawing arrows between the columns. Below is an example of a completed chart, using the information contained in "Drought Among the Maasai" on pages 8-9. Use this as a model for the other Looking at Levels charts in this Grade Aid.

The Brain	The Person	The Group
Child's temperament	Mom's belief that she should care for only when fussing Mom's feeding behavior Mom's stress level	Nomads = dependent on naturally occurring resources (e.g., water) Extended families

On September 11, 2001, Al Queda terrorists flew planes into the World Trade Center and the Pentagon. Name some of the factors, at each of the **three levels**, that may have influenced the terrorists' decision to do this. Draw arrows indicating how events at the different levels may interact.

The Brain	The Person	The Group

Name some of the factors, at each of the **three levels**, that influenced your decision to attend college. Draw arrows indicating how events at the different levels may have interacted to influence your decision.

The Brain	The Person	The Group

TRY PRACTICE TEST #1 NOW!
GOOD LUCK!

Psychology Then and Now

The Evolution of a Science

Fill in the following chart. Who are the key people and what are the key ideas of each school of psychology? Which **level(s) of analysis** does each theory concentrate on most?

School of Thought	Key People	Key Ideas	Levels of Analysis (Brain, Person, Group)
Structuralism			
Functionalism			
Gestalt psychology			
Psychodynamic theory			
Behaviorism			
Humanistic psychology			
Cognitive psychology			
Cognitive neuroscience			
Evolutionary psychology			

In October, 2002, two snipers terrorized the Washington, D.C. area, killing 10 people and injuring 3 more. In the days after the snipers were caught, numerous TV shows hosted specials about them. Suppose that the following psychologists were asked to participate in one of these special broadcasts. How would each of them explain the snipers' actions?

Psychologist	Explanations
Psychodynamic theorist	
Behaviorist	
Humanistic psychologist	
Cognitive psychologist	
Cognitive neuroscientist	
Evolutionary psychologist	

GO SURFING ...

... to put faces with the names and to find out more about your favorite psychologists.

Some places to start are:

♦ http://elvers.stjoe.udayton.edu/history/welcome.htm
This site allows you to search by birthday (do you have the same birthday as any famous psychologist?), name, and category. Although some of the trivia questions on the site aren't covered in this chapter of your textbook, others are. Test yourself!

♦ http://www.ship.edu/~cgboeree/historyofpsych.html
This site is an e-book, written by Dr. C. George Boeree at Shippensburg University. It tells more about the very early days of psychology. Scroll down for more recent happenings.

♦ http://www.cwu.edu/~warren/today.html
This site includes over 3100 events. Chances are good that something important happened today in the history of psychology. Find out!

♦ http://psych.athabascau.ca/html/aupr/history.shtml
This site, sponsored by Athabascu University, has tons of links for various schools of psychology and famous psychologists.

WHAT KIND OF PSYCHOLOGIST ARE YOU?

Choose the option that you feel is the best by circling one letter for each question.

1.   Human beings are driven by:
   a.   irrational passions.
   b.   external events.
   c.   brain-based mental processes.
   d.   their desire to be the best they can be.
   e.   instincts.

2.   We can best learn about humankind by studying:
   a.   people's dreams.
   b.   people's behaviors.
   c.   people's brains.
   d.   model humans.
   e.   animals.

3.   How do parents most influence their children?
   a.   By causing pain, which becomes hidden and will be uncovered later
   b.   By rewarding and punishing their children
   c.   By providing a model for future relationships
   d.   By providing a good environment to help them develop to their fullest potential
   e.   By passing on their genetics

4.   Humans:
   a.   are basically aggressive.
   b.   can be bad or good, depending on their environments.
   c.   are basically rational, reasoning beings.
   d.   are basically good, although some may be corrupted by bad experiences in life.
   e.   are basically selfish and driven to reproduce.

5.   Mental illness:
   a.   results from repressed pain.
   b.   results from negative experiences.
   c.   results from negative thoughts.
   d.   results from a person not being valued unconditionally.
   e.   is inborn, a result of bad genetics.

6.   What kind of evidence is needed to prove a psychological fact?
   a.   Anecdotal evidence from cases of people seeing psychologists
   b.   Behaviors, observed in lab settings
   c.   Evidence of brain functioning (e.g., from a brain scan)
   d.   Anecdotal evidence from cases of exceptional human beings
   e.   Evidence that a certain phenomenon exists in multiple cultures

Compare your answers on the previous page with those at the end of this Grade Aid to find out what kind of psychologist you are. (Although you could probably take a good guess as to which theory is represented by each letter!) Do you agree with your results?

When did the interest in **mental processes** and **behavior** start? Who started it? _____
_____
_____

Was this the same time that the field of **psychology** started? Why or why not? _____
_____
_____

When did **psychology** begin and who started it? _____
_____
_____

How did the schools of **structuralism** and **functionalism** differ? _____
_____
_____

Has **functionalism** made any contributions to psychology that endure until today? If so, what are they? _____
_____
_____

How are **structuralism** and **Gestalt psychology** similar and different? _____
_____
_____

How is **Gestalt psychology** related to current psychological research? _____
_____
_____

What are the drawbacks to **psychodynamic theory** (as proposed by **Freud**)?_____
_____
_____

List some of the positive contributions of **psychodynamic theory**:

1. _____

2. _____

3. _____

4. _____

5. _____

Behaviorists pointed out that the consequences of person's behavior influence whether the behavior is repeated. If the consequences are good, then a person will be more likely to repeat a behavior. If the consequences are bad, then a person will be less likely to repeat it.

Describe a situation in which you were more or less likely to do something because you had previously experienced the consequences of that behavior. _____
_____
_____

How do you think **humanistic psychology** has influenced many of the therapies now used? (You can check your answers in Chapter 12.) _____
_____
_____

The **cognitive revolution** led to a tremendous change in American psychology. Before the **cognitive revolution**, the predominant theory had been **behaviorism**. Afterwards, it became **cognitive psychology**. How are **cognitive psychology** and **behaviorism** different?
_____
_____

What effects have new technologies, such as **brain-scanning** equipment, had on the field?
_____
_____

How is **evolutionary psychology** similar to **functionalism**? _____
_____
_____

How does **evolutionary psychology** differ from **functionalism**? _____
_____
_____

What evidence do **evolutionary psychologists** look for? Why? _____
_____
_____

What is the fundamental limitation of **evolutionary psychology**? _____

The Psychological Way: What Today's Psychologists Do

Do you know any **psychologists**? If so, what do they do? _____
_____

Kosslyn and Rosenberg identify three main types of psychologists: **clinical/counseling psychologists**, **academic psychologists**, and **applied psychologists**. For each of these types of psychologists, give a job description and the degrees they have.

Type of Psychologists	Job Description	Degree
Clinical/counseling psychologists		
Academic psychologists		
Applied psychologists		

The following are jobs related to **psychology**. Describe each of these jobs and the degrees these professionals must have.

Job	Job Description	Degree(s)
Psychiatrist		
Social worker		
Psychiatric nurse		

Students often say that they want to be **clinical** or **counseling psychologists** so they can "help people." What skills do you think a **clinical** or **counseling psychologist** must have, in addition to this motivation? _____

_____

What difficulties do you think **clinical** or **counseling psychologists** might face? _____

_____

_____

How might recent health care developments (such as the increase in managed care) affect **clinical** and **counseling psychologists**?_____

_____

_____

GO SURFING ...

... to find out all the different specialties within psychology. (Your book lists only a few.) A look at the divisions of the American Psychology Association (APA) will give you an idea of all the different subfields. Here is the official APA website: http://www.apa.org/. Follow the Quick Link to Divisions.

List some subfields not mentioned in your textbook here:

_____

_____

_____

Do any of them sound especially interesting to you? Which ones?

_____

_____

Visit your school's website and discover what types of **psychologists** are on the faculty. Below, list some of the professors and their specialties. Keep this for later reference, especially if you are considering a major in psychology!

Professor	Specialty

You may wonder what your professors do all day—after all, they only teach a few classes a week and hold a few office hours, right? You might be surprised! Here are just a few of the things that professors do. Take a guess about how many hours a week they spend on each task. Then, ask your psychology professor for his or her estimate.

Task	Your Estimate	Your Professor's Estimate
Teaching (including preparing for class, in-class time, grading, consulting with students, and holding office hours)		
Research/scholarly activity (including planning and conducting studies, writing studies for publication, and other writing projects—like your textbook!)		
Service (work on university and psychology-related committees, presentations in various venues, and service in community organizations)		
Advising students (formally and informally)		

How do the jobs of **academic** and **applied psychologists** differ? How are they similar?

_____

_____

Where might each of these types of **applied psychologists** look for jobs? What kind of companies might they work for? What would they be doing?

Type of Applied Psychologist	Job Possibilities	Companies	Job Description
Cognitive psychologist			
Developmental psychologist			
Human factors psychologist			
Industrial/ organizational psychologist			
Personality psychologist			
Physiological psychologist			
School (educational) psychologist			
Social psychologist			
Sport psychologist			

GO SURFING ...

... to find out what the job outlooks are for various types of psychologists with different degrees. Use this to fill out the chart below. Some places to start are:

♦ http://www.bls.gov/oco/home.htm
Allows you to search by occupation. Be sure to notice all the pecialties of psychology.
♦ http://online.onetcenter.org/
Provides information about the working environments and tasks of various jobs, including psychologists.
♦ www.apa.org
Use the APA search engine to find out what recent psychology majors and psychology Ph.D.'s are doing with their degrees.

Type of Psychologists	Working Environment (e.g., setting, salary)
Clinical/counseling psychologists	
Academic psychologists	
Applied psychologists	

If you were going to be a **psychologist**, what type would you want to be? Why? _____
_____

Would you have a preferred subfield (developmental, social, personality, etc.)? _____
_____

What is the job outlook like for this type of psychologist? _____
_____

What type of degree would you need to be this type of psychologist? _____

What could you do with a bachelor's degree in psychology? _____
_____
_____

Looking at Levels

Here are some commonly heard statements. Take a guess as to whether these statements are true or false. Then, check your book (page references provided) to see if you were right.

Statement	Your Guess	Fact
If someone talks about suicide, she just wants attention. (p. 424)	TRUE FALSE	TRUE FALSE
People become homosexual because they were mistreated as children. (p. 282)	TRUE FALSE	TRUE FALSE
Opposites attract. (p. 504)	TRUE FALSE	TRUE FALSE

For one of the examples listed in the above chart, name some of the factors, at each of the **three levels**, that may be influential. Draw arrows indicating how events at the different levels may interact.

The Brain	The Person	The Group

TRY PRACTICE TEST #2 NOW!
GOOD LUCK!

The Research Process:
How We Find Things Out

The Scientific Method

Step 1 of the scientific method is to specify a problem. What does "problem" mean, in this context?

_____

_____

_____

Where do you think scientists get their "problems"? _____

_____

_____

Name some problems or questions you have that would be suitable for psychological research:

- **Problem #1:** _____

  _____

- **Problem #2:** _____

  _____

- **Problem #3:** _____

  _____

- **Problem #4:** _____

  _____

Step 2 of the scientific method is to observe events. What does this mean to scientists? _____

_____

_____

_____

_____

What does it mean for a scientist to **replicate** a study? _____

_____

_____

_____

Why do psychologists prefer to use numerical measurements? _____

_____

_____

_____

What are the two kinds of events in which psychologists are interested?

- _____

- _____

Look at the problems or questions you listed above, under Step 1. What kind of events could you observe for each of these?

- **Problem #1:** _____

  _____

- **Problem #2:** _____

  _____

- **Problem #3:** _____

  _____

♦   **Problem #4:** _____

_____

Step 3 of the scientific method is to form a **hypothesis**. What is a **hypothesis**? _____

_____

_____

_____

What is the opposite of a **variable**? _____

Can you think of an example? _____

Look at the problems or questions you listed above, under Step 1. Do you have a hypothesis about each of these?

♦   **Problem #1:** _____

_____

♦   **Problem #2:** _____

_____

♦   **Problem #3:** _____

_____

♦   **Problem #4:** _____

_____

Step 4 of the scientific method is to test the **hypothesis**. How does a researcher do this?

_____

_____

_____

_____

What is an **operational definition**? _____

_____

_____

_____

_____

How is an **operational definition** different from any other type of definition? _____

_____

_____

_____

Offer an **operational definition** for one of the **variables** in the problems you listed in Step 1:

♦   **Problem #1:** _____

_____

♦   **Problem #2:** _____

_____

♦   **Problem #3:** _____

_____

♦   **Problem #4:** _____

_____

Step 5 of the scientific method is to formulate a **theory**. Compare and contrast hypotheses and theories in the table below.

	Hypotheses	Theories
Similarities		
Differences		

Step 6 of the scientific method is to test a **theory**. How can a **theory** be supported? _____

_____

_____

_____

What happens when a **theory** is supported? _____

_____

What leads to a **theory** being rejected? _____

_____

_____

_____

What does it mean for a theory to be **falsifiable**? _____

_____

_____

_____

The Psychologist's Toolbox: Techniques of Scientific Research

Name one advantage and one disadvantage for each of the following types of **research**.

Technique	Advantage	Disadvantage
Experimentation		
Quasi-experimentation		
Correlational research		
Naturalistic observation		
Case studies		
Surveys		

For each of the following hypotheses, indicate the **independent variable (IV)** and the **dependent variable (DV)** and think of one possible **confound**. If you have trouble remembering which variable is the **IV** and which is the **DV**, try using the following sentence to help:

The ___(dependent variable)___ is dependent on the ___(independent variable)___.

◆ Children who are abused during childhood will have lower self-esteem in adulthood than will children who are not abused.
   IV = _____
   DV = _____
   Possible confound = _____

◆ College seniors have better study skills than do freshmen.
   IV = _____
   DV = _____
   Possible confound = _____

◆ The more children watch TV, the less intelligent they are.
   IV = _____
   DV = _____
   Possible confound = _____

◆ Lawyers are more devious than psychologists.
   IV = _____
   DV = _____
   Possible confound = _____

- Lawyers make more money than psychologists.

  IV = _____

  DV = _____

  Possible confound = _____

- The happier people are with their jobs, the more hours they will work.

  IV = _____

  DV = _____

  Possible confound = _____

- Catholics are more likely to vote Republican than are non-Catholics.

  IV = _____

  DV = _____

  Possible confound = _____

- The more religious people are, the less they will be afraid of death.

  IV = _____

  DV = _____

  Possible confound = _____

- People who are underweight live longer than people who are overweight.

  IV = _____

  DV = _____

  Possible confound = _____

- People who have more than 12 years of education are less likely to get Alzheimer's disease than people who have 12 or fewer years of education.

  IV = _____

  DV = _____

  Possible confound = _____

Describe two ways that researchers can avoid **confounds** in experimental research.

- _____
  _____
  _____
  _____
  _____

- _____
  _____
  _____
  _____
  _____

How is a **quasi-experimental design** like an **experiment**? _____
_____
_____

How is a **quasi-experimental design** different from an **experiment**? _____
_____
_____

A **correlation coefficient** is a number between _____ and _____. The sign of
the **correlation coefficient** indicates _____, while the number indicates
_____.

On the blank grids below, draw space below, draw scatterplots and lines showing the following
correlations:

♦   -.70
♦   +.30

♦   -1.0
♦   +.90

-.70

-1.0

+.30

+.90

Find 10 adult friends (or classmates or family members) to serve as participants in a study. Ask them:

♦ *How many hours per week do you watch sports games (on average)?*
♦ *How many hours per week do you work out (on average)?*

Record the data in the chart below.

Participant	Hours Watching Sports	Hours Working Out
#1		
#2		
#3		
#4		
#5		
#6		
#7		
#8		
#9		
#10		

Now, graph your data on the blank grid below.

Hours Working Out

Hours Watching Sports

Based on your results, does it appear that there is a correlation between watching sports and working out? _____ What size and direction would you estimate the correlation to be? _____

GO SURFING ...

...at http://faculty.vassar.edu/lowry/VassarStats.html
- Choose the link for "correlation and regression" on the left.
- Then scroll down and choose "direct-entry version" under "basic linear correlation and regression."
- At the pop-up screen, enter 10. Follow the directions that appear.
- The correlation coefficient will be abbreviated as r in the results.

What **correlation coefficient** did you obtain at this site? _____

How accurate was your prediction? _____

What factors influenced the size of the **correlation coefficient**? _____
_____

Why might a researcher want to conduct **descriptive research**, given that it does not say anything about a relationship between two variables? _____
_____
_____

Can you think of a person or type of person (besides those described in the book) who might be a good subject for a **case study**? _____
_____
_____

Under what circumstances might a **case study** be particularly useful? _____
_____
_____

What are some of the difficulties with using **surveys** to collect data?

◆ _____

◆ _____

◆ _____

◆ _____

◆ _____

◆ _____

Be a Critical Consumer of Psychology

What does it mean to say that something is **valid**? _____
_____
_____

Give your own example of a test or measurement that lacks **validity**. Explain your example.
_____
_____

Provide an example of a measure that is **reliable** and one that is unreliable.

◆ **Reliable:** _____
_____

◆ **Unreliable:** _____
_____

Name and describe, in your own words, two sources of **bias** in a research study:

◆ _____
_____
_____
_____

◆ _____
_____
_____
_____

How can a researcher unintentionally affect the results of a study? _____
_____
_____
_____
_____

What can a researcher do to ensure that he or she *doesn't* affect the results of a study? _____
_____
_____
_____
_____

Go to the health or science section of a newspaper and find a brief article about a research study. Obviously, the study was summarized for inclusion in the paper. What questions about the study does the article leave you with? What is the significance of each of these unanswered questions?

♦   **Question:** _____
    _____

    Importance: _____
    _____

♦   **Question:** _____
    _____

    Importance: _____
    _____

♦   **Question:** _____
    _____

    Importance: _____
    _____

What is **pseudopsychology**? _____
_____
_____
_____
_____

Why is ESP not necessarily **pseudopsychology**? _____
_____
_____
_____
_____

Ethics: Doing It Right

GO SURFING ...

... to find out more about the controversy about whether Nazi research should be used. Here is a starting point: *The ethics of using medical data from Nazi experiments*, by Baruch Cohen, at http://www.jlaw.com/Articles/NaziMedEx.html.

The Nazis conducted horrific studies on Holocaust victims. List some of those studies here:

_____

_____

Some people argue that the results of these studies should be used, if appropriate. Again, surf the web. Then, summarize this position. What do *you* think? Should data collected in an unethical way ever be used? Under what conditions? Why or why not?

_____

_____

Briefly summarize, *in your own words*, the five general **ethical principles** adopted by the APA for psychologists:

PRINCIPLE A:

_____

_____

_____

PRINCIPLE B:

_____

_____

_____

PRINCIPLE C:

_____

_____

_____

PRINCIPLE D:

_____

_____

_____

PRINCIPLE E:

_____

_____

_____

Now, suppose that you are a member of your school's **institutional review board** (IRB). Consider the following situations. What are the ethical considerations for each of them?

SITUATION #1: Dr. August plans to study the effects of competition on ability to solve math problems. Half of the participants will be told that he wants to see what approach they take in solving math problems. The other half will be told that he wants to see which person chooses the best approach.

Ethical considerations: _____

_____

_____

SITUATION #2: Dr. Schwartz plans to compare the intellectual skills of retired people to those of sophomores. To recruit sophomores, she plans to arrange for volunteers to receive an A in their psychology course and for nonvolunteers to have their grades lowered. To recruit retired people, she plans to go to a retirement community each evening next week, knock at people's doors, and ask them to work some puzzles without explaining all of the details of the study, because she thinks that most of the retirees would not understand.

Ethical considerations: _____

_____

_____

SITUATION #3: To study self-esteem in children, Dr. Ayers plans to have 8-year-olds draw pictures of themselves and their friends and to answer some questions. He plans to ask a teacher friend to let him test some of his students.

Ethical considerations: _____

_____

_____

Name three specific things that it would be unethical for a clinical psychologist to do. Explain which of the general **ethical principles** applies to each situation.

Unethical Action	Related General Ethical Principle

Looking at Levels

How can psychologists justify trying new treatments on people instead of using established treatments? Consider the factors at the **three levels** that might influence psychologists' decisions. Draw arrows between the factors to indicate how they may interact.

The Brain	The Person	The Group

TRY PRACTICE TEST #3 NOW!
GOOD LUCK!

After You Read . . . Practice Tests

PRACTICE TEST #1:
THE SCIENCE OF PSYCHOLOGY

True/False Questions
Circle TRUE or FALSE for each of the following statements.

1.   TRUE   FALSE   Psychologists want to predict and control behavior. (p. 5)

2.   TRUE   FALSE   Psychology is a science. (p. 4)

3.   TRUE   FALSE   Psychology does not study observable behaviors. (p. 5)

4.   TRUE   FALSE   The level of the brain never influences the level of the group. (p. 8)

5.   TRUE   FALSE   Relationships would be events at the level of the group. (p. 7)

Multiple-Choice Questions
For each question, circle the letter of the best answer.

1.   Psychology is defined by the authors as the science of _____. (p. 4)
    a.   mental processes and behavior
    b.   behavior and emotions
    c.   human and animal behavior
    d.   normal and deviant behavior

2.   Which of the following is NOT a mental process? (p. 4)
    a.   Thinking
    b.   Memorizing
    c.   Feeling happy
    d.   Jumping for joy

3.   Talking involves _____. (pp. 4-6)
    a.   a behavior
    b.   a mental process
    c.   the level of the brain
    d.   all of the above

4.	Which of the following questions would be LEAST likely to be answered by a psychologist? (pp. 4-6)
	a.	How do people store memories?
	b.	Are there basic human rights?
	c.	Are personalities more influenced by genetics or the environment?
	d.	How would damage to the frontal lobes affect a person's thinking?

5.	How does psychology differ from philosophy? (p. 10)
	a.	Psychologists are interested in the study of behavior, whereas philosophers are interested in the study of mental processes.
	b.	Psychologists are interested in the study of mental processes, whereas philosophers are interested in the study of behaviors.
	c.	Psychologists use logic and data to answer questions, whereas philosophers use only logic to answer questions.
	d.	Psychologists use data to answer questions, whereas philosophers use logic.

6.	The four goals of psychology are to _____. (p. 5)
	a.	predict, describe, explain, control
	b.	predict, contribute, describe, answer
	c.	theorize, control, describe, explain
	d.	describe, explain, hypothesize, answer

7.	At the level of the _____, psychologists focus on beliefs, desires, and feelings. (p. 6)
	a.	brain
	b.	person
	c.	group
	d.	culture

8.	Which of the following is NOT likely to happen? (pp. 6-7)
	a.	Events at the level of the person affect events at the level of the brain.
	b.	Events at the level of the group affect events at the level of the brain.
	c.	Events at the level of the person affect events at the level of the group.
	d.	All are likely to happen.

9.	The brain damage that a person suffered during a car accident would be an event at _____. (pp. 6-7)
	a.	the level of the brain
	b.	the level of the person
	c.	the level of the group
	d.	all three levels

10.	Among the Maasai, the infants who were most likely to survive the drought were the ones who were _____. (p. 8)
	a.	calm and cooperative
	b.	testy and demanding
	c.	small in size
	d.	cared for by a single person

PRACTICE TEST #2:
PSYCHOLOGY THEN AND NOW

Fill-in-the-Blank Questions

Fill in each blank in the paragraphs below with a word from the word bank.

WORD BANK	
behavior	information processing
behaviorism	introspection
brain	mental processes
brain scans	philosophy
cognitive	physiology
cognitive neuroscience	psychodynamic
computer	psychology
evolutionary	science
functionalism	structuralism
Gestalt	unconscious drives

In 1879, Wilhelm Wundt established the first _____ laboratory in Leipzig, Germany. This new field shared its interests with _____; however, because it is a _____, its methods are more similar to those of _____. Over time, the field has evolved and many theories have emerged. Wundt's school of psychology was called _____. These psychologists used _____ as the primary method of data collection. Other schools of psychology with European roots include _____ psychology, which takes its name from the German word for "whole," and Freud's _____ school, which focused on people's _____.

William James brought psychology to America. His school of psychology, _____, was strongly influenced by the theories of Charles Darwin, as was the more recent school of _____ psychology. However, the predominant school of psychology in the United States in the early 20th century was _____. As its name suggests, this school focused primarily on people's _____. In fact, _____ were not much studied by American psychologists until after the _____ revolution in the 1950s. Many psychologists taking this perspective used a metaphor of the brain as a _____ to study human _____. Recent technologies, such as _____, have been important in the development of _____, which blends cognitive psychology with neuroscience (the study of the _____). (p. 10-17)

Matching Questions

Match each name with the school of thought. Write the correct letter in the blank on the left.

_____1.   Wilhelm Wundt (p. 10)   a.   Psychodynamic theory

_____2.   Max Wertheimer (p. 12)   b.   Cognitive psychology

_____3.   William James (p. 12)   c.   Gestalt psychology

_____4.   Sigmund Freud (p. 13)   d.   Behaviorism

_____5.   James B. Watson (p. 14)   e.   Structuralism

_____6.   Carl Rogers (p. 15)   f.   Evolutionary psychology

_____7.   Herbert Simon (p. 15)   g.   Functionalism

_____8.   David Buss (p. 16)   h.   Humanism

Matching Questions

Match the type of psychologist or other professional with the activities that individual will typically engage in. Write the correct letter in the space at the left.

_____1.   Clinical psychologist (p. 17)   a.   Prescribes medication

_____2.   Clinical neuropsychologist (p. 19)   b.   Studies individual differences in preferences

_____3.   Counseling psychologist (p. 19)   c.   Studies thinking, memory, and related topics

_____4.   Psychiatrist (p. 19)   d.   Diagnoses the effects of brain damage

_____5.   Social worker (p. 19)   e.   Studies biological structures and functions related to psychological phenomena

_____6.   Psychiatric nurse (p. 19)   f.   Teaches and conducts research

_____7.   Academic psychologist (p. 20)   g.   Helps people with serious problems

_____8.   Developmental psychologist (p. 20)   h.   Helps athletes improve performance

_____9.   Cognitive psychologist (p. 20)   i.   Studies how groups function

_____10.	Social psychologist (p. 20)	j.	Works with educators to help children in schools
_____11.	Personality psychologist (p. 20)	k.	Helps people with normal stressors
_____12.	Human factors psychologist (p. 20)	l.	Focuses on using psychology in the workplace
_____13.	Applied psychologist (p. 20)	m.	Has an M.S.N. with specialization and works closely with medical doctors
_____14.	Physiological psychologist (p. 21)	n.	Studies how people's mental processes and behavior change during life
_____15.	Industrial/organizational psychologist (p. 21)	o.	Has an M.S.W. degree and frequently works with families
_____16.	Sport psychologist (p. 21)	p.	Tries to solve practical problems
_____17.	School psychologist (p. 21)	q.	Tries to improve products so they can be used more effectively

Multiple-Choice Questions

For each question, circle the letter of the best answer.

1. Psychodynamic psychologists focused primarily on the level of the _____. (p. 13)
    a. brain
    b. person
    c. group
    d. all of the above

2. The key idea of Gestalt theory is that _____. (p. 12)
    a. the whole is greater than the sum of its parts
    b. some individuals possess characteristics that enable them to survive and reproduce more successfully than others
    c. only directly observable behavior should be the subject matter of psychology
    d. behavior is driven by mental processes often hidden from conscious awareness

3. According to behaviorists, people behave in certain ways because _____ _____. (p. 14)
    a. they are reinforced for their behaviors
    b. they want to
    c. it is part of the basic human desire to self-actualize
    d. they unconsciously wish to be successful

4.   Helping people achieve self-actualization is a goal of _____ psychologists. (p. 15)
    a.   behavioral
    b.   humanistic
    c.   Gestalt
    d.   cognitive

5.   The universality of certain behaviors is the best evidence for _____ psychology. (p. 16-17)
    a.   behavioral
    b.   evolutionary
    c.   humanistic
    d.   cognitive

6.   Gestalt psychology has influenced the modern study of _____. (p. 12)
    a.   perception
    b.   the brain
    c.   memory
    d.   psychotherapy

7.   Which of the following is NOT one of the long-term influences of Freud's psychodynamic theory? (p. 14)
    a.   The idea that some mental processes are hidden from awareness
    b.   The creation of new approaches to treating psychological problems
    c.   Attention to certain kinds of observations, like tip-of-the-tongue phenomena
    d.   An emphasis on cultural relativism

8.   How are behaviorism and cognitive psychology different? (p. 15)
    a.   Behaviorism relies on the scientific method, whereas cognitive psychology does not.
    b.   Mental processes play no part in behaviorism, whereas they are central to cognitive psychology.
    c.   Behaviorists do not believe that there is such a thing as mental illness, whereas cognitive psychologists do.
    d.   Cognitive psychologists attach no importance to social experiences, whereas behaviorists do.

9.   Which of the following has NOT been influenced by behaviorism? (p. 15)
    a.   Recognition of need for rigor in psychological studies
    b.   Education
    c.   Psychotherapy
    d.   Neuro-imaging technologies

10.   Psychiatrists are able to _____, and most psychologists are not. (p. 19)
    a.   prescribe drugs
    b.   sleep with their patients
    c.   use psychotherapy
    d.   work in a hospital setting

11. Which of the following professionals would be least likely to perform psychotherapy?
(p. 20)
   a.   Psychiatrist
   b.   Counseling psychologist
   c.   Social psychologist
   d.   Social worker

12. How are academic and applied psychology different? (pp. 19-21)
   a.   There are many subspecialties of academic psychology (developmental, social, etc.), whereas there are none for applied psychology.
   b.   Applied psychologists do research, whereas academic psychologists do not.
   c.   Academic psychologists do research, whereas applied psychologists do not.
   d.   By definition, applied psychologists help to solve specific practical problems, whereas academic psychologists may study practical or theoretical problems.

13. In which location would you be LEAST likely to find an applied psychologist?
(p. 20)
   a.   A company
   b.   A school
   c.   A government office
   d.   A college

14. How are clinical and counseling psychology different? (pp. 17-19)
   a.   Clinical psychologists tend to use behavioral therapies, whereas counseling psychologists are more likely to use psychotherapy.
   b.   Clinical psychologists will prescribe medications, whereas counseling psychologists don't.
   c.   Clinical psychologists have Ph.D.s, whereas counseling psychologists have only master's degrees.
   d.   Clinical psychologists would be more likely to deal with people with mental disorders, whereas counseling psychologists deal with issues that we all face.

15. Which of the following is NOT typically a function of an academic psychologist?
(p. 20)
   a.   Teaching
   b.   Counseling students about personal problems
   c.   Advising students about their classes
   d.   Conducting research

PRACTICE TEST #3:
THE RESEARCH PROCESS

True/False Questions
Circle TRUE or FALSE for each of the following statements.

1. TRUE   FALSE   In correlational research, the researcher controls the situation. (p. 28)

2. TRUE   FALSE   A quasi-experimental design is similar to an experimental design in that it involves comparing groups. (p. 28)

3. TRUE   FALSE   The sign of a correlation will tell you if two variables vary in the same or opposite directions. (p. 28)

4. TRUE   FALSE   Case studies may sometimes involve experimentation, but with only a single subject. (p. 30)

5. TRUE   FALSE   Random assignment involves selecting participants for a study randomly. (p. 27)

6. TRUE   FALSE   Correlations can help you establish that one variable causes another. (p. 28)

7. TRUE   FALSE   Not all psychological research involves examining relationships between two variables. (p. 29)

8. TRUE   FALSE   Confounds help to clarify the results of a study. (p. 27)

9. TRUE   FALSE   In a double-blind study, the participants are not aware of the predictions of the study. (p. 35)

10. TRUE   FALSE   A study can be reliable but not valid. (p. 32)

Matching Questions

Match each description with the appropriate step of the scientific method for doing research. Write the correct letter in the space at the left.

_____1.   Step 1 (p. 23)   a.   Specify operational definitions

_____2.   Step 2 (pp. 23-24)   b.   Find a research question

_____3.   Step 3 (p. 24)   c.   Compare outcomes to theory

_____4.   Step 4 (p. 24)   d.   Develop an idea about what might happen

_____5.   Step 5 (p. 25)   e.   Develop a set of ideas to explain observations

_____6.   Step 6 (p. 25)   f.   Collect data

Matching Questions

Match each situation with the general ethical principle it violates. Write the correct letter in the space at the left.

_____1.   Beneficence and Nonmaleficence (p. 38)   a.   Falsifying some data

_____2.   Fidelity and Responsibility (p. 38)   b.   Overburdening a student assistant with work, to the point that the assistant becomes ill

_____3.   Integrity (p. 38)   c.   Making disparaging remarks about homosexuality during a group therapy session at which several homosexual members are present

_____4.   Justice (p. 38)   d.   Providing therapy to both spouses during a messy divorce, without telling either spouse

_____5.   Respect for People's Rights and Dignity (p. 38)   e.   Deciding not to hire a young female applicant to be a new professor because she may need maternity leave soon

Multiple-Choice Questions

For each question, circle the letter of the best answer.

1.   Amy has just read about a study that she finds very interesting. Unfortunately, the researchers do not provide many details about how they collected their data. As a result, Amy is unable to _____ the study. (p. 24)
   a.   validate
   b.   copy
   c.   replicate
   d.   repeat

2.   Which of the following is not a variable? (p. 24)
   a.   Height
   b.   The value of pi
   c.   Batting averages
   d.   The number of phone calls people make per day

3.   Leslie is trying to decide how to collect data on college students' motivation. She is considering asking open-ended questions in individual interview settings. Which of the following is most likely to be a problem if Leslie uses this method? (pp. 30-31)
   a.   Maximizing the accuracy of people's responses
   b.   Developing operational definitions
   c.   The falsifiability of the theory
   d.   Eliminating confounds

4.   Jesika is interested in studying whether first-year college students' reading habits predict their writing abilities. She has decided to measure writing ability by asking students to self-report their grades in Freshman Composition. Jesika has established _____ for her _____. (pp. 24-26)
   a.   an operational definition; independent variable
   b.   confound; study
   c.   an operational definition; dependent variable
   d.   a variable; study

5.   Hypotheses and theories are similar in that both _____. (p. 25)
   a.   produce predictions
   b.   are rooted in a web of facts and concepts
   c.   apply only to specific studies
   d.   are tentative ideas

6.   How are hypotheses and theories related to each other? (p. 25)
   a.   They are the same thing.
   b.   Hypotheses are tested in studies; the results of these studies are then woven together into theories.
   c.   Hypotheses produce predictions, whereas theories report conclusions.
   c.   Hypotheses may be either correct or incorrect; theories are always correct.

7. Although it is impossible to directly observe emotions, researchers can learn about them by
_____. (p. 24)
   a. testing hypotheses
   b. observing things that directly correlate to emotions, such as facial expressions
   c. replicating others' studies
   d. asking subjects

8. By "problem," psychologists mean _____. (p. 23)
   a. a conflict
   b. a question they want to answer
   c. an occurrence of a particular phenomenon
   d. an unsolved dilemma

9. A good theory is falsifiable, meaning that _____. (p. 25)
   a. it is possible to reject the theory if the predictions are not confirmed
   b. is never wrong
   c. has not yet been rejected
   d. makes correct predictions

10. Pete was interested in whether training students in memory techniques really improved their memory. He randomly assigned students in his class to one of two groups. One group received memory training, and the other did not. A week later, Pete tested the students' memory. This technique is most likely to be an example of
_____. (p. 27)
   a. an experiment
   b. a quasi-experiment
   c. a correlation
   d. a case study

11. In the study described in #10 above, the independent variable is _____. (p. 26)
   a. memory
   b. memory training
   c. Pete
   d. students' intelligence

12. A possible confounding variable in the study described in #10 is _____.
(p. 27)
   a. the amount of sleep the students have had recently
   b. students' memory
   c. students' memory training
   d. Pete

13. The group that did not receive training in the study in #10 above would be called
_____. (p. 27)
   a. the control group
   b. naïve participants
   c. the experimental group
   d. confounding subjects

14. A quasi-experiment is different from an experiment in that _____.
    (p. 28)
    a. it does not involve comparing groups
    b. it does not involve random assignment
    c. it does not involve collecting data
    d. it has fewer confounds

15. Which of the following indicates the *weakest* correlation? (p. 28)
    a. -.29
    b. -.78
    c. 1.6
    d. .16

16. Gail is conducting a study comparing a placebo with a prescription medicine for allergies. As she administers the allergy medicine, Gail says to the study participant, "I'm sure you will be feeling well soon." She says nothing to the participants who receive the placebo. This is an example of _____. (p. 34)
    a. response bias
    b. sampling bias
    c. lack of ethics
    d. experimenter expectancy

17. To avoid a situation like that in #16, Gail could use _____. (p. 35)
    a. a double-blind study
    b. a quasi-experimental design to study those already using the medicine
    c. random assignment
    d. a survey

18. Which of the following is NOT a potential difficulty associated with the use of surveys? (pp. 30-31)
    a. People may lie, especially about sensitive material.
    b. What people say and what they do may be different.
    c. Not everyone who is asked to fill out a survey does.
    d. They are expensive.

19. Greg takes his temperature once and gets 96.7° F. Five minutes later, he takes it again and gets 98.1°. Five minutes after that, he gets a reading of 99.2°. Greg's thermometer apparently _____. (p. 32)
    a. lacks validity
    b. lacks reliability
    c. lacks validity but not reliability
    d. has both validity and reliability

20. When researchers combine results from different studies into one larger study, the method is called _____. (p. 31)
   a.   a big study
   b.   a meta-analysis
   c.   an experiment
   d.   a quasi-experiment

21. Before a study commences, participants must provide _____; after the study, they must be _____. (p. 37)
   a.. a debriefing; informed
   b.   informed consent; debriefed
   c.   an affidavit; paid
   d.   a contract; reimbursed

22. Informed consent must include _____. (p. 37)
   a.   a description of what the participants will be asked to do
   b.   a description of any risks and benefits of the procedure
   c.   a statement that participants can withdraw from the study at any time without penalty
   d.   all of the above

23. In California (and most other states), if a client threatens the life of another individual, the therapist must _____. (p. 38)
   a.   take steps to protect the individual being threatened
   b.   do nothing – it would be a breech of confidentiality
   c.   place the client under house arrest
   d.   discontinue treatment with the client

24. Research has found that people with schizophrenia benefit greatly if _____. (p. 39)
   a.   they receive psychotherapy
   b.   they are placed in a group home
   c.   they are medicated as soon as they are diagnosed
   d.   they are allowed to leave their jobs

25. Which of the following would be *unethical* for a clinical psychologist to do? (p. 39)
   a.   Use a new technique in therapy after being trained appropriately
   b.   Break confidentiality to tell a person that his/her life has been threatened by a patient of the psychologist
   c.   Engage in sexual relations with a patient
   d.   Advertise his or her services

26. Which of the following would NOT be included in informed consent? (p. 37)
   a.   Information about the risks of the study
   b.   Information about the benefits of the study
   c.   Information about what journal will publish the results of the study
   d.   A notice that the participants can withdraw from the study at any time

27. For animal studies, what is the role of an IRB? (p. 37)
   a. None
   b. To ensure that participants are not mistreated
   c. To ensure that participants are adopted after the study is finished
   d. To prohibit any studies that involve inflicting pain

28. What spurred the development of codes of professional ethics? (p. 36)
   a. A 1996 study of suicidal teens in New York
   b. The Nuremberg trials following World War II
   c. The animal rights movement
   d. The cognitive revolution

29. Who is likely to serve on an IRB? (p. 37)
   a. Psychologists
   b. Representatives from the local community
   c. Clergy
   d. All of the above

30. John received a survey in the mail. He answered every question "yes" and then returned it to the researcher. This is an example of _____. (p. 34)
   a. response bias
   b. sampling bias
   c. experimenter expectancy
   d. lack of reliability

COMPREHENSIVE PRACTICE TEST

True/False Questions

Circle TRUE or FALSE for each of the following statements.

1. TRUE   FALSE   The founder of psychology was Sigmund Freud. (p. 10)

2. TRUE   FALSE   Early behaviorists focused on mental processes. (p. 14)

3. TRUE   FALSE   Humanistic psychology emphasizes free will and personal growth. (p. 15)

4. TRUE   FALSE   Evolutionary theories are easy to test. (p. 17)

5. TRUE   FALSE   Clinical psychologists must have a Ph.D. to practice psychology. (p. 19)

6. TRUE   FALSE   William James established the first psychological laboratory in the United States. (p. 12)

7. TRUE   FALSE   Psychologists want to know how to control people's behavior. (p. 5)

8. TRUE   FALSE   In some states, clinical psychologists can prescribe medications. (p. 19)

9. TRUE   FALSE   Developmental psychologists do psychotherapy with children. (p. 20)

10. TRUE   FALSE   Correlation equals causation. (p. 29)

Matching Questions

Choose the motto or quote that best describes each theory. Write the matching letter in the space to the left.

_____1.   Structuralism   (p. 10)   a.   "The whole is more than just the sum of its parts."

_____2.   Functionalism (p. 11)   b.   "Be all you can be."

_____3.   Gestalt psychology (p. 12)   c.   "Tell me about your mother."

_____4.   Psychodynamic theory (p. 13)   d.   "The mind is what the brain does."

_____5.   Behaviorism (p. 14)   e.   "The real question is not whether machines think but whether men do."

_____6.   Cognitive psychology (p. 15)   f.   "The brain can be explained by natural selection."

_____7.   Cognitive neuroscience (p. 16)   g.   "The human mind is like a computer."

_____8.   Humanistic psychology (p. 15)   h.   "What is that for?"

_____9.   Evolutionary psychology (p. 16)   i.   "Look within."

Matching Questions

Match the research technique with the best description. Write the correct letter in the space to the left.

_____ 1.   Experiment (p. 26)   a.   Involves looking in real-world habitats

_____ 2.   Quasi-experiment (p. 28)   b.   Does not examine the relationship between variables

_____ 3.   Correlational research (p. 28) c.   Uses random assignment

_____ 4.   Case study (p. 30)   d.   Is limited by participants' honesty

_____ 5.   Naturalistic observation (p. 30) e.   Could be a comparison of males and females on some variable

_____ 6.   Surveys (p. 30)   f.   Does not prove causation

_____ 7.   Descriptive research (p. 29)   g.   Is difficult to generalize from

Identification Questions

Identify the following as positive or negative correlations. Circle the correct answer. (p. 28)

1.   POSITIVE   NEGATIVE   As clouds gather, temperature drops.

2.   POSITIVE   NEGATIVE   As inflation increases, interest rates drop.

3.   POSITIVE   NEGATIVE   As children age, they grow taller.

4.   POSITIVE   NEGATIVE   As hours spent studying decrease, grades decrease.

5.   POSITIVE   NEGATIVE   As alcohol consumption increases, motor control decreases.

Identification Questions

Identify the dependent variable (DV) and the independent variable (IV) in each of the following hypotheses. Write the correct answer in the space provided. (p. 26)

1. The more water you drink, the less likely you are to have kidney stones.
   IV = _____
   DV = _____

2. Rats are bigger than mice.
   IV = _____
   DV = _____

3. Female gymnasts are more likely to be anorexic than other females of the same age.
   IV = _____
   DV = _____

4. Students who complete their study guide activities will have better grades than those who don't.
   IV = _____
   DV = _____

5. Parents who have books in their homes are more likely to have children who like to read.
   IV = _____
   DV = _____

Multiple-Choice Questions

For each question, circle letter of the best answer.

1.   Psychologists who focus on culture study events at the level of the _____. (p. 7)
   a.   brain
   b.   person
   c.   group
   d.   neuron

2.   Among the Maasai, the difficult babies were more likely to survive the drought than were the easy babies because they _____. (p. 8)
   a.   were healthier
   b.   were older
   c.   had better immune systems
   d.   were more demanding

3.   The first formal movement in psychology was _____. (p. 10)
   a.   behaviorism
   b.   structuralism
   c.   psychoanalysis
   d.   functionalism

4.   The problem with the research method of introspection was that _____.
   (p. 10)
   a.   its results couldn't be verified
   b.   it relied on expensive equipment that most psychologists couldn't afford
   c.   it ignored the level of the group
   d.   it didn't focus on mental processes

5.   It was the _____ who led us to realize that the observation of animals could provide clues to human behavior. (p. 12)
   a.   structuralists
   b.   functionalists
   c.   behaviorists
   d.   psychoanalysts

6.   Which of the following would behaviorists be LEAST interested in studying? (p. 14)
   a.   Environmental antecedents
   b.   Unconscious processes
   c.   Stimulus-response associations
   d.   Reinforcements

7. The cognitive neuroscience approach considers events at all three levels of analysis, but with a primary focus on the _____. (p. 16)
   a. brain
   b. group
   c. person
   d. interactions of the three levels

8. Which professional would need the LEAST amount of education to get a job? (p. 19)
   a. A psychiatrist
   b. A social worker
   c. An academic psychologist
   d. A clinical psychologist

9. A _____ studies individual differences in preferences and inclinations. (p. 20)
   a. social psychologist
   b. personality psychologist
   c. neuropsychologist
   d. developmental psychologist

10. A therapist may engage in sexual relations with his/her client _____. (p. 39)
    a. if he/she knew the client before therapy
    b. if he/she terminates therapy
    c. if the client is being seen for a nonemotional, behavioral problem
    d. never

11. Which of the following statements comparing various schools of psychology is FALSE? (pp. 11-17)
    a. Functionalism is similar to evolutionary psychology in that they both were influenced by Darwin.
    b. Cognitive psychology is similar to psychodynamic theory in that they both focus on mental processes.
    c. Psychodynamic theory is similar to evolutionary psychology in that both are hard to test.
    d. Humanistic psychology is similar to evolutionary psychology in that both view humans as generally good.

12. Which of the following is an event at the level of the person? (p. 7)
    a. Brain injury following a fall from a cliff
    b. The decision to use drugs
    c. Exposure to the media
    d. World War II

13. How do the levels of analysis interact? (p. 8)
    a. Each level interacts with the next "bigger" level (e.g., the brain impacts the person, and the person impacts the group).
    b. Each level interacts with the next "smaller" level (e.g., the person impacts the brain, and the group impacts the person).
    c. All levels interact once.
    d. All levels interact continuously.

14. Which of the following disciplines has LEAST influenced psychology? (pp. 10-17)
    a. English
    b. Computer science
    c. Biology
    d. Philosophy

15. Which of the following is a FALSE statement about the roots of modern psychology? (p. 15)
    a. The scientific standards set by behaviorists are still used today.
    b. Gestalt psychology has influenced the modern study of perception.
    c. The humanistic view of people has influenced modern therapy.
    d. The behaviorists' view that behavior is driven by mental processes is still applicable today.

16. Which school of psychology used introspection? (p. 10)
    a. Functionalism
    b. Structuralism
    c. Gestalt psychology
    d. Behaviorism

17. Which list shows the schools of psychology in order of their development (from earliest to latest)? (pp. 11-17)
    a. Psychodynamic, cognitive, evolutionary, behaviorism
    b. Functionalism, behaviorism, cognitive neuroscience, evolutionary
    c. Structuralism, Gestalt, cognitive neuroscience, humanistic
    d. Humanistic, Gestalt, psychodynamic, evolutionary

18. Which of the following schools of psychology did NOT originate in Europe? (p. 14)
    a. Gestalt psychology
    b. Structuralism
    c. Behaviorism
    d. Psychodynamic theory

19. Evolutionary psychology is difficult to study because _____. (p. 17)
    a. we don't know much about what our ancestors were like
    b. most people are resistant to the idea that humans had primate ancestors
    c. people will not admit to their baser instincts
    d. it is not important to today's psychologists

20. Which of the following people is most likely to be working as an applied psychologist? (p. 20)
   a.   Humpty, who studies how people adjust to prostheses
   b.   Jack and Jill, who counsel people who have suffered serious traumas
   c.   Little Miss Muffet, who studies why people are more afraid of spiders than cars
   d.   Old King Cole, who teaches Introduction to Psychology at Harvard

21. A tentative idea that might explain a set of observations is a(n) _____. (p. 24)
   a.   theory
   b.   variable
   c.   hypothesis
   d.   prediction

22. Dr. Speramental is interested in studying the effects of caffeine on memory in lab rats. In his experiment, the independent variable is _____ and the dependent variable is _____. (p. 26)
   a.   the rats; caffeine
   b.   caffeine; memory
   c.   memory; the rats
   d.   memory; caffeine

23. To test his hypothesis, Dr. Speramental decides to inject one group of rats with caffeine every day for a week, but to leave the other group alone. At the end of the week, he will measure the rats' memory for a maze they had previously learned. To avoid a confound, Dr. Speramental should probably _____. (p. 27)
   a.   inject all the rats, some with caffeine and some with water
   b.   use a correlational study
   c.   allow only one group of rats to learn the maze before the injections
   d.   groom the rats every day

24. Dr. Figerout is interested in whether a new teaching technique she learned at a conference is an effective means of making her classroom presentations more interesting to students. To test her hypothesis that the new technique is more effective, she uses her old technique with her 8:00 a.m. class and her new technique with her 11:00 a.m. class. What is one confound in this study? (p. 27)
   a.   The students
   b.   The old technique
   c.   The time of day
   d.   The new technique

25. If interested in studying the differences between two existing groups (e.g., those with depression and those without), a researcher would have to use a(n) _____. (p. 28)
   a.   correlational study
   b.   meta-analysis
   c.   experiment
   d.   quasi-experiment

26. Which of the following correlations has the greatest predictive value? (p. 28)
    a. 2.3
    b. -.76
    c. 0
    d. .54

27. Which of the following techniques offers the greatest control? (p. 27)
    a. An experiment
    b. A case study
    c. A quasi-experiment
    d. Naturalistic observation

28. A technique that combines the results from different studies is a(n) _____. (p. 31)
    a. case study
    b. experiment
    c. meta-analysis
    d. naturalistic observation

29. If a study can be replicated, it is said to be _____. (p. 32)
    a. confounded
    b. reliable
    c. explicated
    d. valid

30. Children typically give the same response over and over again, without regard for the questions asked. This type of bias is called _____. (p. 34)
    a. sampling bias
    b. age bias
    c. population bias
    d. response bias

31. The first step in the scientific method is _____. (p. 23)
    a. forming a hypothesis
    b. replication
    c. systematically observing events
    d. specifying a problem

32. The variable a researcher manipulates is called the _____ variable. (p. 26)
    a. independent
    b. hypothetical
    c. dependent
    d. confounding

33. Which of the following correlation coefficients would probably best describe the relationship between how sociable people are and how much time they spend at a party? (p. 28)
   a. 0.2
   b. 1.7
   c. 0.8
   d. -0.2

34. In a _____ experiment, neither the participant nor the investigator knows the predictions of the experiment or the condition to which the participant has been assigned. (p. 35)
   a. single-blind
   b. completely confounded
   c. double-blind
   d. quasi-experimental

15. If you replicated another researcher's study, you would be _____ it. (p. 24)
   a. critiquing
   b. praising
   c. repeating
   d. building upon

Essay Questions
Answer each question in the space provided.

1. How might a researcher come to understand depression at the levels of the brain, the person, and the group? _____

   _____

   _____

   _____

   _____

   _____

   _____

   _____

   _____

2. How might an evolutionary psychologist, a psychodynamic theorist, and a behaviorist interpret a child's fearfulness at being separated from his or her mother? _____

   _____

   _____

   _____

   _____

   _____

   _____

   _____

   _____

3.   Why would it be a bad idea for an academic psychologist who has clinical training to also work in the counseling center at the school at which he or she teaches? _____

_____

_____

_____

_____

_____

_____

4.   How might a psychiatrist, a psychologist, and a social worker each approach a client suffering from an eating disorder? _____

_____

_____

_____

_____

_____

_____

_____

_____

_____

_____

5.   Design a study to investigate the influence of morality on willingness to cheat in an academic setting. Identify the independent and dependent variables, and discuss the ethical considerations of such a study. _____

_____

_____

_____

_____

_____

_____

_____

_____

_____

_____

_____

_____

_____

_____

_____

_____

_____

6.	Discuss each of the following sources of error in a study, including the stage of the research process at which it arises and its possible effects:
	♦	Sampling bias
	♦	Response bias
	♦	Experimenter expectancy effects

_____
_____
_____
_____
_____
_____
_____
_____
_____
_____

7.	Provide examples of studies for which you would be likely to use correlational, quasi-experimental, and experimental research designs. Why would each design be most appropriate for that study?

_____
_____
_____
_____
_____
_____
_____
_____
_____
_____
_____
_____
_____
_____
_____

8.	What kinds of problems must you be careful to avoid when using surveys? _____

_____
_____
_____
_____
_____
_____
_____
_____
_____

61

9.　　If you had your choice, what type of research design would you want to use? Why?_____

_____
_____
_____
_____
_____
_____
_____
_____
_____
_____

10.　　Think of a situation in which you might be tempted to use statistics to "lie" about your
　　　research data. Describe. _____

_____
_____
_____
_____
_____
_____
_____
_____
_____

When You Are Finished . . . Puzzle It Out

Across

2. Interview after study completed
5. Founded first psychological lab
7. Outside conscious awareness
9. Consistency
11. Subset of larger population
13. Aspect of situation that can change
16. Entire set of relevant people
17. Difference in DV due to IV
18. Developed psychotherapy
19. Study focusing on one individual

Down

1. Science of mental processes and behavior
3. "Whole"
4. Set of questions
6. Step 5 of the scientific method is to formulate this
8. Objective observations
9. Always answering "yes" or "no"
10. Said people don't have "thoughts"
12. Outwardly observable acts
14. First American psychologist
15. Founded client-centered therapy

Puzzle created with Puzzlemaster at DiscoverySchool.com.

Chapter 2
The Biology of Mind and Behavior:
The Brain in Action

Before You Read . . .

Have you ever known anyone who has suffered brain damage ... perhaps someone who has had a stroke or has Alzheimer's disease? How did this damage affect the person's functioning?

In this chapter, you will learn the basics of how the brain works, beginning with the basic cell of the nervous system: the neuron. Communication within the brain and across the nervous system is an electrochemical process that results in neurotransmitters being released into the synapses between neurons. You will also learn how the brain and the nervous system are organized.

The chapter also discusses two other systems of the body that interact with our brains to keep our bodies healthy: the neuroendocrine system and the immune system. You will discover how researchers have learned about the brain, by using neuroimaging, and by studying the effects of effects of lesions and strokes. Finally, the chapter ends with a discussion of genetic influences on behavior, and the dynamic interaction of genes and the environment.

Chapter Objectives

After reading this chapter, you should be able to:

♦   Describe how neurons work.

♦   Explain how chemicals allow neurons to communicate and what happens if healthy neurons can no longer communicate.

♦   Name and describe the major parts of the brain and the nervous system and their functions.

♦   Understand how the functions of the two sides of the brain differ.

♦   Name and explain the techniques used to study the brain.

♦   Describe the role of genes in behavior, and discuss how genes and the environment interact as the brain develops and functions.

♦   Explain what *heritability* means and how evolution shaped the functions of the brain.

As You Read ... Term Identification

Make flashcards using the following terms as you go. Use the definitions in the margins of this chapter for help. If you write the definitions in your own words, though, you will remember them better!

Action potential

Active interaction

Adaptation

Adoption study

Agonist

All-or-none law

Amygdala

Antagonist

Autonomic nervous system (ANS)

Axon

Basal ganglia

Behavioral genetics

Brain circuit

Brainstem

Cell body

Cell membrane

Central nervous system (CNS)

Cerebellum

Cerebral cortex

Cerebral hemisphere

Complex inheritance

Computer-assisted tomography (CT)

Corpus callosum

Cortisol

Dendrite

Deoxyribonucleic acid (DNA)

Dizygotic

Electroencephalogram

Electroencephalograph (EEG)

Endogenous cannabinoids

Estrogen

Evocative (or reactive) interaction

Evolution

Forebrain

Frontal lobe

Functional magnetic resonance imaging (fMRI)

Gene

Genotype

Glial cell

Gyrus

Heritability

Hindbrain

Hippocampus

Hormone

Hypothalamus

Interneuron

Ion

Lesion

Limbic system

Lobes

Magnetic resonance imaging (MRI)

Medulla

Mendelian inheritance

Meninges

Microelectrode

Midbrain

Monozygotic

Motor neuron

Motor strip

Myelin

Natural selection

Neuroendocrine system

Neuroimaging

Neuromodulator

Neuron

Neurotransmitter

Occipital lobe

Parasympathetic nervous system

Parietal lobe

Passive interaction

Peripheral nervous system (PNS)

Phenotype

Pituitary gland

Plasticity

Pons

Positron emission tomography (PET)

Pruning

Receptor

Reflex

Resting potential

Reticular formation

Reuptake
Selective serotonin reuptake inhibitor (SSRI)
Sensory neuron
Skeletal system
Somatosensory strip
Spinal cord
Split-brain patient
Stroke
Subcortical structure
Sulcus

Sympathetic nervous system
Synapse
Synaptic cleft
Temporal lobe
Terminal button
Testosterone
Thalamus
Transcranial magnetic stimulation (TMS)
Twin study

As You Read . . . Questions and Exercises

Brain Circuits: Making Connections

The Neuron: A Powerful Computer

For each of the following types of neurons, provide a definition and an example.

Type of Neuron	Definition
Sensory neuron	
Motor neuron	
Interneuron	

In addition to approximately 100 billion neurons, the brain also contains 10 times as many
_____ cells, which fill the gaps between neurons and have the following functions:

◆ _____

◆ _____

◆ _____

◆ _____

What are brain circuits, and how do they work? _____

_____

_____

_____

Think of an analogy for brain circuits that will help you to remember them and their functions.
Describe it. _____

_____

_____

_____

_____

In the space below, draw a picture of two connecting neurons.

Label each part of your drawing with the correct number from the chart below. Also, provide the function of each part of the **neuron**.

	Neural Structure	Function
1	Cell membrane	
2	Cell body	
3	Dendrites	
4	Axon	
5	Myelin sheath	
6	Terminals (terminal branches)	
7	Terminal buttons	
8	Synapse	
9	Synaptic cleft	
10	Receptor sites	
11	Neurotransmitters	

What is the **all-or-none law**? _____
_____
_____
_____
_____

Neurotransmitters and Neuromodulators: Bridging the Gap

GO SURFING ...

... at http://faculty.washington.edu/chudler/synapse.html to read more about (and see pictures of) how an action potential travels. Go to the notes page at http://faculty.washington.edu/chudler/shell/notes1.html and let your professor know what you thought about this page! (Just type in your professor's e-mail address instead of your own.)

Describe the difference in the functions of **neurotransmitters** and **neuromodulators**.

Neurotransmitters	Neuromodulators

When neurotransmitters or neuromodulators **bind** to receptors, they can have one of two effects. Explain each:

♦   **Excitatory:** _____

_____

_____

♦   **Inhibitory:** _____

_____

_____

What happens to any extra **neurotransmitter** that is released by the terminal buttons, but not taken up by receptors? _____

_____

_____

_____

_____

_____

Describe three ways that drugs may affect **neurotransmitters**:

♦ _____
_____
_____
_____

♦ _____
_____
_____
_____

♦ _____
_____
_____

Looking at Levels

Michael J. Fox quit working on his successful TV series *Spin City*, citing his fight against Parkinson's disease and his need to spend more time with his family as the primary reasons. Describe how Parkinson's disease has affected Fox at the various levels of functioning. Use arrows to indicate how factors at the different levels may interact with each other.

The Brain	The Person	The Group

TRY PRACTICE TEST #1 NOW!
GOOD LUCK!

The Nervous System:
An Orchestra With Many Members

Overview

Together, the brain and the **spinal cord** make up the **central nervous system (CNS)**. What are the functions of the spinal cord?

◆ _____

◆ _____

◆ _____

Explain how **reflexes** work. _____

_____

_____

_____

_____

The **CNS** hooks into the **peripheral nervous system (PNS)**, which has two parts: the **autonomic nervous system** and the **skeletal nervous system**. In the chart below, for each system, identify the muscles controlled, the appearance of these muscles, and other characteristics of these muscles.

	Autonomic Nervous System	Skeletal System
Muscles controlled		
Appearance of muscles controlled		
Other characteristics of muscles controlled		

The **autonomic nervous system (ANS)** also has two parts: the **sympathetic nervous system** and the **parasympathetic nervous system**. Provide the characteristics of each in the chart below.

	Sympathetic Nervous System	Parasympathetic Nervous System
What is the purpose of the system?		
What activates the system?		
What are the effects of activation of the system?		

If you could see inside someone's skull, what would you see (in order from the outside in)? Name and describe each feature.

♦ _____

_____

♦ _____

_____

Under all this, you would see two **cerebral hemispheres**.

♦ Why are these parts called hemispheres? _____

_____

_____

♦ What does each hemisphere do? _____

_____

_____

Each hemisphere is divided into **four lobes**. Give the location of each of the lobes. (The answer is given for the **temporal lobes**.)

	Occipital	Temporal	Parietal	Frontal
Location		At the temples		

Why is the **cerebral cortex** so "crumpled up"? _____

_____

_____

_____

_____

The Cerebral Cortex: The Seat of the Mind

Complete the following chart, indicating the function and the result of the four types of lobes in the brain.

	Function	Result of Damage to This Part
Occipital lobes		
Temporal lobes		
Parietal lobes		
Frontal lobes		

The Dual Brain: Thinking with Both Barrels

Who are **split-brain patients**? What information can studies of split-brain patients provide?

_____

_____

_____

_____

Mark an X in the column headed "left" or "right" to indicate the **hemisphere** in which each function typically takes place.

Function	Left	Right
Captures the details of shapes		
Carries out most aspects of language		
Makes the pitch of a voice rise at the end of a question		
Extracts the metaphors and allusions of language		
Recognizes the overall shape of objects		
Registers the literal meaning of a message		

Why must generalizations about the specializations of each **hemisphere** be made cautiously?

_____
_____
_____
_____
_____

If you had to suffer damage to one **hemisphere**, which one would it be? Why? _____

_____
_____
_____
_____
_____

GO SURFING ...

... http://faculty.washington.edu/chudler/rightl.html to determine how strong your hand preference is. Take one of the Handedness Questionnaires. How strong is your hand preference?

_____
_____

What is the relationship between handedness and hemispheric specialization? Go to http://faculty.washington.edu/chudler/split.html and then briefly explain here. _____

_____

_____

_____

_____

_____

Beneath the Cortex: The Inner Brain

For each **brain part** in the chart below, explain its function and then provide an example of when you use this brain part in your life.

Brain Part	Function	Example of Use
Thalamus		
Hypothalamus		
Hippocampus		
Amygdala		
Basal ganglia		
Brainstem		
Cerebellum		

The Neuroendocrine System: It's Hormonal

How is the **CNS** related to the **neuroendocrine system**? _____
_____
_____
_____

What are **hormones**? Define in your own words. _____
_____
_____

What role does the **pituitary gland** play in the neuroendocrine system? Explain. _____
_____
_____
_____
_____

What are the effects of the following **hormones**?

Hormone	Effects
Testosterone	
Estrogen	
Cortisol	

In addition to physical effects, hormones (testosterone and estrogen) may have psychological or behavioral effects. Can you think of any psychological or behavioral changes you experienced in adolescence that may have resulted from hormonal changes? _____
_____
_____
_____
_____

Looking at Levels

There is some research to suggest that riding roller coasters may sometimes cause brain damage. Explain the factors at each of the **three levels** of analysis that may be involved in causing such brain damage. Draw arrows to indicate how these factors may interact.

The Brain	The Person	The Group

TRY PRACTICE TEST #2 NOW!
GOOD LUCK!

Probing the Brain

The Damaged Brain: What's Missing?

What are **strokes** and **lesions**, and how do they help scientists understand the brain's functions?

_____
_____
_____
_____
_____
_____
_____

Recording Techniques: The Music of the Cells

The following two techniques record the activity of neurons. For each technique, explain how it works, and list its advantages.

	Description of Technique	Advantages
Electroencephalograph (EEG)		
Single-cell recording		

Neuroimaging: Picturing the Living Brain

How has **neuroimaging** transformed psychology? _____

_____

_____

_____

_____

Stimulation: Tickling the Neurons

In your own words, describe two types of **neural stimulation techniques**.

Technique	Description

GO SURFING...

... at http://www.pbs.org/wgbh/aso/tryit/brain/ to electronically recreate one of Wilder Penfield's studies. What does this activity tell you about how much of the **motor cortex** is devoted to different brain parts? Discuss. _____

_____
_____
_____
_____

Looking at Levels

Consider some ability or talent that you have (e.g., musical talent). List factors at the **three levels** (brain, person, group) that have influenced your ability. Draw arrows to indicate how these factors may interact.

The Brain	The Person	The Group

TRY PRACTICE TEST #3 NOW!
GOOD LUCK!

Genes, Brain, and Environment: The Brain in the World

Genes as Blueprints: Born to Be Wild?

What are the two key ideas of **Mendelian inheritance**?

♦ _____
  _____
  _____

♦ _____
  _____
  _____

Name and describe a characteristic for which you apparently received **recessive alleles** from both of your parents. _____
_____
_____

Name and describe a characteristic for which your **phenotype** demonstrates the **dominant allele** of one parent. _____
_____
_____

Why do some neural connections get **pruned**? _____
_____
_____
_____
_____

Do you think there might be any good results of **pruning**? If so, what would those be? _____
_____
_____
_____

Pruning is one aspect of the brain's **plasticity**, which is its ability to change with experience. Name and briefly describe the other ways that the brain changes with experience:

_____
_____
_____
_____
_____
_____

In what circumstances is **plasticity** most evident?

- ♦ _____
  _____

- ♦ _____
  _____

- ♦ _____
  _____

- ♦ _____
  _____

Give examples from your own life of **passive interaction**, **evocative interaction**, and **active interaction**.

Type of Interaction	Example
Passive	
Evocative	
Active	

Behavioral Genetics

What types of questions might a researcher in **behavioral genetics** ask?

- ♦ _____
  _____

- ♦ _____
  _____

- ♦ _____
  _____

In your own words, define **heritability**. _____

_____

_____

_____

_____

_____

Describe the following types of studies, which allow researchers to study the relative contributions of genes and environment to a particular trait.

♦   **Twin studies:** _____

_____

_____

_____

_____

♦   **Adoption studies:**_____

_____

_____

_____

_____

Evolution and the Brain: The Best of All Possible Brains?

Consider the giraffe, the elephant, and the human. What characteristics of each species may have evolved over time (been reproduced over and over again) because they ensured survival and helped the animals adapt to their environment?

Animal	Characteristic	Reason for Adaptation
Giraffe		
Elephant		
Human		

Looking at Levels

Some Mormons and Muslims *do* drink, and some become alcoholics. Considering the **levels of analysis**, what might lead an individual whose religious convictions do not allow drinking to drink anyway? Draw arrows to indicate how events at the different levels may interact to allow this.

The Brain	The Person	The Group

TRY PRACTICE TEST #4 NOW!
GOOD LUCK!

After You Read . . . Thinking Back

1. What must researchers do to ensure that their use of animals in research settings is ethical?

    _____
    _____
    _____
    _____
    _____
    _____
    _____
    _____

2. Of the different schools of psychology discussed in Chapter 1, which ones do you think rely the most on the brain research described in this chapter? Why? _____

    _____
    _____
    _____
    _____
    _____

3. Which schools do you think rely the least on this research? Why? _____

    _____
    _____
    _____
    _____

4. Explain how a neuropsychologist might use experimental, quasi-experimental, and correlational research designs.

    ◆   **Experimental:** _____

        _____
        _____
        _____

    ◆   **Quasi-experimental:** _____

        _____
        _____
        _____

    ◆   **Correlational:** _____

        _____
        _____
        _____

5.	What are some of the difficulties with using case studies to make conclusions about brain functioning? _____
_____
_____
_____

After You Read . . . Practice Tests

PRACTICE TEST #1:
BRAIN CIRCUITS

Fill-in-the-Blank Questions
Fill in each blank in the paragraph below with a word from the word bank.

WORD BANK	
excitatory	neurotransmitters
glial	reuptake
inhibitory	synapse
neuromodulators	

Communication between neurons takes place at the _____, the place where the axon of the sending neuron comes closest to the receiving neuron. Two types of chemicals are released from the terminal buttons into the synaptic cleft:_____, which are the chemical messengers, and _____, which are chemicals that alter the effects of the neurotransmitters. _____ cells may also influence chemical activity between neurons by producing a substance that either increases or decreases a neuron's sensitivity to input from other neurons. Chemicals that bind to the receptors of the receiving neuron can be _____, causing the receiving neuron to fire; or they can be _____, making the receiving neuron less likely to fire. After being released into the space between neurons, the chemicals are reabsorbed in a process called _____. (pp. 50-52)

Matching Questions

Match the following parts of the neuron with their functions.

_____	1.	Cell body (p. 47)	a.	The sending end of the neuron
_____	2.	Cell membrane (p. 47)	b.	The receiving end of the neuron
_____	3.	Channel (p. 48)	c.	Contains the nucleus
_____	4.	Axon (p. 47)	d.	Contains neurotransmitters or neuromodulators
_____	5.	Terminal button (p. 47)	e.	The skin of the neuron
_____	6.	Dendrite (p. 48)	f.	A small hole in the skin of a neuron

Multiple-Choice Questions

For each question, circle the letter of the best answer.

1. Most of the neurons in the brain are _____. (p. 46)
    a. sensory neurons
    b. motor neurons
    c. channel neurons
    d. interneurons

2. There are ten times as many _____ as there are neurons in the human brain. (p. 47)
    a. glial cells
    b. hormones
    c. blood cells
    d. leukocytes

3. The sending end of the neuron is the _____. (p. 47)
    a. axon
    b. dendrites
    c. cell body
    d. nucleus

4. The _____ of a neuron receive messages from the axons of other neurons. (p. 48)
    a. cell bodies
    b. dendrites
    c. axons
    d. glial cells

5.   During an action potential, _____ ions move into the neuron and _____ ions move out. (p. 48)
    a.   sodium; potassium
    b.   sodium; chloride
    c.   potassium; sodium
    d.   hydrogen; potassium

6.   Neurons obey the _____ law, meaning that if enough stimulation reaches the neuron, it fires. (p. 49)
    a.   excitatory potential
    b.   all-or-none
    c.   sodium-potassium exchange
    d.   dendritic expression

7.   Most axons are covered with _____, a fatty substance that helps impulses travel more quickly. (p. 49)
    a.   glial cells
    b.   sodium
    c.   myelin
    d.   potassium

8.   The gap between sending and receiving neurons is called the _____. (p. 50)
    a.   glial gap
    b.   myelin mile
    c.   synaptic cleft
    d.   brain bridge

9.   Neurotransmitters that make the receiving neuron more likely to fire an action potential are said to be _____ neurotransmitters. (p. 51)
    a.   excitatory
    b.   ignitatory
    c.   inhibitory
    d.   modulatory

10.   Drugs that mimic the effects of a neurotransmitter by activating a particular type of receptor are called _____. (p. 52)
    a.   antagonists
    b.   hormones
    c.   agonists
    d.   neuromodulators

PRACTICE TEST #2:
THE NERVOUS SYSTEM

Matching Questions

Match each of the terms with the appropriate description. Write the correct letter in the space at the left.

_____	1.	Gyri (p. 57)	a.	Creases in the cerebral cortex
_____	2.	Sulci (p. 57)	b.	Controls the smooth muscles and some glandular functions
_____	3.	Central nervous system (p. 54)	c.	Readies an animal to cope with emergencies
_____	4.	Peripheral nervous system (p. 55)	d.	Protective membranes that cover the brain
_____	5.	Autonomic nervous system (p. 55)	e.	Affects the organs one at a time to slow them down after an emergency passes
_____	6.	Skeletal system (p. 56)	f.	Bulges in the cerebral cortex
_____	7.	Sympathetic nervous system (p. 56)	g.	Where most of the brain's mental processes take place
_____	8.	Parasympathetic nervous system (p. 56)	h.	The system of nerves attached to voluntary muscles
_____	9.	Meninges (p. 56)	i.	The brain and spinal cord
_____	10.	Corpus callosum (p. 57)	j.	Links the central nervous system to the organs
_____	11.	Cerebral cortex (p. 57)	k.	Connects the two hemispheres of the brain

Matching Questions

Match the following brain structures with their functions. Write the correct letter in the space at the left.

_____ 1. Thalamus (p. 62)   a. Controls many bodily functions, including eating and drinking, maintaining temperature and blood pressure, and sexual behavior.

_____ 2. Hypothalamus (p. 62)   b. Important in the automatic control of breathing, swallowing, and blood circulation

_____ 3. Hippocampus (p. 62)   c. Involved in planning and producing movement, and in forming habits

_____ 4. Amygdala (p. 63)   d. Involved in coordinated motor movements

_____ 5. Basal ganglia (p. 64)   e. Relay station in the brain; also involved in attention and sleep control

_____ 6. Medulla (p. 64)   f. A bridge connecting the brainstem and cerebellum

_____ 7. Reticular formation (p. 64)   g. Plays a role in expressing and reading emotions such as fear and anger

_____ 8. Pons (p. 65)   h. Plays a key role in the storage of new memories

_____ 9. Cerebellum (p. 65)   i. Plays a key role in arousal and alertness

Matching Questions

Match the following terms with their descriptions. Write the correct letter in the space at the left.

_____ 1. Testosterone (p. 66)   a. Causes breasts to develop in women

_____ 2. Estrogen (p. 66)   b. The "master gland" of the endocrine system

_____ 3. Cortisol (p. 66)   c. Causes males to develop facial hair and build up muscle

_____ 4. Pituitary gland (p. 66)   d. Helps the body cope when under stress by breaking down protein and fat into sugar

Multiple-Choice Questions

For each question, circle the letter of the best answer.

1. Which of the following could you expect to experience when your sympathetic nervous system kicks in? (p. 56)
    a. Impaired vision
    b. Sweaty palms
    c. Decreased heart rate
    d. Decreased respiration

2. The central nervous system is composed of the _____. (p. 54)
    a. brain and spinal cord
    b. sympathetic and parasympathetic systems
    c. limbic and hippolimbic systems
    d. sensory and motor neurons

3. Reflexes are initiated by the _____. (p. 54)
    a. cerebral cortex
    b. spinal cord
    c. occipital lobe
    d. hypothalamus

4. When you clench your fist, you are using your _____system. (pp. 55-56)
    a. skeletal
    b. hypothalamic
    c. sympathetic nervous
    d. parasympathetic nervous

5.   The two major divisions of the autonomic nervous system are the _____. (p. 56)
      a.   brain and spinal cord
      b.   skeletal and muscular systems
      c.   sympathetic and parasympathetic systems
      d.   forebrain and midbrain

6.   The creases in the cerebral cortex are called _____. (p. 57)
      a.   sulci
      b.   collosi
      c.   gyri
      d.   ventricles

7.   Chemicals that are produced by glands and that can act as neuromodulators are called
      _____. (p. 65)
      a.   neurotransmitters
      b.   hormones
      c.   leukocytes
      d.   cerebral fluids

8.   The male hormone associated with puberty is _____, and the female
      hormone associated with puberty is _____. (p. 66)
      a.   testosterone; estrogen
      b.   cortisol; estrogen
      c.   estrogen; testosterone
      d.   testosterone; cortisol

9.   The "master gland" of the endocrine system is the _____ gland. (p. 65)
      a.   pineal
      b.   thalamus
      c.   thyroid
      d.   pituitary

10.   The "gray matter" is the _____. (p. 57)
      a.   gyri
      b.   cortex
      c.   ventricles
      d.   subcortical structures

PRACTICE TEST #3:
PROBING THE BRAIN

Fill-in-the-Blank Questions
Fill in the blanks with words from the word bank.

WORD BANK	
computer-assisted tomography (CT)	magnetic resonance imaging (MRI)
functional magnetic resonance	neuroimaging techniques
Imaging (fMRI)	positron emission tomography (PET)

Because they produce an actual picture of neuronal structure and function, brain-scanning

techniques are referred to as _____. _____ is the

oldest technique and involves taking a series of X-rays and building up a three-dimensional image,

slice by slice. _____ makes use of the magnetic properties of different

atoms, producing an even sharper image. When _____ is used, small amounts of

radiation are introduced into the blood, which is then taken up into different brain areas to show

how hard neurons are working. The most popular type of neuroimaging today is _____

_____, which reveals functioning by detecting oxygen usage in the brain. (pp. 69-71)

Multiple-Choice Questions
For each question, circle the letter of the best answer.

1.   The most frequent source of damage to the brain is a(n) _____. (p. 68)
    a.   aneurysm
    b.   stroke
    c.   lesion
    d.   EEG

2.   EEG stands for _____. (p. 68)
    a.   electroencephalograph
    b.   excitatory encephalogram
    c.   electric event graphing
    d.   entrance and exit graphing

3.   Which of the following provides a visual picture of brain structures? (p. 69)
      a.   MRI
      b.   MEG
      c.   EEG
      d.   TMS

4.   A lesion is a _____. (p. 68)
      a.   burst blood vessel
      b.   malignant tumor
      c.   region of impaired tissue
      d.   disruption of brain function

5.   Cathy suffers a stroke that causes her to lose her short-term memory. The doctors are eager
      to ascertain exactly where the damage occurred. They will most likely use
      _____. (p. 70)
      a.   single-cell recording
      b.   X-rays
      c.   MRI
      d.   fMRI

6.   Penfield and his colleagues delivered mild electricity to different parts of the brains of people
      about to undergo brain operations. From their findings, they concluded that people
      experience different images, memories, and feelings depending on the area in the brain that
      is stimulated. One problem with this technique is that _____.
      (p. 71)
      a.   it is dangerous to the patient
      b.   researchers can't be sure whether the memories are real or fabricated
      c.   different people have different kinds of memories
      d.   it is very expensive

7.   When doctors study structural damage to the brain, they _____.
      (p. 69)
      a.   examine which parts of the brain are responsible for body function
      b.   use single-cell recording
      c.   examine which areas of the brain are performing below par
      d.   examine which areas of the brain are affected by an injury

8.   When he was 8 months old, Christian was in a car accident. To assess his brain activity after
      the accident, Christian's doctors probably used _____. (p. 70)
      a.   transcranial magnetic stimulation
      b.   near infrared spectroscopy
      c.   a natural experiment
      d.   positron emission tomography

9. _____ show that certain neurons respond to some words but not to others. (pp. 68-69)

    a.   EEGs

    b.   PET scans

    c.   Single-cell recordings

    d.   fMRIs

10. MRIs provide information about _____, whereas fMRIs provide information about _____. (pp. 69-70)

    a.   the function of brain parts, the structure of the brain.

    b.   brain activity, the damage that has occurred to certain parts of the brain.

    c.   what specific neurons do, the function of brain parts.

    d.   brain structure, the brain at work.

PRACTICE TEST #4:
GENES, BRAIN, AND ENVIRONMENT

True/False Questions
Circle TRUE or FALSE for each of the following statements.

1. TRUE FALSE A gene is a stretch of DNA that produces a specific protein. (p. 73)

2. TRUE FALSE Many genes keep working throughout a person's life. (p. 75)

3. TRUE FALSE There were fewer connections in your brain at birth than you have now. (pp. 74-75)

4. TRUE FALSE Neural connections are destroyed but not formed as we experience the world. (p. 75)

5. TRUE FALSE Genes and the environment are two interlocking systems working together. (p. 76)

6. TRUE FALSE Genes can be "turned on" to produce proteins and other substances. (pp. 75-76)

Multiple-Choice Questions
For each question, circle the letter of the best answer.

1. Genes produce _____, which in turn form(s) the building blocks of our bodies. (p. 76)
    a. DNA
    b. fats
    c. proteins
    d. sugars

2. The process by which certain neural connections are eliminated is called _____. (p. 75)
    a. cutting
    b. pruning
    c. lesioning
    d. ablating

3. A protein that is produced at the "instruction" of genes is said to be _____. (p. 76)
    a. pruned
    b. expressed
    c. turned on
    d. stimulated

4. A famous pianist introduces her child to the piano at the age of 2, in an example of
    _____ interaction. (p. 76)
    a. passive
    b. active
    c. evocative
    d. reactive

5. Difficult babies tend to elicit punitive reactions from their caregivers. This is an example of
    a(n) _____ interaction. (p. 76)
    a. passive
    b. active
    c. evocative
    d. reactive

6. Saying that intelligence is 50% heritable means _____. (p. 78)
    a. you get 50% of your intelligence from your mom, and 50% from your dad
    b. you get 50% of your intelligence from your parents, and 50% from the
        environment
    c. in a specific environment, 50% of the variability in intelligence among people is
        due to genetics
    d. in a specific environment, 50% of people are intelligent and 50% are not

7. Which two people would have the most similar genes? (p. 78)
    a. A parent and child
    b. A pair of monozygotic twins
    c. Two siblings born at different times
    d. A pair of dizygotic twins

8. Plasticity refers to _____. (p. 75)
    a. the soft spots on an infant's head
    b. the fact that people are born with few neural connections
    c. the ability of the brain to change with experience
    d. the fluid-filled parts at the center of the brain

9. Suppose that snakes with better camouflage are less likely to be eaten by birds and therefore,
    are more likely to reproduce. In this example, better camouflage can be termed
    _____. (p. 79)
    a. an adaptation
    b. evolution
    c. natural selection
    d. an accident

10. A child's height is not necessarily the same as that of either of his/her parents. The most
    likely reason for this is _____. (p. 73)
    a. height is an example of a trait that is subject to complex inheritance
    b. height is an example of a trait that is subject to Mendelian inheritance
    c. the child may be adopted
    d. the child is malnourished

COMPREHENSIVE PRACTICE TEST

True/False Questions

Circle TRUE or FALSE for each of the following statements.

1.   TRUE   FALSE   A neuron can fire at different strengths. (p. 49)

2.   TRUE   FALSE   Antagonist drugs block particular receptors. (p. 52)

3.   TRUE   FALSE   The sympathetic and parasympathetic systems always work against one another. (p. 56)

4.   TRUE   FALSE   An EEG allows researchers to observe brain structure. (p. 68)

5.   TRUE   FALSE   Adult brains can create new neurons. (p. 75)

Multiple-Choice Questions

For each question, circle the letter for the best answer.

1.   Which of the following is NOT a type of neuron? (pp. 46-47)
      a.   Sensory neuron
      b.   Interneuron
      c.   Motor neuron
      d.   Glial neuron

2.   If enough stimulation reaches a neuron, it _____. (p. 48)
      a.   fires
      b.   becomes chemically neutral
      c.   stops firing
      d.   dies

3.   During an action potential, _____ is actively pushed out of the neuron. (p. 48)
      a.   potassium
      b.   chloride
      c.   sodium
      d.   bromine

4.   Multiple sclerosis causes _____ to deteriorate, resulting in impaired sensation, loss of vision, and paralysis. (p. 49)
      a.   interneurons
      b.   myelin
      c.   sensory neurons
      d.   glial cells

5.   The process by which a surplus of neurotransmitter is reabsorbed back into the sending neuron is called _____. (p. 52)
      a.   reuptake
      b.   reusage
      c.   reabsorption
      d.   removal

6.   The peripheral nervous system is composed of the _____. (p. 55)
      a.   brain and spinal cord
      b.   sympathetic and parasympathetic systems
      c.   skeletal and autonomic divisions
      d.   midbrain and the hindbrain

7.   When under stress, our _____ prepares us for "fight or flight." (p. 56)
      a.   spinal cord
      b.   skeletal system
      c.   reticular formation
      d.   sympathetic system

8.   The two halves of the brain are connected by the _____. (p. 57)
      a.   glial connection
      b.   corpus callosum
      c.   brain bridge
      d.   midbrain

9.   Damage to the _____ lobes causes partial or complete blindness. (p. 58)
      a.   occipital
      b.   parietal
      c.   temporal
      d.   frontal

10.   The somatosensory strip is found in the _____ lobes. (p. 58)
      a.   occipital
      b.   parietal
      c.   temporal
      d.   frontal

11.   The subcortical region of the brain that coordinates inputs from sensory and motor systems and plays a crucial role in attention is the _____. (p. 62)
      a.   cerebral cortex
      b.   thalamus
      c.   cerebellum
      d.   hypothalamus

12. Damage to the _____ would most likely result in difficulty in planning and producing movement. (p. 64)
   a. cerebral cortex
   b. thalamus
   c. basal ganglia
   d. hippocampus

13. Farah signed up for a sleep study, and the neurologist attached wires to her head. Most likely, the neurologist plans to make a _____ of the electrical activity in Farah's brain as she descends through the sleep stages. (p. 69)
   a. transcranial recording
   b. magnetic resonance image
   c. electroencephalogram
   d. neuroimage

14. A gene is a stretch of DNA that produces a specific _____. (p. 73)
   a. fatty acid
   b. neuromodulator
   c. neurotransmitter
   d. protein

15. The theory of _____ asserts that more genes arise in a population if those genes allow an organism to have more offspring. (p. 79)
   a. genetic selection
   b. Darwinism
   c. natural selection
   d. adaptation

Essay Questions
Answer each of the questions in the space provided.

1. Explain the passage of the electrical signal along the axon. _____
   _____
   _____
   _____
   _____
   _____
   _____
   _____

2. Explain how the sympathetic and parasympathetic nervous systems are effective in an immediate emergency, but less effective in situations of chronic stress. _____

_____
_____
_____
_____
_____
_____
_____
_____
_____

3. If a picture of a fork were flashed to the left visual field of a person whose corpus callosum had been split, what would he see? What would be the best way for him to "tell" you what he was seeing? Explain your answer. _____

_____
_____
_____
_____
_____
_____
_____

4. Why is it misleading to attribute any differences in intelligence among groups of people to genetics? _____

_____
_____
_____
_____
_____

5. Discuss the functions of myelin. _____

_____
_____
_____
_____

6. Suppose you had to give up one part of your brain. Which part would you give up, and why? Which part(s) could you definitely not live without? _____

_____
_____
_____
_____
_____

7. Animal models allow researchers to study the effects of brain lesions on behavior. Discuss the ethical dilemmas involved in such research. Do the pros outweigh the cons?

    _____
    _____
    _____
    _____
    _____
    _____
    _____
    _____

8. What is plasticity? Why is it important? What can people do, if anything, to improve plasticity? _____

    _____
    _____
    _____
    _____
    _____
    _____
    _____
    _____

9. Researchers have mapped out the entire genetic code for humans. We could one day know whether we carry the gene for a particular illness, whether we will eventually develop an illness that could kill us, and whether we could possibly pass a gene onto a child   who would then be at risk for the illness. Do we want this much information? Why or why not? How might the information be abused and by whom? _____

    _____
    _____
    _____
    _____
    _____
    _____
    _____

10. What are passive, evocative, and active interactions between genes and the environment? Give an example of each from your own life. _____

    _____
    _____
    _____
    _____
    _____
    _____
    _____
    _____

When You Are Finished . . . Puzzle It Out

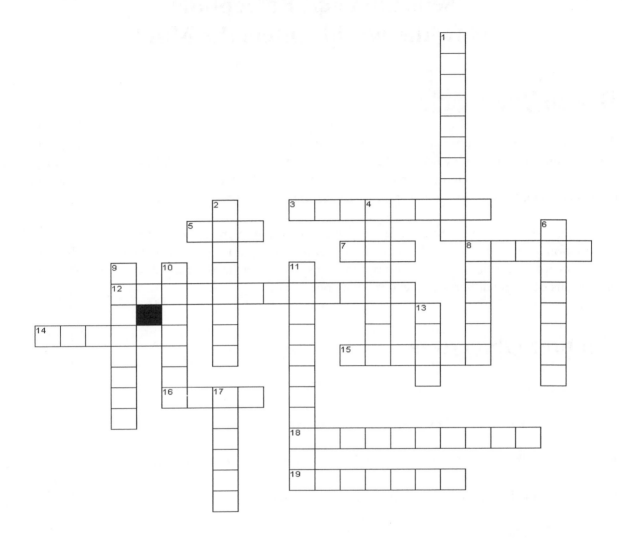

Across

3. Involved in emotions like anger
5. Technique measuring blood flow in brain
7. Includes the spinal cord and brain
8. Four parts of each hemisphere
12. Amount of variability due to genetics
14. Helps impulses travel faster down an axon
15. Basic unit of the nervous system
16. Bulges in the cortex
18. Molding of brain by experience
19. Place where two neurons meet

Down

1. Fill gaps between neurons
2. Charge of resting potential
4. Individual's genetic code
6. From the Greek word for "tree"
8. Region of impaired tissue
9. Often thought of as a switching center
10. Elimination of neural connections
11. Critical to making new memories
13. Blocks reuptake of serotonin
17. Automatic response to an event

Puzzle created with Puzzlemaker at DiscoverySchool.com.

Chapter 3
Sensation and Perception:
How the World Enters the Mind

Before You Read . . .

Why is your significant other always able to spot the deer at the side of the road when you don't? Why does food taste funny when you have a cold? In this chapter, you will learn how you come to understand the world around you through your senses. Understanding the world depends not only upon sensation, but also upon perception, or your brain's interpretation of the incoming stimuli.

The chapter starts with in-depth coverage of two senses: vision and hearing. Less detailed information is presented about the other senses: smell, taste, and the somasthetic senses (those that have to do with sensing your body and position in space). Finally, the chapter concludes with discussions of magnetic sense and extrasensory perception.

Chapter Objectives

After reading this chapter, you should be able to:

♦   Define sensation and explain how it differs from perception.

♦   Explain how people see, including the sensations of color, shape, and motion.

♦   Describe how people make sense of what they see.

♦   Define attention.

♦   Explain how ears normally register sound.

♦   Describe how the sense of smell works.

♦   Describe how the sense of taste works.

♦   Explain how we sense our bodies.

♦   Understand the evidence for the existence of magnetic sense and extrasensory perception (ESP).

As You Read . . . Term Identification

Make flashcards using the following terms as you go. Use the definitions in the margins of this chapter for help. If you write the definitions in your own words, though, you will remember them better!

Absolute threshold
Accommodation
Afterimage
Amplitude
Attention
Attentional blink
Bias
Binocular cues
Bottom-up processing
Categorical perception
Chemical senses
Cocktail party phenomenon
Color blindness
Color constancy
Conduction deafness
Cones
Cornea
Dark adaptation
Dichotic listening
Double pain
Endorphins
Extrasensory perception (ESP)
Figure
Fovea
Frequency
Frequency theory
Gate control
Gestalt laws of organization
Ground
Hair cells
Iris
Just-noticeable difference (JND)
Kinesthetic sense
Loudness
Monocular static cues
Motion cues

Nerve deafness
Opponent cells
Opponent process theory of color vision
Optic nerve
Paradoxical cold
Perception
Perceptual constancy
Perceptual set
Pheromones
Pitch
Place theory
Pop-out
Psychophysics
Pupil
Repetition blindness
Retina
Retinal disparity
Rods
Selective attention
Sensation
Sensitivity
Shape constancy
Signal detection theory
Size constancy
Somasthetic senses
Speech segmentation problem
Taste buds
Texture gradients
Threshold
Top-down processing
Transduction
Trichromatic theory of color vision
Vestibular sense
Wavelength
Weber's law

As You Read . . . Questions and Exercises

Vision

Name and describe the two phases of **visual perception**.

♦ _____
_____
_____
_____
_____

♦ _____
_____
_____
_____
_____

Visual Sensation: More Than Meets the Eye

Define each of the following terms, and give an example of how it could be important in your life.

Term	Definition	Personal Example
Threshold		
Absolute threshold		
Just-noticeable difference (JND)		

What is the goal of **signal detection theory**? _____
_____
_____

There are two key concepts that explain why **signals** are detected or missed. Define each of these concepts. Then, explain how these concepts could be used in ensuring that airport security personnel detect any dangerous materials during screening procedures.

Concept	Definition	Impact in Airport Security Screening
Sensitivity		
Bias		

What is **light**? _____

_____

Define the following terms:

♦ **Amplitude:** _____

_____

_____

♦ **Frequency:** _____

_____

_____

♦ **Wavelength:** _____

_____

_____

Name the color of light with the **lowest frequency** and **longest wavelength**: _____

Name the color of light with the **highest frequency** and **shortest wavelength**: _____

GO SURFING ...

... at http://kidshealth.org/misc_pages/bodyworks/eye.html to see how the eye works. Then, explain the steps involved in **transduction**, or the conversion of electromagnetic energy into nerve impulses by describing what each part of the eye does.

♦   The **iris** _____ .

♦   The **pupil** _____ .

♦   The **cornea** _____ .

♦   The **lens** _____ .

♦   The **retina** _____ .

♦   The **fovea** _____ .

Why does everything look gray at night? _____

_____

_____

_____

_____

_____

GO SURFING ...

... at http://faculty.washington.edu/chudler/chvision.html, and do the experiments on finding your **blind spot**. Why do you have a **blind spot**? _____

_____

_____

_____

_____

_____

What allows the process of **dark adaptation** to occur?

♦ _____
_____
_____

♦ _____
_____
_____

What are the **three types of cells** that assist in transforming light into neural impulses? Explain what each type of cell does.

♦ _____
_____
_____

♦ _____
_____
_____

♦ _____
_____
_____

Name and briefly describe the three ways that **colors** can vary.

♦ _____
_____
_____

♦ _____
_____
_____

♦ _____
_____
_____

Recent research has supported the **trichromatic theory of color vision** with some modifications. Fill in the blanks in the following paragraph.

This theory says that we can see different hues because we have three different types of cones. Each type is *most* sensitive to a different range of wavelengths. So, one type is most sensitive to light seen as _____ and another to light seen as _____ and yet another to light seen as _____.

For each color, there are at least two different types of cones that are sensitive to it, although one type of cone will be *more* sensitive. The brain registers the mixture of the different responses of the three types of cones. However, some materials, such as paint, absorb some light. As a result, not all light is reflected. Only the wavelengths that are

_____, not absorbed, reach our eyes. But there is more to seeing color than this theory can explain. The **opponent process theory of color vision** provides another factor. This theory says that the presence of one color of a pair inhibits the perception of the other color. The opponent pairs are red/_____,

yellow/_____, and black/_____.

Why might one person call a **color** "green" and another person call the color "blue-green"? _____

_____

_____

_____

_____

GO SURFING ...

... at http://faculty.washington.edu/chudler/chvision.html. Scroll down to the section on visual illusions and do the activities on **afterimages**. Why can't we see the blue and yellow separately when a mixture of light of those colors enters our eyes? _____

_____

_____

_____

_____

GO SURFING ...

... at http://colorlab.wickline.org/colorblind/colorlab/, and see what colors would look like if you had different forms of color blindness.

Do you know anyone who has **color blindness**? If so, what form does it take? _____
_____
_____

Who is most likely to have **color blindness**? _____

What causes **color blindness**?

♦ _____

♦ _____

What implications would it have in your life if you were **color-blind**? (For example, the author of this study guide once had a karate instructor who was color-blind and could not identify the different colored belts of his students!) _____
_____
_____
_____
_____
_____

First Steps of Visual Perception: Organizing the World

In Operation Iraqi Freedom, how might the United States armed forces take advantage of research on separating **figure** from **ground**? _____
_____
_____

Why do you see your desk as a desk, even though it is likely covered by papers and other objects?
_____
_____
_____
_____

How does learning affect your **perception**? _____
_____
_____
_____
_____
_____
_____

Perceptual constancy is the perception of the characteristics of objects as the same even though the sensory information striking the eyes changes. Give a personal example of each of the following types of constancy.

Type of Constancy	Example
Size constancy	
Shape constancy	
Color constancy	

To perceive the world as three-dimensional, the brain uses different types of cues. Briefly describe, and provide an example of each of the following types of **cues**.

Type of Cue	Description	Example
Binocular cues	Cues that come from both eyes working together.	
Retinal disparity		
Monocular cues	Cues that come from only one eye.	
Texture gradient		
Linear perspective (foreshortening)		
Occlusion cue		
Motion cues		
Motion parallax		

GO SURFING ...

... at http://psych.hanover.edu/Krantz/SizeConstancy/index.html to see more about size constancy. Be sure to play with the interactive figure. What are the three cues that you use to determine if the size of an object is constant? Name and briefly describe.

♦ _____

♦ _____

♦ _____

What are two of the **cues** that help you to perceive whether an object is coming closer to you?

♦ _____

♦ _____

GO SURFING ...

... at http://faculty.washington.edu/chudler/chvision.html. Scroll down and take a look at the visual illusions there. Some other good sites for viewing illusions are:
♦ www.sandlotscience.com
♦ http://www.optillusions.com/

Which **illusions** are your favorites? Describe a few and explain how they work.

Illusion (Name and Draw)	Explanation

Visual Perception: Recognition and Identification

There are two major neural pathways in the brain:

♦   **The "what" pathway,** which _____
_____
_____

♦   **The "where pathway,** which _____
_____
_____

What is involved in the final stages of **perceptual processing**? _____
_____
_____
_____
_____
_____
_____

Give the definition and an example of each of the following.

Type of Processing	Description	Example
Bottom-up processing		
Top-down processing		

How do **bottom-up** and **top-down processing** interact? _____
_____
_____
_____
_____
_____
_____

What are **perceptual expectancies**, and where do they come from?_____
_____
_____
_____
_____
_____
_____

Kosslyn proposes that the brain uses two different ways to **code space**. Describe each of these two ways, and identify the hemisphere primarily responsible.

Method of Coding Space	Description	Hemisphere
Categorical spatial relations		
Coordinate spatial relations		

There are two reasons why people **pay attention** to something. How does each work?

Reason for Attention	How It Works
Pop-out	
Voluntary (vigilance)	

Name a factor at each of the **levels of analysis** that helps to explain **attention**.

♦   **Level of the brain:** _____
_____
_____

♦   **Level of the person:** _____
_____
_____

♦   **Level of the group:**_____
_____
_____

How is it possible for some **blind people to see**? _____
_____
_____
_____
_____

Define each phenomenon and give an example of how it may affect an editor's job.

Phenomenon	Definition	Effect on Editor
Repetition blindness		
Attentional blink		

Looking at Levels

What body parts do you find most attractive in others? Analyze your **preferences** at each of the **three levels**. Draw arrows to indicate how factors at the different levels may interact.

The Brain	The Person	The Group

TRY PRACTICE TEST #1 NOW!
GOOD LUCK!

Hearing

Auditory Sensation: If a Tree Falls, but Nobody Hears It, Is There a Sound?

Why do some people's ears emit **sounds**, some so loud that others can hear them?

_____
_____
_____
_____

Why can't we **hear** anything in outer space? _____
_____
_____
_____

Name and describe the two phases of **auditory processing**.

♦   _____
      _____
      _____
      _____
      _____

♦   _____
      _____
      _____
      _____
      _____

If a tree falls in the forest but nobody hears it, is there a sound? Explain your answer. _____
_____
_____
_____

GO SURFING ...

... at http://kidshealth.org/misc_pages/bodyworks/ear.html to see how the ear works. Then, describe the steps involved in **auditory processing.**

♦   **Waves** _____ .

♦   The **eardrum**_____ .

♦   The **three bones in the middle ear (hammer, anvil, and stirrup)** _____
_____ .

♦   The **basilar membrane**_____ .

♦   **Hair cells sticking up from the basilar membrane** _____
_____ .

There are two main theories about the way the **basilar membrane** converts pressure waves to sound: **frequency theory** and **place theory.** Which of these theories appears to be correct? Explain the theory. _____
_____
_____
_____
_____

First Steps of Auditory Perception: Organizing the Auditory World

The first column of this chart lists some of the ways that **vision** and **hearing** are similar. In the other two columns, explain how each idea relates specifically to vision and hearing.

Similarity	... As Applied to Vision	... As Applied to Hearing
Reliance on Gestalt laws		
Use of categorical perception		
Use of two sensory organs (e.g., two eyes or two ears)		
Use of many different cues		

How important is **awareness** to the **processing of sound**? _____

_____

_____

_____

_____

_____

Auditory Perception: Recognition and Identification

What is the **cocktail party phenomenon**? _____

_____

_____

Can people learn when they aren't paying attention? Why or why not? _____

_____

_____

Looking at Levels

Explain how, at the **levels of the brain, the person, and the group**, Beethoven was able to become one of the greatest composers, despite the fact that he was deaf. Draw arrows to indicate how events at the different levels may have interacted.

The Brain	The Person	The Group

TRY PRACTICE TEST #2 NOW!
GOOD LUCK!

Sensing and Perceiving in Other Ways

Smell: A Nose for News?

What are the two **chemical senses**? _____

Why are they called that? _____
_____
_____

What are some characteristics of people who are particularly good at **identifying smells**?

◆ _____

◆ _____

Explain the steps involved in **olfaction**:

◆ **Molecules** _____.

◆ **Receptors** _____.

What are the two major neural tracks by which odor signals can travel into the brain:

♦ _____

♦ _____

Female **pheromones** can attract men. In one study, women who wore perfume mixed with a female pheromone reported:

♦ _____

♦ _____

♦ _____

♦ _____

Would you ever wear a **pheromone**? Why or why not? _____
_____
_____
_____
_____

Taste: The Mouth Has It

Where can **taste buds** be found? _____
_____

What is the relationship between **smell** and **taste**? _____
_____
_____

Somasthetic Senses: Not Just Skin Deep

Briefly describe each of the **somasthetic senses** in the chart below. Identify the receptors for each sense.

Sense	Description/Definition	Sense Receptors
Kinesthetic sense		
Vestibular sense		
Touch		
Temperature		

What are the two different kinds of **pain**?

◆ _____

◆ _____

Explain the role of **bottom-up** and **top-down processing** in the perception of **pain**.

Bottom-Up Processing	Top-Down Processing

Research indicates that people differ widely in the amount of pain that they can withstand. Do you think that you have a **low** or **high pain threshold**? _____

_____
_____
_____
_____

Other Senses

What impact would it have on the medical field if it were discovered that humans respond to **magnetic fields** as strongly as do birds? _____

_____

_____

_____

Briefly describe each of the following forms of **extrasensory perception (ESP)**.

Form	Description
Telepathy	
Clairvoyance	
Precognition	
Psychokinesis (PK)	

What are the three reasons why most psychologists are **skeptical** about **ESP**?

♦ _____

♦ _____

♦ _____

Looking at Levels

Given that some cultures hold less rigid standards about body odor, would you expect the effects of **pheromones** to be stronger in those cultures? Explain why or why not, at the **levels of the brain, the person, and the group**. Draw arrows to indicate how events at the different levels may interact.

The Brain	The Person	The Group

TRY PRACTICE TEST #3 NOW!
GOOD LUCK!

After You Read . . . Thinking Back

1. What is the relationship between the **sense organs** and **neural impulses in the brain**?

    _____

    _____

    _____

    _____

    _____

    _____

2. In Chapter 1, you learned about **evolutionary psychology**. Give some examples of how evolutionary psychologists might explain aspects of sensation and perception. (For example, what would an evolutionary psychologist say is the purpose of pain?)

    ◆   _____

        _____

        _____

    ◆   _____

        _____

        _____

        _____

    ◆   _____

        _____

        _____

        _____

    ◆   _____

        _____

        _____

3. In Chapter 1, you learned about the importance of **replication** to scientific research. Why is the ability to replicate studies on ESP so important? Why does the failure to replicate studies make psychologists so skeptical about ESP? _____

    _____

    _____

    _____

    _____

    _____

    _____

4.   Despite the differences between the **sense organs**, there are many similarities in how different kinds of sensory information is processed in the **brain**. Give some examples.

◆   _____
_____
_____

◆   _____
_____
_____

◆   _____
_____
_____

After You Read . . . Practice Tests

PRACTICE TEST #1:
VISION

Matching Questions

For each figure, indicate which Gestalt law of organization is at work. Write the correct letter in the space at the left. (p. 98)

_____	1. **XX XX XX XX**	a. Proximity
		b. Continuity
_____	2. **XXXXxxxx**	c. Similarity
		d. Closure
_____	3.	

_____   4.   _ _ _ _ _ _ _ _ _ _ _

Multiple-Choice Questions

For each question, circle the letter of the best answer.

1. The willingness to report noticing a stimulus is called _____. (p. 90)
    a. sensitivity
    b. reactivity
    c. bias
    d. vigilance

2. Weber's law states that _____. (p. 90)
    a. a neuron must only be stimulated slightly to fire
    b. to notice a stimulus, one must attend to the event
    c. individual differences determine which signals are perceived and which are not
    d. a constant percentage of a magnitude change is necessary to detect a difference

3.   Red light has a _____ frequency and a _____ wavelength. (p. 91)
      a.   high; short
      b.   low; short
      c.   high; long
      d.   low; long

4.   The conversion of electromagnetic energy (light) into nerve impulses is called
      _____. (p. 91)
      a.   accommodation
      b.   transduction
      c.   opponent processing
      d.   trichromation

5.   There are three types of cones in the eye, which correspond to three wavelengths of light.
      Which of the following is a wavelength for which there is NOT a unique type of cone?
      (p. 95)
      a.   Yellow
      b.   Green
      c.   Violet
      d.   Blue

6.   An object is camouflaged when _____ and _____ are similar.
      (p. 97)
      a.   hue; saturation
      b.   saturation; intensity
      c.   brightness; hue
      d.   figure; ground

7.   Which of the following is NOT an effect that helps to make the world seem stable, despite
      changes in the images striking the retina? (p. 99)
      a.   Size constancy
      b.   Color constancy
      c.   Figure constancy
      d.   Shape constancy

8.   A stroke that affects the bottom parts of the temporal lobes impairs a person's ability to
      _____. (p. 102)
      a.   perceive depth
      b.   see colors
      c.   recognize objects by sight
      d.   register locations

9.   The words in bold in the text of your book stand out because of _____. (p. 105)
      a.   bias
      b.   selectivity
      c.   vigilance
      d.   pop-out

10. Greg walked out of the room for a few minutes during the World Series. When he came back, he was able to immediately understand what had been going on, based on his extensive knowledge of baseball. This is an example of _____. (p. 103)
    a.   bottom-up processing
    b.   top-down processing
    c.   perceptual set
    d.   selective attention

PRACTICE TEST #2:
HEARING

Multiple-Choice Questions

For each question, circle the letter of the best answer.

1.   We are most sensitive to the frequencies of _____. (p. 110)
    a.   music
    b.   a baby's cry
    c.   speech
    d.   a dog's bark

2.   If you emit a humming sound from your ears, it probably _____. (p. 109)
    a.   acts like sonar to help you locate the objects around you
    b.   impairs your hearing
    c.   is feedback from the brain to the ear
    d.   is your ear sending signals to your brain

3.   According to place theory, _____. (p. 111)
    a.   the higher the frequency, the more numerous the neural firings
    b.   different frequencies activate different places on the basilar membrane
    c.   different sounds will activate different parts of the eardrum
    d.   the direction of the sound will indicate how well it is heard

4.   Rods and cones in vision are analogous to _____ in auditory processing. (p. 111)
    a.   the eardrum
    b.   the hammer, anvil, and stirrup
    c.   the auditory canal
    d.   hair cells on the basilar membrane

5.   Which of the following is the pathway that a sound sensation takes in the ear? (p. 110-111)
    a.   cochlea → basilar membrane → eardrum → bones in the middle ear
    b.   eardrum → bones in the middle ear → basilar membrane → auditory nerve
    c.   eardrum → basilar membrane → bones in the middle ear → auditory nerve
    d.   bones in the middle ear → eardrum → cochlea → auditory nerve

6.   The theory that best explains how we hear sounds at a high frequency is the _____ theory. (p. 110)
    a.   place
    b.   opponent-processing
    c.   frequency
    d.   tonotopic

7.   Nerve deafness occurs when the _____ is/are damaged. (p. 112)
        a.   bones in the middle ear
        b.   eardrum
        c.   hair cells
        d.   auditory nerve

8.   The process by which we distinguish the sounds we want to hear (figure) from background
        noise (ground) is called _____. (p. 112)
        a.   tonotopic processing
        b.   opponent-processing analysis
        c.   frequency processing
        d.   auditory scene analysis

9.   In auditory perception, Gestalt laws explain how _____. (p. 112)
        a.   you determine where the beginnings and endings of words are
        b.   you know what to pay attention to
        c.   sounds "pop out" at you
        d.   people locate sounds

10.   To distinguish figure from ground in auditory processing, you _____.
        (p. 112)
        a.   conduct an auditory scene analysis
        b.   pay close attention
        c.   use cues from both of your ears
        d.   rely on tonotopic organization of auditory information

11.   Having two ears _____. (p. 113)
        a.   allows us to categorize perception better
        b.   helps us to assess the distance of a sound source
        c.   helps us to identify a sound more easily
        d.   balances our heads

12.   Because we have two ears, there are important differences in the sound stimuli that reach
        the ears including _____. (p. 113)
        a.   the difference in the phase of the sound waves
        b.   the difference in loudness of the sound
        c.   the difference in when sound waves reach each ear
        d.   all of the above

13.   Suppose that you are at a party, talking to a friend, when all of a sudden you hear someone
        several feet away say your name. This is an example of _____. (p. 114)
        a.   Gestalt laws of processing
        b.   absolute pitch
        c.   plasticity
        d.   the cocktail party phenomenon

14. Studies of dichotic listening indicate that _____. (p. 114)
    a.   attention is required for hearing
    b.   people hear with a single ear at a time
    c.   people "fill in" sounds that they didn't hear
    d.   even when not paying attention, people register some information from an unattended ear

15. If you are in the middle of a telephone conversation and your partner's speech is disrupted by the dog barking, you will _____. (p. 113)
    a.   probably still understand what your partner said, because of the phonemic restoration effect
    b.   have to ask your partner to repeat the disrupted words
    c.   probably still understand what your partner said, because you have two ears
    d.   not understand your partner at all because attention is required for hearing

PRACTICE TEST #3:
SENSING AND PERCEIVING IN OTHER WAYS

True/False Questions
Circle TRUE or FALSE for each of the following statements.

1.   TRUE   FALSE   Once burned and lost, taste buds never regenerate. (p. 118)

2.   TRUE   FALSE   Sensitivity to taste diminishes as we age. (p. 118)

3.   TRUE   FALSE   Taste buds are found on the tongue, in the throat, and inside the cheeks. (pp. 117-118)

4.   TRUE   FALSE   There are five types of taste buds: sweet, sour, salty, bitter, and spicy. (p. 118)

5.   TRUE   FALSE   Bitter tastes are best detected in the front of your mouth. (p. 118)

6.   TRUE   FALSE   All kinds of taste buds can be found in most locations on the tongue. (p. 118)

7.   TRUE   FALSE   One type of cell that senses balance information can be found in the inner ear. (p. 119)

8.   TRUE   FALSE   The more cortex devoted to a particular area of the skin, the more sensitive to touch that area is. (p. 119)

9.   TRUE   FALSE   The mix-and-match principle means that we can feel more types of sensations than we have receptors for. (p. 119)

10.   TRUE   FALSE   Magnetic fields can disrupt spatial learning in mice. (p. 121)

Matching Questions

Match the following types of extrasensory perception with their definitions. (p. 121)

_____1.   Telepathy   a.   The ability to move objects without touching them

_____2.   Clairvoyance   b.   The ability to foretell future events

_____3.   Precognition   c.   The ability to send and transmit thoughts mind-to-mind

_____4.   Psychokinesis   d.   The ability to know about events directly, without using the ordinary sense or reading someone's mind

Multiple-Choice Questions

For each question, circle the letter of the best answer.

1.   Who is likely to be best at distinguishing among different smells? (p. 116)
    a.   An elderly person
    b.   A man
    c.   A 20-year-old, female college student
    d.   A 5-year-old girl

2.   Pheromones are similar to hormones in that they _____. (p. 117)
    a.   modulate the functions of various organs
    b.   are released inside the body
    c.   are released by the pituary gland
    d.   are sensed by the nose

3.   In one study, participants who wore pheromones reported _____. (p. 117)
    a.   having more sex
    b.   feeling sexier
    c.   having more informal dates
    d.   engaging in masturbation more often

4.   The reason that smells can evoke strong emotions is that _____. (p. 116)
    a.   one neural track sends signals about odors to the thalamus.
    b.   one neural track sends signals about odors to the limbic system.
    c.   both a and b
    d.   neither a nor b

5.   Free nerve endings in the mouth are irritated by _____. (p. 118)
    a.   salty food
    b.   bitter food
    c.   spicy food
    d.   sweet food

6.   Being able to clap your hands together without looking at them is made possible by the
        _____ sense. (p. 118)
        a.   magnetic
        b.   kinesthetic
        c.   vestibular
        d.   limbic

7.   Damage to the _____ can cause disruption in a person's vestibular sense. (p. 119)
        a.   inner ear
        b.   occipital lobe
        c.   somasthetic nerve
        d.   thalamus

8.   The role of top-down processing in the perception of pain is shown in _____.
        (p. 120)
        a.   acupuncture
        b.   the placebo effect
        c.   double pain
        d.   paradoxical cold

9.   The gate control mechanism may explain _____. (p. 120)
        a.   why some people are more sensitive to pain than others
        b.   how hypnosis can control pain
        c.   why the menstrual cycle can influence pain perception
        d.   how the vestibular sense works

10.   Which of the following is one reason why most psychologists are skeptical about ESP?
        (p. 121)
        a.   Studies that have been found to support ESP are difficult to replicate.
        b.   The brain mechanisms underlying ESP are unknown.
        c.   It is unknown what form ESP signals might take.
        d.   All of the above

COMPREHENSIVE PRACTICE TEST

True/False Questions

Circle TRUE or FALSE for each of the following statements.

1.   TRUE   FALSE   Top-down processing is guided by knowledge, expectations, or beliefs. (p. 103)

2.   TRUE   FALSE   It is only late in visual processing that what we see becomes meaningful. (p. 102)

3.   TRUE   FALSE   Rods are extraordinarily sensitive to light and color. (p. 92)

4.   TRUE   FALSE   Most color blindness is present from birth. (p. 96)

5.   TRUE   FALSE   Binocular cues arise from the eyes working separately. (p. 99)

6.   TRUE   FALSE   Repetition blindness results when the visual system is "locked up" for a brief period of time. (p. 106)

7.   TRUE   FALSE   If a tree falls in the forest and nobody hears it, no sound is produced. (p. 110)

8.   TRUE   FALSE   Distinct spots on the skin register hot or cold stimuli. (p. 119)

9.   TRUE   FALSE   Most adults are not very good at identifying odors. (p. 116)

10.   TRUE   FALSE   Endorphins cause people to be more sensitive to pain. (p. 120)

Identification

Identify the following experiences as involving mainly bottom-up or top-down processing. (p. 103)

Experience	Bottom-up or Top-down?
Unexpectedly seeing a friend walking down the street.	
"Hearing" strange noises in the night when you're alone in the house but nothing is there.	
Tasting something new for the first time.	
Thinking you recognize a friend you are expecting in a passing group of strangers.	

Multiple-Choice Questions

For each question, circle the letter of the best answer.

1. While watching television, sometimes Jeffrey hears his mother calling his name and sometimes he doesn't. _____ seeks to explain why. (p. 90)
   a. Signal detection theory
   b. JND theory
   c. Weber's law
   d. Absolute threshold theory

2. It would take you longer to identify a seahorse pictured in a barn setting than one pictured in an ocean setting. This is an example of _____. (p. 104)
   a. a Gestalt law
   b. perceptual set
   c. selective attention
   d. pop-out

3. The study of the relation between physical events and the corresponding experience of those events is called _____. (p. 89)
   a. psychophysics
   b. psychosensation
   c. astrophysics
   d. psychoperception

4. Jamal is lifting a 10-lb weight; Joel is lifting a 5-lb weight. If it takes an additional 2 pounds to make Jamal's weight feel heavier, then it will only take an additional 1 pound to make Joel's weight feel heavier. The theory that best explains this is _____. (p. 90)
   a. Gestalt's law of grouping
   b. the opponent process theory
   c. sensory adaptation
   d. Weber's law

5. Gestalt laws of organization describe _____. (p. 97)
   a. what people pay attention to and what they don't
   b. how the brain organizes input from the sense organs
   c. how people mix colors
   d. why odors evoke strong memories

6.   An advertiser creates a billboard, with a neon-colored product shown against a black-and-white background. The advertiser is using _____ to draw the audience's attention. (p. 105)
        a.   selectivity
        b.   bias
        c.   pop-out
        d.   Weber's law

7.   The automatic adjustment of the eye in order to see things at different distances is called _____. (p. 91)
        a.   accommodation
        b.   transduction
        c.   induction
        d.   adaption

8.   Which of the following pairs of color is NOT an opponent pair? (p. 95)
        a.   Red/green
        b.   Black/white
        c.   Yellow/blue
        d.   Orange/brown

9.   Most color-blind people are unable to distinguish _____. (p. 96)
        a.   red from green
        b.   red from yellow
        c.   yellow from blue
        d.   any colors

10.   One of the neural tracks that leaves the olfactory bulb passes through the _____, which is particularly involved in memory. (p. 116)
        a.   hypothalamus
        b.   hindbrain
        c.   thalamus
        d.   forebrain

11.   The ability to foretell future events is called _____. (p. 121)
        a.   telepathy
        b.   precognition
        c.   clairvoyance
        d.   psychokinesis

12.   The immediate experience of the basic properties of an object or event that occurs when a receptor is stimulated is called _____. (p. 88)
        a.   sensation
        b.   processing
        c.   perception
        d.   accommodation

13. Perception is the process by which _____. (p. 88)
   a.   stimuli are detected
   b.   stimuli are transformed into neural activity
   c.   stimuli are organized and interpreted
   d.   nerve cells fire in an organized fashion

14. Matthew couldn't hear many of the tones presented during a hearing test because they were below his _____. (p. 89)
   a.   absolute threshold
   b.   difference threshold
   c.   subliminal threshold
   d.   amplitude threshold

15. An airline pilot must have great auditory _____ in order to say when she detects an odd noise over the sound of the jet engines. (p. 90)
   a.   bias
   b.   sensitivity
   c.   accommodation
   d.   opponent-processing

Essay Questions

Answer each of the following questions in the space provided.

1. What are the two stages of processing sensory input from the outside world? _____

   _____
   _____
   _____
   _____
   _____
   _____
   _____
   _____
   _____

2. Explain how bottom-up and top-down processing would help you to understand a language you never heard before. _____

   _____
   _____
   _____
   _____
   _____
   _____
   _____
   _____

3. Explain why most people cannot confuse green and red or blue and yellow. _____

    _____
    _____
    _____
    _____
    _____
    _____
    _____

4. Explain how repetition blindness and attentional blink can affect the proofreading of your own papers. How can you overcome them? _____

    _____
    _____
    _____
    _____
    _____
    _____
    _____

5. If you could choose one sense to enhance, which would it be? If you had to sacrifice one sense, which would you choose? Which sense do you think will be the most important to you in your future career? Why? _____

    _____
    _____
    _____
    _____
    _____
    _____
    _____

6. Given that perception is subjective, and possibly dependent upon each person's unique genetic make-up, how can there be objective definitions of colors (e.g., blue)? _____

    _____
    _____
    _____
    _____
    _____
    _____
    _____

7. Books and movies about blind individuals gaining sight do not always paint a happy picture. What would be some problems with regaining your sight if you were previously blind? Would it be worth it? _____

_____

_____

_____

_____

_____

_____

_____

8. If a deaf person is in a forest when a tree falls, does the falling tree make a sound? Why or why not? _____

_____

_____

_____

_____

_____

_____

_____

9. Discuss the evidence for and against ESP. _____

_____

_____

_____

_____

_____

_____

_____

10. How could you tell whether an infant has depth perception? Explain.

_____

_____

_____

_____

_____

_____

_____

_____

When You Are Finished . . . Puzzle It Out

Across

3. Opening in eye that light goes through
4. Defect in curvature of cornea
6. Where optic nerve exits retina
11. When stimuli strong enough to notice
14. When different stimuli are obvious
17. Painkilling chemicals produced in the brain
19. Sensitive to different tastes
20. Retinal cells that register only gray

Down

1. Central region of retina
2. Person's willingness to report stimuli
5. Just discovered receptor in eye
7. Like hormones, but outside the body
8. Focusing on particular information
9. Rate at which light waves move past a particular point
10. Sense registering limp body posture
12. Set of characteristics corresponding to an object
13. Opponent color of red
15. Processing guided by knowledge
16. Leftover from previous visual perception
18. Strength of a sound

Puzzle created with Puzzlemaker at DiscoverySchool.com.

Chapter 4
Learning:
How Experience Changes Us

Before You Read . . .

In this chapter, you will discover the different ways that people learn. With classical conditioning, you learn by associating two things together. If you have ever gotten sick from something you ate or drank and now get nauseous just at the smell of that food or drink, you have experienced **classical conditioning**!

With **operant conditioning**, you also learn by association, but this time you are associating the behavior and its consequence. For example, if you have learned that using this Grade Aid improves your exam performance, you have learned through operant conditioning. In this chapter, you will learn how behaviors are established and extinguished with classical and operant conditioning.

You will also learn that people can learn just by watching others; this is called **observational learning**. This type of learning explains why parents must watch their language so carefully around their children (lest their children pick up any curse words). In addition, the chapter introduces **cognitive learning**, which is involved in learning complex tasks. Not surprisingly, cognitive learning involves cognitive processes such as memory and reasoning, which are covered in more depth in the next two chapters.

Chapter Objectives

After reading this chapter, you should be able to:

♦   Define classical conditioning, and trace its history.

♦   Name some common examples of classical conditioning in daily life.

♦   Define operant conditioning, and explain how it occurs.

♦   Name some common examples of operant conditioning in daily life.

♦   For both classical and operant conditioning, explain the principles of extinction, spontaneous recovery, generalization, and discrimination.

♦   Explain the brain functions involved in both classical and operant conditioning.

♦ Explain cognitive learning.

♦ Define insight learning.

♦ Explain how watching others can help people learn and why some models are better than others.

♦ Differentiate among the different forms of learning.

As You Read . . . Term Identification

Make flashcards using the following terms as you go. Use the definitions in the margins of this chapter for help. If you write the definitions in your own words, though, you will remember them better!

Acquisition
Avoidance learning
Behavior modification
Biological preparedness
Classical conditioning
Cognitive learning
Conditioned emotional response (CER)
Conditioned response (CR)
Conditioned stimulus (CS)
Continuous reinforcement
Contrapreparedness
Delayed reinforcement
Discrimination
Discriminative stimulus
Extinction (in classical conditioning)
Extinction (in operant conditioning)
Fixed interval schedule
Fixed ratio schedule
Food aversion (taste aversion)
Generalization
Habituation
Immediate reinforcement
Insight learning
Interval schedule
Latent learning
Law of Effect
Learning

Negative punishment
Negative reinforcement
Observational learning
Operant conditioning
Partial reinforcement
Phobia
Positive punishment
Positive reinforcement
Primary reinforcer
Ratio schedule
Reinforcement
Reinforcer
Response contingency
Secondary reinforcer
Shaping
Spontaneous recovery (in classical conditioning)
Spontaneous recovery (in operant conditioning)
Stimulus discrimination
Stimulus generalization
Successive approximations
Unconditioned response (UR)
Unconditioned stimulus (US)
Variable interval schedule
Variable ratio schedule

As You Read . . . Questions and Exercises

How does the text define learning? _____
_____

Which of the following are examples of learning? Circle YES or NO as appropriate.

Originally published in Rocklin, T. (1987). Defining learning: Two classroom activities. Teaching of Psychology, 14, 228-229. Reprinted with permission of the publisher and author.

1. YES NO The cessation of thumb-sucking by an infant.

2. YES NO The acquisition of language in children.

3. YES NO A computer program generates random opening moves for its first 100 chess games and tabulates the outcomes of those games. Starting with the 101st game, the computer uses those tabulations to influence its choice of opening moves.

4. YES NO A worm is placed in a T maze. The left arm of the maze is brightly lit and dry; the right arm is dim and moist. On the first 10 trials, the worm turns right seven times. On the next 10 trials, the worm turns right all 10 times.

5. YES NO Ethel stays up late the night before the October GRE administration and consumes large quantities of licit and illicit pharmacological agents. Her combined (verbal plus quantitative) score is 410. The night before the December GRE administration, she goes to bed early after a wholesome dinner and a glass of milk. Her score increases to 1210. Is her change in pretest regimen due to learning?

6. YES NO A previously psychotic patient is given Dr. K's patented phrenological surgery and no longer exhibits any psychotic behaviors.

7. YES NO A lanky zinnia plant is pinched back and begins to grow denser foliage and flowers.

8. YES NO MYCIN is a computer program that does a rather good job of diagnosing human infections by consulting a large database of rules it has been given. If we add another rule to the database, has MYCIN learned something?

9. YES NO After pondering over a difficult puzzle for hours, Jane finally figures it out. From that point on, she can solve all similar puzzles in the time it takes her to read them.

10. YES NO After 30 years of smoking two packs a day, Zeb throws away his cigarettes and never smokes again.

Pavlov's Experiments

In Pavlov's initial experiment, in which he paired a tone with the presentation of food, the _____ was the **unconditioned stimulus**, the _____ was the **unconditioned response**; the _____ was the **conditioned stimulus**, and the _____ was the **conditioned response**.

Practice identifying the US, CS, UR, and CR using these examples.

1. Your professor slams her book down every day when she gets to her desk, so that you now wince when you see her walk in the door.
   US: _____ CS: _____ UR: _____ CR: _____

2. Jack always smokes when he is in someone's car at school. When his mother picks him up for fall break, Jack immediately reaches for a cigarette when he gets in the car (even though he doesn't want his mother to know he smokes!).
   US: _____ CS: _____ UR: _____ CR: _____

3. Mandi once got sick after eating Chinese food (because she was allergic to the MSG in it). Now, even the smell of Chinese food makes her sick.
   US: _____ CS: _____ UR: _____ CR: _____

4. Marketing researchers have found that men are more likely to buy a car after viewing advertisements showing attractive women sitting on the car.
   US: _____ CS: _____ UR: _____ CR: _____

5. John successfully quit drinking alcohol by participating in an Antabuse treatment program.
   US: _____ CS: _____ UR: _____ CR: _____

6. Ader and Cohen's rats died after drinking flavored water, even after they were *not* injected with an immune-suppressing drug.
   US: _____ CS: _____ UR: _____ CR: _____

7. Marcia was once a victim in a bank robbery in which a robber pulled a gun from his inside coat pocket and held it to her face. Now, she jumps every time she sees a man put his hand into his inside coat pocket.
   US: _____ CS: _____ UR: _____ CR: _____

8. On her 21st birthday, Teri drank too much tequila and got sick. Now, whenever she sees a tequila bottle, she feels nauseous.
   US: _____ CS: _____ UR: _____ CR: _____

9. Every Sunday, Robin visits his mother, who makes him a delicious, 6-course meal. Now, every time he pulls into his mother's driveway, Robin's mouth begins to water.

US: _____ CS: _____ UR: _____ CR: _____

10. Each time she meets with her boss, Michelle gets berated for having done something wrong. Now, whenever she even sees her boss, Michelle flinches.

US: _____ CS: _____ UR: _____ CR: _____

GO SURFING ...

... at Fullerton College's interactive demonstration of **classical conditioning**: http://www.uwm.edu/~johnchay/cc.htm. Try conditioning the dog to salivate to a light. Click on each of the boxes to present that stimulus. The lines on the salivation bar represent the frequency of salivating.

In this situation, what is ...

♦ the US? _____

♦ the CS? _____

♦ the UR? _____

♦ the CR? _____

What did you do to try to **condition** the dog to salivate to a light? _____
_____
_____

How many **trials** (or pairings) did it take for the dog to salivate before the food was presented? ____

If you stopped presenting the food and only presented the light, what happened? _____
_____
_____

Now, what happens if you again present the food and the light together? _____
_____
_____

Try doing this a few different times. Is there anything that you can do to make the salivation occur for more trials, even without the food? _____
_____

What is **conditioning**? _____
_____

When is the **CS** presented: before, after or at the same time as the **US**? Why is this important?
_____
_____

Classical Conditioning: How It Works

What is **avoidance learning?** _____
_____
_____

How was **avoidance learning** discovered? _____
_____
_____

What was the significance of the **Little Albert** study? _____
_____
_____

Some stimuli are easier to **condition** than others. Fill in the chart below with several examples.

Some stimuli that organisms seem to be biologically prepared to be conditioned to	Some stimuli that organisms seem to be contraprepared to be conditioned to

Why might it be easier to **condition** some stimuli than others? _____
_____
_____

When was **extinction** shown in the interactive demonstration you did earlier?

 ♦ What did you do to cause the **extinction**? _____
 _____

 ♦ What did the dog do when the behavior had been **extinguished**? _____
 _____

When was **spontaneous recovery** shown in the interactive demonstration you did earlier?

♦   What did you do to cause **spontaneous recovery**?_____
_____

♦   What did the dog's behavior look like at this point? _____
_____

How might you demonstrate **stimulus generalization** in a study like the one in the interactive demonstration you did earlier?

♦   What types of stimuli might the dog **generalize** to? _____
_____

♦   What would the dog's behavior look like at this point? _____
_____

Why might dogs (or people) **generalize** stimuli? _____
_____
_____

How might you demonstrate **stimulus discrimination** in a study like the one in the interactive demonstration you did earlier?

♦   What type of stimuli might the dog **discriminate** between?_____
_____

♦   What would the dog's behavior look like at this point? _____
_____

♦   What might you do to help the dog **discriminate** between stimuli? _____
_____

In your own words, summarize the three pieces of evidence that indicate that **cognitive processes** are involved in learning (contrary to what strict behaviorists would say):

♦   _____

♦   _____

♦   _____

There are three distinct brain areas and processes involved in **classical conditioning**. What are they?

Brain Part(s)	Function(s)

In your own words, explain why a **classically conditioned response** will never *really* be extinguished. _____

_____

_____

If this is true, then what is **extinction**? _____

_____

In your own words, explain how the brain is involved in **extinction.** _____

_____

Describe what would have happened to **Little Albert** had his amygdala been removed. What if only the central nucleus of the amygdala had been removed? _____

_____

_____

Classical Conditioning Applied

In your own words, explain how **classical conditioning** is involved in some drug overdoses.

_____

_____

How is **classical conditioning** used as a therapeutic technique? _____

_____

_____

Have you ever experienced a **taste aversion** to a particular food or drink? If so, explain. (If not, think of a friend's taste aversion and explain that.) _____

_____

_____

In your example of a taste aversion, identify the following components of **classical conditioning**:

- ◆ US: _____
- ◆ CS: _____
- ◆ UR: _____
- ◆ CR: _____

In Ader and Cohen's study, identify the following components of **classical conditioning**:

- ◆ US: _____
- ◆ CS: _____
- ◆ UR: _____
- ◆ CR: _____

What was the significance of Ader and Cohen's study?

- ◆ _____

- ◆ _____

Describe an example of **classical conditioning** in your own life (other than those listed above).

_____
_____
_____

In this example, identify the following components of **classical conditioning**:

- ◆ US: _____
- ◆ CS: _____
- ◆ UR: _____
- ◆ CR: _____

Looking at Levels

Some chemotherapy patients develop anticipatory nausea from being in the hospital or seeing other stimuli. In this example, identify the following components of **classical conditioning**:

- ◆ US: _____

- ◆ CS: _____

- ◆ UR: _____

- ◆ CR: _____

Explain the factors that operate at **each of the levels** to influence whether someone develops anticipatory nausea. Use arrows to show how events at the different levels may interact.

The Brain	The Person	The Group

Do you think you are more **autonomically reactive** than other people? Why or why not?

_____

_____

TRY PRACTICE TEST #1 NOW!
GOOD LUCK!

Operant Conditioning

The Roots of Operant Conditioning: Its Discovery and How It Works

Distinguish between **operant** and **classical conditioning**. _____

_____

_____

_____

What does the word "operant" mean? _____

_____

_____

What is the **Law of Effect**? _____
_____
_____

How did Thorndike develop the **Law of Effect**? _____
_____
_____
_____

GO SURFING ...

... at Fullerton College's interactive demonstration of operant conditioning:
http://www.uwm.edu/~johnchay/oc.htm. This is a computerized model of a **Skinner box**.
Familiarize yourself with all of its different parts.

In this model, identify the following components of **operant conditioning**:

♦   the stimulus: _____

♦   the response: _____

♦   the consequence: _____

What happens when you push the button to **reinforce** the pigeon? _____
_____
_____
_____

What do the displayed numbers mean? _____
_____
_____

One of the most successful treatments for autism is based on operant conditioning. Search (on www.google.com or another good search engine) for "applied behavioral analysis" and "autism." Here is a good starting link: http://members.tripod.com/RSaffran/aba.html. You can also search by the name "O. Ivar Lovaas," the pioneer in the field. How his childhood influenced him in developing this technique is particularly interesting.

Describe how applied behavioral analysis (ABA) is used with autistic children. _____

_____

_____

_____

_____

_____

_____

_____

_____

_____

Principles of Operant Conditioning

The difference between **classical** and **operant conditioning** is exemplified in how responses are described as coming about.

♦ In classical conditioning, responses are _____, indicatiing that they are usually reflexive and involuntary.

♦ In operant conditioning, responses are _____, indicating that they are usually voluntary.

What would happen if the pigeon (in the interactive model you investigated) didn't like food pellets?

_____

_____

What is the difference between **reinforcement** and **punishment**?

_____

_____

In the terms **positive reinforcement**, **positive punishment**, **negative reinforcement**, and **negative reinforcement**, the words "positive" and "negative" do not refer to whether something is *good* or *bad*. Instead, what do the words mean in this context?

♦ positive = _____

♦ negative = _____

Within each cell of this table, write the type of feedback that would result from a combination of that action and that effect. Then, think of an example to illustrate each type of feedback.

Action / Effect	Giving a stimulus	Removing or withholding a stimulus
To increase behavior		
To decrease behavior		

What type of feedback is involved in these situations: **positive reinforcement (PR)**, **positive punishment (PP)**, **negative reinforcement (NR)**, or **negative punishment (NP)**?

1. _____ Your professor says that your class's performance on the last exam was so good that she is canceling your cumulative final exam.

2. _____ Your boss yells at you because you came late to work.

3. _____ You clean your dorm room before your mother visits so that she won't nag you.

4. _____ Your grades are so bad that the coach takes away your basketball scholarship.

5. _____ Your professor praises your excellent term paper.

6. _____ You have found from past experience that smoking reduces your anxiety, so you light up right before your final exam.

7. _____ Your professor gives you an F because you cheated.

8. _____ You get a bonus at work for going above and beyond the call of duty!

9. _____ Your coach has you run an additional 15 minutes for every pass you miss during practice.

10. _____ Your girlfriend refuses to kiss you because you smoke. (She says you taste like an ashtray!)

11. _____ Your professor has an attendance policy in which you lose four points for each unexcused absence.

12. _____ Your child gives you a hug every time you read her a bedtime story.

Describe three problems with using spanking as a means to control a child's behavior.

♦ _____

♦ _____

♦ _____

If you had children, would you spank them (as a form of **discipline**)? Why or why not?
_____
_____
_____

If you do plan (or do) use spanking as a form of **discipline**, list four things you could do to make them more effective.

♦ _____

♦ _____

♦ _____

♦ _____

Describe at least two alternatives to spanking that you could use to control a child's behavior.

♦ _____
_____

♦ _____
_____

In the list below, circle the **secondary reinforcers**:

Food	**Money**	**Attention**	**Praise**	**Sex**
Promotion	**Good grades**	**Water**	**Pain relief**	**Raises**

Using the principles of **immediate** and **delayed reinforcement**, explain why exercising is so difficult for some people to do. _____
_____
_____
_____

Beyond Basic Reinforcement

Give an original example of **generalization** as it relates to operant conditioning. _____
_____
_____
_____

Give an original example of **discrimination** as it relates to operant conditioning. _____
_____
_____
_____

Underline the discriminative stimulus in each of the following situations:

- ◆ Jessica is sure to dress up and put her make-up on when she knows she will be seeing her boyfriend.

- ◆ Judy's dog, Cosmo, starts wagging his tail and jumping around whenever Judy comes home.

- ◆ You do all the assigned reading when you know that there will be a quiz.

- ◆ David is careful to use polite language when his son is present.

GO SURFING…

… at the computerized model of the **Skinner box** that you visited earlier
(http://www.uwm.edu/~johnchay/oc.htm).

Shape the pigeon's behavior to get it to peck at the lever. How did you do this? _____
_____
_____

What type of **reinforcement schedule** did you use initially? _____
_____

Why might this be a good schedule to use initially? _____
_____
_____

Next, try using a **fixed ratio schedule** for several minutes. Reinforce the pigeon for every 6th peck.
What happens to the pigeon's other behaviors as you do this? _____
_____
_____

Graph the results of using the **fixed ratio schedule**.

**Frequency
of
Pecking**

Time

Now, **extinguish** the behavior. How did you do this? _____

_____

_____

Now, restart the exercise and try using a **variable interval schedule** of reinforcement. How did you do this? _____

_____

Graph the results of using the **variable interval schedule**.

**Frequency
of
Pecking**

Time

Do the same thing using a **fixed interval schedule** of reinforcement. Graph your results below.

**Frequency
of
Pecking**

Time

Finally, try using a **variable ratio schedule** of reinforcement. Graph your results below.

```
Frequency
   of
Pecking    │
           │
           │
           │
           │
           │
           │
           │
           │
           └────────────────────────────────
                                         Time
```

After the pecking behavior is well-established using this schedule, try **extinguishing** the behavior. What happens, especially in comparison to extinguishing the pecking behavior following **a fixed ratio schedule**? _____

_____

Now, restart the program. Try using **continuous reinforcement** to encourage the pigeon to flap its wings. What happens, especially in comparison to reinforcing pecking? _____

_____

_____

What does this tell you about the relative frequency of pecking versus flapping in pigeons?

_____

_____

Do you think you could **shape** a more complicated behavior in the pigeon (such as a peck followed by a flap)? If so, how would you do it? _____

_____

_____

Consider pigeons that were not immediately reinforced for their behaviors. (You can try it in the computer model, if you like!) These pigeons had to figure out what caused the food pellet to (eventually) appear. Was it the pecking? Was it because they walked in a circle? Explain how **delayed reinforcement** can help us to understand superstitious behaviors not only among pigeons but among humans as well. _____

_____

_____

_____

_____

_____

160

Which schedule of **reinforcement** . . .

- ♦ is most resistant to extinction? _____

- ♦ causes exhaustion? _____

- ♦ results in slow but consistent responding? _____

- ♦ causes an individual to slow down right after reinforcement? _____

Describe how you could use **shaping** techniques to teach your roommate to clean up the room. What **successive approximations** would you reward? What schedule of reinforcement would you use? Explain. _____
_____
_____
_____
_____
_____
_____
_____

GO SURFING...

... at The Adaptive Mind Center (http://epsych.msstate.edu/adaptive/index.html) to try another interactive model of **operant conditioning**.

What type of reinforcement schedule is being used in each of the following situations: **fixed ratio (FR), fixed interval (FI), variable ratio (VR)**, or **variable interval (VI)**?

1. _____ Picking up your paycheck at the end of each week

2. _____ Factory worker being paid for every three dresses she makes

3. _____ Slot machines at a gambling casino

4. _____ Calling a friend and getting no answer and then continuing to call until you reach her

5. _____ Buying lottery tickets

6. _____ A strawberry picker being paid per pints picked

7. _____ Looking at your watch repeatedly during a lecture until its ends

8. _____ Checking for mail repeatedly, assuming that the mailman comes at a different time each day

9. _____ Asking people out on dates

10. _____ Checking your e-mail

11. _____ Giving yourself a break from studying after every 30 minutes

12. _____ Getting your favorite cookies (which must bake for exactly seven minutes) from the oven

The Learning Brain

Learning by **operant conditioning** involves two phases. Different brain structures and neurotransmitters are involved in each phase. Fill in the following table to indicate which brain parts and neurotransmitters are involved in each phase of the learning process.

Brain Parts & Neuro-transmitters / Phase	Brain Parts Involved	Neurotransmitters Involved
#1: Individual learns when to do a certain behavior.		
#2: Individual learns the stimulus-response association (i.e., what the effect of the behavior is).		

List the similarities between **classical** and **operant conditioning**:

♦ _____

♦ _____

♦ _____

♦ _____

Given these similarities, how do we know that **classical** and **operant conditioning** are different? (Or, do we?) _____
_____
_____

Looking at Levels

If you could alter the behavior of one of your professors, what behavior would you alter and how would you accomplish it? Describe what would happen at the **levels of the brain, the person, and the group** throughout the process. Use arrows to indicate how events at the different levels may interact.

The Brain	The Person	The Group

What do the interactions you identified indicate about your role in creating the most beneficial learning environment? Explain. _____
_____
_____
_____

TRY PRACTICE TEST #2 NOW!
GOOD LUCK!

Cognitive and Social Learning

Cognitive Learning

In what ways **are latent learning** and **observational learning** similar? _____
_____
_____
_____
_____
_____
_____
_____

Give examples from your own experience of **latent learning**. Is most of what we learn not evident at first? What does the educational setting typically require of students? _____

_____

_____

_____

_____

_____

_____

_____

Insight Learning

GO SURFING ...

... at http://www.xsiq.com/content/demonstration/board_psychology2.htm to run an animated version of the Köhler's study. Also, take a look at some real pictures of Köhler's work at: http://elvers.stjoe.udayton.edu/history/history.asp?RURL=http://elvers.stjoe.udayton.edu/%20% 20history/people/Kohler.html. (Yes, the URL is *very* long!) At the latter site, read some of the commentaries on Köhler's work.

Do you have any other interpretations for Köhler's findings, besides that the chimps had **insights**?

_____

_____

_____

Do you think that *all* animals can have **insights**, or is this ability limited to certain species?

_____

_____

_____

Have you ever had an **"aha"** experience, when things finally fell into place for you? If so, explain.

_____

_____

_____

Observational Learning/ Learning from Models

Think about your role models. For each type listed below, identify at least one behavior that your models engage in. Then, complete the following chart, indicating whether or not you imitate the behavior and listing factors that promote and discourage imitation.

Role Models	Behavior	Do You Imitate This Behavior?	Factors Promoting Imitation	Factors Discouraging Imitation
Your parents				
Your siblings				
Other, older relatives				
Peers				
Your teachers/coaches				
Celebrities				

Looking at Levels

Besides the use of drugs, children and adolescents also imitate a number of **prosocial behaviors** displayed by their parents. Consider your own behaviors. Do any of them appear to have derived from imitation of your parents? Explain how, at the **levels of the brain, the person, and the group**. Use arrows to indicate how events at the different levels may interact.

The Brain	The Person	The Group

TRY PRACTICE TEST #3 NOW!
GOOD LUCK!

Conclusion

What type of **learning** is involved in each of the following examples?

1. _____ Max was a genius who didn't speak until he was 3. When asked why not, he said, "I didn't have anything important to say until then."

2. _____ You have been attending class all semester, but suddenly one day, you finally understand statistics!

3. _____ You have noticed that your boss is always in a bad mood on Fridays, so you have learned to avoid him on those days.

4. _____ You have watched your roommate all semester and noticed that her study techniques have gotten her good grades. You begin using those techniques yourself.

5. _____ The cafeteria food at your school is awful, and you feel sick every time you just walk in the building.

166

6. _____ Bobby's dad exhibits road rage and frequently curses at other drivers. One time, when he sees an upcoming roadblock, Bobby shouts the same expletives.

7. _____ You are returning to your hometown after a long absence, but you find you can still navigate the roads as if you never left.

8. _____ Your professor spits when he gets excited. Unfortunately, you sit in the front row. Now, whenever his voice starts to rise, you keep your head down.

9. _____ You went to church every Sunday with your parents. They thought you didn't pay any attention, until one night you are watching *Jeopardy* with them and correctly answer all the questions in the religion category.

10. _____ You have been struggling with how to organize your thesis. One day, while you are taking a shower, the answer suddenly comes to you.

11. _____ Your boyfriend is so pleased that you have stopped smoking that he gives you a massage each day you don't light up. You love the massages, so you refrain from smoking.

12. _____ Despite your requests to the contrary, your roommate persists in burning aromatherapy candles that aggravate your allergies. Now, you begin coughing and sneezing as soon as you walk in the room, whether or not the candles are lit.

How could you use **classical, operant,** and/or **social learning** principles in each of the following situations? (Surf around on the Web if you can't think of any ideas yourself!)

1. After graduation, you take a job as a computer salesperson. Your income depends almost entirely on your sales commissions. (Your base pay is very low.) How could you use learning principles to assist you in generating sales? _____
_____
_____
_____
_____
_____
_____
_____

2. You are the parent of a four-year-old who still isn't potty-trained. How could you use learning principles to encourage him to use the potty? _____

_____

_____

_____

_____

_____

_____

3. Think of your favorite teacher of all time. How did he or she use learning principles in teaching? _____

_____

_____

_____

_____

_____

_____

4. Suppose that you get a job as a manager in a restaurant. How could you use your knowledge of learning principles in your management of others? _____

_____

_____

_____

_____

_____

_____

After You Read . . . Thinking Back

1.   The Little Albert study is considered a classic study in the field of psychology and has led to many important findings. Yet, it would not be allowed by institutional review boards today. Do you think the field of psychology will be hindered by these ethical restraints? Should ethical standards be revised? _____
      _____
      _____
      _____

2.   Can you think of situations in which either classically or operantly conditioning an individual or group would be unethical? How might individuals in positions of authority get reluctant followers to do what they want them to do, using learning principles? _____
      _____
      _____
      _____

3.   Which of the learning theories in this chapter fall into the category of behaviorism?
      _____

      How can you remember this, given the content of the theories and the term "behaviorism"?
      _____
      _____

      What were the lasting impacts of behaviorism (from Chapter 1)? _____
      _____
      _____

4.   Tolman and Honzik's discovery of **cognitive maps** in rats was one factor that led to the end of the reign of behaviorism (as the predominant school of thought in psychology). Why?
      _____
      _____

5.   What followed the fall of behaviorism (from Chapter 1)? How would Tolman's studies contribute to this? _____
      _____
      _____

6.   The first phase of operant conditioning involves the hippocampus. What are the other functions of the hippocampus? How are all these functions similar? _____
      _____
      _____

7.   In classical conditioning, extinction involves the frontal lobe's active suppression of the amygdala's response. What are the other functions of the frontal lobes? How are all these functions similar? _____
      _____

After You Read . . . Practice Tests

PRACTICE TEST #1:
CLASSICAL CONDITIONING

Matching Questions

Match each of the following terms with its definition. Write the correct answer in the space at the left.

_____ 1.   Acquisition (p. 130)

a.   CS repeatedly presented without US

_____ 2.   Avoidance learning (p. 131)

b.   Initial learning

_____ 3.   Biological preparedness (p. 132)

c.   CR re-appearing after extinction

_____ 4.   Contrapreparedness (p. 132)

d.   Responding only to the CS and not to similar stimuli

_____ 5.   Conditioned emotional response (CER) (p. 132)

e.   Pairing of a CS and an unpleasant US that leads to later avoidance of the CS

_____ 6.   Extinction (p. 133)

f.   Irrational fear of a specific object or stimulus

_____ 7.   Phobia (p. 131)

g.   Reason it is easier to condition fear snakes than babies

_____ 8.   Spontaneous recovery (p. 133)

h.   Inability to condition some stimuli

_____ 9.   Stimulus generalization (p. 134)

i.   Responding to stimuli similar to the original CS

_____ 10.   Stimulus discrimination (p. 134)

j.   An emotional response elicited by a previously neutral stimulus

Multiple-Choice Questions

For each question, circle the letter of the best answer.

1.   Suppose that when you had your wisdom teeth extracted, the procedure was very painful and complicated. Now, whenever you pass by the oral surgeon's office, you flinch. Your flinching response is a(n) _____. (p. 130)
    a.   unconditioned stimulus
    b.   conditioned stimulus
    c.   conditioned response
    d.   example of biological preparedness

2.   In the previous question, an unpleasant stimulus (pain) was paired with a neutral stimulus (the oral surgeon's office). As a result, you will probably _____. (p. 132)
      a.   become depressed
      b.   become angry
      c.   approach the oral surgeon's office
      d.   avoid the oral surgeon's office

3.   Which of the following situations would be most likely to result in a conditioned response? (p. 134)
      a.   When the CS follows the US
      b.   When the CS and the US are presented at the same time
      c.   When the US follows the CS immediately
      d.   When the US follows the CS after an interval

4.   According to the principle of contrapreparedness, which of the following stimuli would it probably be most difficult to condition someone to fear? (p. 132)
      a.   Rats
      b.   Spiders
      c.   Heights
      d.   Blocks

5.   Which of the following theories is usually used to explain the phenomena of biological preparedness and contrapreparedness? (p. 132)
      a.   Evolutionary
      b.   Psychodynamic
      c.   Humanistic
      d.   Cognitive

6.   Which of the following phenomena indicates that classical conditioning is a relatively *permanent* form of learning? (p. 134)
      a.   Initial acquisition
      b.   Biological preparedness
      c.   Stimulus generalization
      d.   Spontaneous recovery

7.   If the _____ were removed from the brain, one could not learn to fear through classical conditioning. (p. 135)
      a.   auditory cortex
      b.   visual cortex
      c.   hypothalamus
      d.   amygdala

8.   The Little Albert study is important because it showed _____. (p. 131)
      a.   avoidance learning
      b.   how unethical some researchers were in the past
      c.   how fear can lead to phobias
      d.   how to extinguish fears

9.   Which of the following is NOT evidence for the fact that cognitive processes are involved in classical conditioning? (pp. 134-135)
     a.   You can condition someone to salivate in response to a mental image of food.
     b.   Backward conditioning is ineffective.
     c.   It is difficult to condition a fear of inanimate objects.
     d.   You can only condition fear to a light if the light provides information about an upcoming event.

10. Classical conditioning is the basis for a treatment technique in which
     _____. (p. 136)
     a.   the therapist listens to the patient's thoughts and reflects them back to the patient
     b.   a person is gradually and repetitively exposed to what she fears
     c.   a person is provided with positive role models
     d.   the therapist explores the patient's past, especially her relationship with her mother

11. Suppose that you ring the dinner bell to get your family to come to dinner. You always feed your dog, Apollo, at the same time. So, whenever Apollo hears the dinner bell ring, he begins to drool. Later, your son breaks both of his legs and can't get out of bed without your help. You give him a different bell to ring whenever he needs you. At first, Apollo will probably _____. (p. 134)
     a.   ignore your son's bell
     b.   drool whenever your son's bell rings
     c.   stop drooling whenever the dinner bell rings
     d.   drool all the time because he is so confused

12. After awhile, Apollo begins to drool only when the dinner bell rings. This is because he has experienced _____. (p. 134)
     a.   stimulus generalization
     b.   stimulus discrimination
     c.   spontaneous recovery
     d.   extinction

13. After his puppy years are over, the vet tells you that Apollo needs to go on a diet because he is gaining too much weight. As a result, you feed him just one meal a day (at breakfast). At dinner time, which is when you ring the dinner bell, he doesn't get to eat. At first, Apollo _____, but then after a while he _____. (p. 134)
     a.   begs for food; experiences spontaneous recovery
     b.   drools in response to the dinner bell; experiences extinction
     c.   doesn't drool in response to the dinner bell; starts drooling again in response to the dinner bell
     d.   experiences discrimination; begins drooling in response to the dinner bell again

14. After several years, your bell breaks from overuse. You take it into the Bell Shop to have it fixed (after all, it's an heirloom), but it takes several months for the shop to fix it. When you finally get it back, you can expect Apollo to _____ because _____. (p. 134)
    a. drool when it is sounded; he is experiencing spontaneous recovery
    b. not drool when it is sounded; his behavior has already been extinguished
    c. drool when he hears any bell (even the doorbell!); he is generalizing
    d. drool when it is sounded; he thinks he isn't on the diet any more

15. Researchers have discovered that fast-tempo music generally makes people feel happier. They have also found that when people are happy, they tend to buy more things. As a result, you frequently hear fast-tempo music played in stores. In this case, marketing executives are relying on shoppers to pair the US of _____ with the CS of _____. (p. 130)
    a. music; stores
    b. stores; happiness
    c. happiness; music
    d. stores; music

PRACTICE TEST #2:
OPERANT CONDITIONING

Fill-In-The-Blank Questions

Fill in each blank with a word from the word bank.

WORD BANK	
acetylcholine discrimination dopamine	hippocampus nucleus accumbens

To learn, we must first identify the appropriate situation in which to make a response, a process called _____ . This process takes place in the _____, where the neurotransmitter _____ helps us to decide which stimuli should be grouped together. Next, we learn which consequences follow which responses, an association that takes place in the _____, which is behind the amygdala. In this part of the brain, the neurotransmitter _____ seems particularly important. (p. 151)

Multiple-Choice Questions

For each question, circle the letter of the best answer.

1. Negative reinforcement is the _____ of an unpleasant stimulus; negative reinforcement _____ the probability of a behavior occurring again. (p. 144)
    a. presentation; increases
    b. removal; increases
    c. presentation; decreases
    d. removal; decreases

2. Which of the following is NOT a characteristic of effective punishment? (p. 144)
    a. It occurs immediately.
    b. It is moderately aversive.
    c. It is consistent.
    d. It is physical.

3. To be most effective, punishment should be accompanied by _____. (p. 145)
    a. generalization of pain
    b. discrimination among schedules of reinforcement
    c. reinforcement of alternative behavior
    d. removal of privileges

4. Bob has learned to be respectful to his parents, as he is reinforced for polite behaviors. He is also respectful to all older individuals, demonstrating the concept of _____. (p. 147)
    a. generalization
    b. discrimination
    c. extinction
    d. secondary reinforcement

5. Bob is not, however, very polite with his friends, demonstrating the concept of _____. (p. 147)
    a. generalization
    b. extinction
    c. discrimination
    d. secondary reinforcement

6. Tara begs for candy every time her mother takes her to the store, a request to which her mother usually gives in. One day, her mother decides no longer to give Tara candy when she begs. What is Tara's likely response? (p. 150)
    a. She will hit her mother.
    b. She will stop begging immediately.
    c. She will beg harder at first, but then eventually stop begging.
    d. She will start crying instead of begging.

7. To teach her daughter to say "Mommy," Clara first rewarded her for putting her lips together to make the "m" sound, then for saying "ma," then for saying "mama," and then for saying "mommy." The earlier behaviors that eventually led to the desired one are called _____. (p. 148)
    a. successive approximations
    b. simple steps
    c. discriminative stimuli
    d. partial reinforcers

8. A quiz every Friday is an example of a _____ schedule of reinforcement. (p. 149)
    a. fixed interval
    b. fixed ratio
    c. variable interval
    d. variable ratio

9. Which of the following is a *primary* reinforcer? (p. 145)
    a. Grades
    b. Food
    c. Money
    d. Praise

10. Walter Mischel and colleagues found that 4-year-olds' responses to
_____ predicted their achievement during adolescence.
   a.   positive reinforcement
   b.   delayed reinforcement
   c.   negative punishment
   d.   interval schedules of reinforcement

PRACTICE TEST #3:
COGNITIVE AND SOCIAL LEARNING

True/False Questions
Circle TRUE or FALSE for each of the following statements.

1. TRUE   FALSE   Köhler discovered that chimps have cognitive maps. (p. 155)

2. TRUE   FALSE   One of Bandura's most famous studies involved Bobo dolls. (p. 157)

3. TRUE   FALSE   Children will imitate all adults. (p. 158)

4. TRUE   FALSE   The process of observational learning is involved in learning social norms. (p. 158)

5. TRUE   FALSE   Tolman and Honzik's work with rats demonstrated that cognitive processes are at work in learning. (p. 154)

Multiple-Choice Questions
For each question, circle the letter of the best answer.

1. Which of the following is NOT a form of cognitive learning? (pp. 154-155)
    a. Salivating when you think of a lemon
    b. Learning how to drive a car
    c. Memorizing the names of your classmates
    d. Evaluating the differences among the choices in this question

2. Tolman and Honzik's rats developed _____ to use later when they were motivated to find their way around the maze. (p. 155)
    a. insight
    b. cognitive maps
    c. neural networks
    d. conditioned responses

3. Latent learning refers to _____. (p. 155)
    a. learning information later in life
    b. learning information by observing someone else
    c. acquiring information through memorization
    d. learning but not displaying the learned behavior immediately

4. The study of learning focuses on the _____ of information; in contrast, the study of memory focuses on the _____ of information. (p. 155)
    a. retention; acquisition
    b. acquisition; retention
    c. generalization; discrimination
    d. discrimination; generalization

5. Robin has been struggling for a week to understand how to calculate standard deviations. While he is taking a shower one day, the answer suddenly comes to him. This is called _____. (p. 155)
    a. latent learning
    b. insight
    c. observational learning
    d. cognitive learning

6. Learning that is not dependent on reinforcement, occurs in a social context, and involves voluntary behaviors is called _____. (p. 156)
    a. latent learning
    b. observational learning
    c. classical conditioning
    d. insight learning

7. Albert Bandura is the psychologist who developed _____. (p. 156)
    a. social learning theory
    b. classical conditioning
    c. cognitive mapping
    d. the latent hypothesis

8. Your professor is trying to memorize the names of all the students in your class, although she doesn't show any observable signs of learning. This is an example of _____. (p. 155)
    a. social learning
    b. modeling
    c. latent learning
    d. insight learning

9. Which of the following is NOT a characteristic of a model to which a person is likely to attend? (p. 158)
    a. Kind
    b. Expert in the field
    c. High status
    d. Socially powerful

10. Researchers have found that adolescents will model their parents' use of drugs if _____. (p. 159)
    a. their parents are honest with them about their use of drugs
    b. the drugs are "soft" (e.g., marijuana), not "hard" (e.g., cocaine)
    c. their friends are also using drugs
    d. they have a positive relationship with their parents

COMPREHENSIVE PRACTICE TEST

True/False Questions

Circle TRUE or FALSE for each of the following statements.

1. TRUE   FALSE   The unconditioned response to the unconditioned stimulus is usually a reflex. (p. 130)

2. TRUE   FALSE   Any phobia can be classically conditioned. (p. 132)

3. TRUE   FALSE   Once classical conditioning has occurred, the stimulus-response association never completely vanishes. (p. 134)

4. TRUE   FALSE   Food aversions require only one pairing of the CS and the US. (p. 136)

5. TRUE   FALSE   Negative reinforcement and punishment are the same concepts. (p. 144)

6. TRUE   FALSE   A behavior established by partial reinforcement schedule is more resistant to extinction. (p. 149)

7. TRUE   FALSE   Classical conditioning and operant conditioning are really the same concept. (p. 151)

8. TRUE   FALSE   Powerful, high-status models are more influential than other models. (p. 158)

9. TRUE   FALSE   Cognitive maps demonstrate the effectiveness of insight learning. (p. 155)

10. TRUE   FALSE   Children's ability to delay reinforcement predicts their later social competence. (p. 146)

Multiple-Choice Questions

For each question, circle the letter of the best answer.

1. A relatively long-term change in behavior that results from experience is called _____. (p. 128)
    a.   learning
    b.   habit
    c.   memory
    d.   observation

2.	Pavlov is to _____ as Skinner is to _____. (pp. 129, 141)
	a.	operant conditioning; classical conditioning
	b.	classical conditioning; operant conditioning
	c.	observational learning; operant conditioning
	d.	classical conditioning; observational learning

3.	Avoidance learning occurs when a(n) _____is paired with a CS and the organism tries to avoid the CS. (p. 131)
	a.	neutral stimulus
	b.	conditioned emotional response
	c.	reinforcement
	d.	unpleasant US

4.	It is easier to condition a fear of spiders than a fear of flowers because of _____. (p. 132)
	a.	conditioned emotional responses
	b.	biological preparedness
	c.	latent learning
	d.	generalization

5.	When Quinn learns to write on paper, but not on walls, he has _____. (p. 147)
	a.	learned to generalize
	b.	learned to discriminate
	c.	experienced extinction
	d.	spontaneously recovered his writing

6.	In classical conditioning, extinction involves _____. (p. 147)
	a.	completely undoing the stimulus-response association
	b.	layering new learning over old learning
	c.	forgetting a stimulus-response association
	d.	not rewarding a behavior any more

7.	Running for shelter when dark clouds threaten rain is an example of _____. (p. 144)
	a.	positive reinforcement
	b.	extinction
	c.	negative reinforcement
	d.	discrimination

8.   At the beginning of the semester, your professor gave extra credit points for class participation. After a few weeks, however, she stopped giving the extra credit points. You noticed that class participation then dropped off, due to _____. However, on the first day back to school after the week-long fall break, the class was once again fully participating, due to _____. (p. 147)
   a.   discrimination; generalization
   b.   extinction; spontaneous recovery
   c.   classical conditioning; latent learning
   d.   discrimination; spontaneous recovery

9.   Food is an example of a _____ reinforcer. (p. 145)
   a.   primary
   b.   positive
   c.   secondary
   d.   negative

10.   Researchers found that children who were able to delay gratification _____. (p. 146)
   a.   were more socially competent as adolescents
   b.   had more friends
   c.   received more positive reinforcement from their parents
   d.   were from higher social classes

11.   In comparison to individuals on a fixed interval schedule, those on a fixed ratio schedule will respond _____. (p. 149)
   a.   more slowly and more consistently
   b.   faster, with a lull right after reinforcement
   c.   more slowly and more inconsistently
   d.   faster, with no pauses in rate of responding

12.   The _____ schedule yields the highest rate of responding. (p. 149)
   a.   fixed interval
   b.   variable interval
   c.   fixed ratio
   d.   variable ratio

13.   Operant conditioning relies on the dopamine-based "reward system" found in the _____. (p. 152)
   a.   frontal lobes
   b.   nucleus accumbens
   c.   hypothalamus
   d.   pituitary gland

14. When researchers block dopamine receptors, animals _____. (p. 151)
    a.   fail to respond to reinforcement
    b.   respond more quickly to reinforcement
    c.   cannot learn which stimuli should be grouped together
    d.   become aggressive toward other animals

15. Jeremy just couldn't understand how to do geometry proofs. One day, after months of trying, Jeremy was riding his bike when suddenly it all became clear—he had found the key to doing proofs! Jeremy's experience is an example of _____. (p. 155)
    a.   latent learning
    b.   observational learning
    c.   insight learning
    d.   classical conditioning

16. Researchers found that adolescents who had good relationships with their drug-using parents _____. (p. 159)
    a.   tried to get their parents to stop using drugs
    b.   also used drugs
    c.   hid their own drug use from their parents
    d.   avoided using drugs

17. Suppose that you wanted to use operant conditioning to teach your child to use the potty. To do this as quickly as possible (because diapers are *so* expensive), which reinforcement schedule should you use at first? (p. 149)
    a.   Continuous
    b.   Fixed interval
    c.   Fixed ratio
    d.   Variable interval

18. Backward pairing in classical conditioning is ineffective because _____. (p. 130)
    a.   punishment is less effective than reinforcement
    b.   the US doesn't warn the individual of the CS
    c.   interval schedules are not as effective as ratio schedules
    d.   it will lead to a phobia

19. Classical conditioning and operant conditioning are _____. (p. 152)
    a.   really the same thing
    b.   different because one involves association and the other doesn't
    c.   different, as demonstrated by the fact that they involve different brain mechanisms
    d.   similar in that they are both governed by the Law of Effect

20.   If you want someone to engage in a complex behavior, you should _____.
       (p. 148)
       a.   use a variable schedule of reinforcement
       b.   use punishment, rather than reinforcement
       c.   be patient; they are probably experiencing latent learning and will demonstrate the
             behavior later
       d.   shape their behavior

Essay Questions
Answer each of the following questions in the space provided.

1.   A positive response to a placebo has typically been attributed to "mind over matter," or the
       individual's belief that he/she will get better. How has research in the area of classical
       conditioning shed light on another possible explanation? _____
       _____
       _____
       _____
       _____
       _____
       _____
       _____
       _____
       _____
       _____

2.   What characteristics of "live" action shows (e.g., *Cops* and *Real TV*) may lead children to
       imitate the violence depicted? What characteristics are less likely to cause them to do so?
       _____
       _____
       _____
       _____
       _____
       _____

3.   If you had to give advice to parents who are trying to "teach" their infant to sleep through
       the night (assuming the child is old enough), what would you tell them to do, and what
       should they expect?
       _____
       _____
       _____
       _____
       _____
       _____
       _____
       _____

4. Explain how operant conditioning, latent learning, and observational learning all interact when a child learns to have a temper tantrum after watching a friend have one.

_____
_____
_____
_____
_____
_____
_____
_____

5. The text clearly explains why physical punishment is a relatively ineffective way of modifying behavior. What role does culture play in the issue of physically disciplining children? As families from other cultures move to the United States, do we have the right to impose our values about discipline on them? How can we balance the knowledge we have about discipline with sensitivity to other cultures?

_____
_____
_____
_____
_____
_____
_____
_____

6. Can classical and operant conditioning be latent? Why or why not? If they _can_ be latent, what does that say about the argument that such learning takes place without cognition?

_____
_____
_____
_____
_____
_____
_____

7. Describe how classical and operant conditioning can be used in clinical treatment.

_____
_____
_____
_____
_____
_____
_____

8. Discuss the evidence for the idea that classical and operant conditioning are different forms of learning. _____

_____

_____

_____

_____

_____

_____

_____

_____

9. Suppose that you owned a company. Given your knowledge of reinforcement schedules, how would you compensate your employees? Why? _____

_____

_____

_____

_____

_____

_____

_____

_____

10. Distinguish between behaviorism (classical and operant conditioning) and cognitive learning.

_____

_____

_____

_____

_____

_____

_____

_____

When You Are Finished . . . Puzzle It Out

Across

3. An "aha" experience
5. Discovered classical conditioning
7. Dogs' salivation in response to food
9. Type of punishment, such as spanking
10. Initial learning of the CR
13. Type of reinforcer, such as food
15. Name of Kohler's chimp
16. Developed a box for pigeons
17. Watson's famous subject
18. Time-based reinforcement schedule

Down

1. Noncontinuous reinforcement
2. Irrational fear
4. Developed the Law of Effect
6. Learning that is not immediately observable
8. Increases likelihood of behavior
11. Emotional response elicited by neutral stimulus
12. Economy based on secondary reinforcement
13. A nonmedicine that acts like one
14. Tolman and Honzik's rats had these in their heads
16. Reinforcing successive approximations

Puzzle created with Puzzlemaker at DiscoverySchool.com.

Chapter 5
Memory: Living With Yesterday

Before You Read . . .

Do you think of yourself as having a good memory or a bad memory? In fact, as you will learn in this chapter, memory is not a single unit or process. Rather, memory consists of multiple memory stores and processes. For example, there are three types of memory stores: sensory memory, short-term memory, and long-term memory (of which there are several different types). To move information into the memory system and then from one store to the next, a person must use different strategies, including encoding and retrieving.

Memory is not just about remembering, but about forgetting, and there are many different reasons why people forget information. In addition to losing information, we can also have false memories and suffer from amnesia. What about repressed memories? Are they real? The chapter attempts to shed some light on this most controversial topic in psychology.

Finally, the chapter ends with information you can use in all your classes: how to improve your memory.

Chapter Objectives

After reading this chapter, you should be able to:

♦ Differentiate between and describe the three different memory stores: sensory memory, short-term memory, and long-term memory.

♦ Describe the different stores within long-term memory, including modality-specific stores, semantic and episodic memory, and explicit and implicit memory.

♦ Explain the concept of working memory and its components.

♦ Discuss the genetic foundations of memory.

♦ Explain how memories are made, stored, and retrieved.

♦ Discuss how memory can be disrupted, including false memories, forgetting, amnesia, and repression.

♦ Provide examples of how memory can be improved, at both storage and retrieval.

As You Read . . . Term Identification

Make flashcards using the following terms as you go. Use the definitions in the margins of this chapter for help. If you write the definitions in your own words, though, you will remember them better!

Amnesia
Anterograde amnesia
Breadth of processing
Central executive
Chunk
Code
Consolidation
Cues
Decay
Depth of processing
Elaborative encoding
Encoding
Encoding failure
Episodic memory
Explicit (declarative) memory
False memories
Flashbulb memory
Forgetting curve
Habit
Implicit (nondeclarative) memory
Incidental learning
Intentional learning
Interference
Long-term memory (LTM)

Memory store
Mnemonic devices
Modality-specific memory stores
Primacy effect
Priming
Proactive interference
Reality monitoring
Recall
Recency effect
Recognition
Rehearsal
Repetition priming
Repressed memories
Retrieval
Retroactive interference
Retrograde amnesia
Semantic memory
Sensory memory (SM)
Short-term memory (STM)
State-dependent retrieval
Storage
Transfer appropriate processing
Working memory (WM)

As You Read . . . Questions and Exercises

Storing Information:
Time and Space Are of the Essence

In the following table, compare and contrast the differences between **sensory**, **short-term**, and **long-term** memory.

	Sensory Memory	Short-Term Memory	Long-Term Memory
What does it hold?			
How much does it hold?			
How long does it hold information?			
Does it have sub-components? If so, what are they?			

For each of the following situations, indicate whether **sensory**, **short-term**, or **long-term memory** is being activated.

Situation	Type of Memory
Trying to remember the names of the states and their capitals	
Believing you hear your name during a loud and busy conference	
Trying to remember a phone number long enough to dial it	
"Committing" a phone number to memory	
Perceiving fleeting visual images as you watch a movie	
Looking at an object for a few seconds before sketching it	

Long-Term Memory: Records of Experience

Draw a picture of the **memory curve**, and indicate where the **primacy effect** and **recency effect** are evident.

On the next page, draw a diagram showing how all the different systems and types of memories are related. (Your drawing should end up looking like an upside-down tree.) Include the following terms:

Memory
Explicit memory
Modality-specific memories
Long-term memory
Implicit memory
Working memory
Sensory store
Priming

Episodic memory
Short-term memory
Habits
Semantic memory
Autobiographical memory
Iconic memory
Echoic memory

Indicate whether memories of the following items are **semantic** or **episodic memories**. If the memory is an episodic memory, identify whether or not it is **autobiographical**.

Item	Type of Memory
Your 16th birthday party	
What you had for breakfast this morning	
The largest country in the world	
The difference between dogs and cats	
The smell of your grandmother's baking	
The first president of the United States	
The meaning of the word "psychology"	
The image of the World Trade Center collapsing	
The square root of 36	
The death of Princess Diana	

Identify the following memories as being either **explicit** or **implicit**.

Memory	Implicit/Explicit
How to ride a bike	
How to spelling the word "psychology"	
The names of the 50 states	
How to tie your shoe	
Your first kiss	
How to walk	

Working Memory: The Thinking Person's Memory

How is **working memory** different from **short-term memory**? _____
_____
_____
_____

Provide three examples from your own life of the use of **working memory**.

- ♦ _____

- ♦ _____

- ♦ _____

Genetic Foundations of Memory

What are **"knockout mice"**? _____
_____
_____
_____

What do **"knockout mice"** tell us about the biological basis of memory? _____
_____
_____
_____

Looking at Levels

Given the negative effects of stress on the **hippocampus**, explain why it is crucial to keep your anxiety level down when studying for and taking an exam, in terms of the **three levels of analysis**. Use arrows to indicate how events at the three levels may interact.

The Brain	The Person	The Group

TRY PRACTICE TEST #1 NOW!
GOOD LUCK!

Encoding and Retrieving Information From Memory

Making Memories

Using the following concepts, explain how you would teach someone to study for an exam in this class: **consolidation, breadth of processing, depth of processing, transfer appropriate processing, elaborative encoding.** _____

_____

_____

_____

_____

_____

_____

_____

_____

In your own words, distinguish between **intentional learning** and **incidental learning**, providing an example of each from your own experience. _____

_____

_____

_____

_____

_____

_____

Describe, in as much detail as you can, how you remember learning about the attack on the World Trade Center on September 11, 2001. _____

_____

_____

_____

_____

_____

_____

_____

_____

_____

Were any other people with you at the time you heard of the terrorist attack? If so, who?

_____

... the people who were present when you first learned of the terrorist attack and record their memories for hearing about it. _____

_____

_____

_____

_____

_____

_____

_____

_____

_____

_____

How does your recall compare to theirs? What does research say about the accuracy (or inaccuracy) of **flashbulb memories**? _____

_____

_____

_____

_____

_____

_____

_____

_____

_____

The Act of Remembering: Reconstructing Buried Cities

How is remembering like **reconstructing** buried cities? Why do Kosslyn and Rosenberg use this analogy? _____

_____

_____

_____

_____

Distinguish between **recognition** and **recall**. Do you do better on essay tests or multiple-choice tests? What does this tell you about your own memory abilities? _____

_____

_____

_____

_____

How can you use what you now know about **cues** and **state-dependent retrieval** to help you study for exams? _____

_____
_____
_____
_____
_____
_____
_____

Looking at Levels

Do you categorize and organize information when trying to remember lists? Why or why not? Are there factors at the level of brain, person, or group that lead you to use or not use such **organizational strategies**? Use arrows to indicate how these factors may interact.

The Brain	The Person	The Group

TRY PRACTICE TEST #2 NOW!
GOOD LUCK!

When Memory Goes Wrong— And What To Do About It

False Memories

When you did the **false memory** experiment in the textbook, did you recall any words that were not on the list? _____

_____

Why do false memories arise? _____

_____
_____
_____
_____

Give an example from your own life of a time when you had difficulty with **reality monitoring**.

_____
_____
_____

Forgetting: Many Ways to Lose It

Identify the type of forgetting that is occurring in each situation: **encoding failure**, **decay**, **retroactive interference**, and **proactive interference**.

Situation	Type of Forgetting
Susan meets several people at a party, but when she bumps into them the next week, she can't remember their names.	
Having just moved last month and memorized her new address, Kristy can't remember her previous address.	
Sam can't remember if he passed a drugstore on the way home from his new job.	
James called his new girlfriend by his old girlfriend's name.	
Sixty-year-old Frank can't remember what his 2nd -grade teacher looked like.	

Amnesia: Not Just Forgetting to Remember

Distinguish between **anterograde** and **retrograde amnesia**. _____
_____
_____
_____
_____
_____

Do you have any memories of your childhood before you were three? Given that memory for events before this age is pretty poor, what do you think accounts for your memories?

_____
_____
_____
_____
_____

Repressed Memories: Real or Imagined?

Explain why events with highly charged emotional content (e.g., abuse) may be forgotten, when such **emotional tone** usually enhances memory. _____

_____

_____

_____

_____

_____

Improving Memory: Tricks and Tools

Using **interactive images**, remember ten items on a grocery list: apples, milk, tissues, hotdogs, cereal, bananas, juice, pasta, green beans, and rice. Study the list for about 1 minute, then cover it up and write as many items as you can remember in the space below.

How many items could you remember? _____

Now, use the **method of loci** to remember this list: asparagus, paper towels, dog food, hamburger, bread, syrup, olives, cookies, peaches, and peanut butter. Again, study the list for about 1 minute, then cover it up and write as many items as you can remember in the space below.

How many items could you remember? _____

Which method worked best for you? Did you experience **interference** in trying to learn the lists? If so, what type of interference did you experience? _____

_____

_____

Can you remember what the five methods the text suggested to enhance **retrieval**? Use what you have learned in this section to memorize the five methods. List your mnemonic devices below:

♦ _____

♦ _____

♦ _____

♦ _____

♦ _____

Looking at Levels

At **the levels of the brain, the person, and the group,** how might **hypnosis** lead an individual to strongly believe in a **false memory**? Use arrows to indicate how events at the different levels may interact.

The Brain	The Person	The Group

What implications does this belief in a false memory have for the use of **hypnosis** in therapy?

_____
_____
_____
_____
_____
_____
_____
_____
_____

TRY PRACTICE TEST #3 NOW!
GOOD LUCK!

After You Read . . . Thinking Back

1. In Chapter 1, you learned about the impact of the cognitive revolution. Certainly, memory research has benefited from the cognitive revolution. However, some of the key studies in memory also contributed to the cognitive revolution. Name two important people and/or studies in memory, and explain how they affected the cognitive revolution._____

    _____

    _____

    _____

    _____

    _____

    _____

2. In Chapter 1, you learned about different kinds of psychological studies, including correlational, quasi-experimental, and experimental studies. Which of these methods lend themselves particularly well to memory studies? Why? _____

    _____

    _____

    _____

    _____

    _____

    _____

3. In Chapter 3, you learned about top-down and bottom-up processing. How does top-down processing affect memory? _____

    _____

    _____

    _____

    _____

    _____

    _____

4. How does bottom-up processing affect memory? _____

    _____

    _____

    _____

    _____

    _____

    _____

5. What is the difference between learning, as described in Chapter 4, and memory? Is there any difference? _____

    _____

    _____

    _____

    _____

After You Read . . . Practice Tests

PRACTICE TEST #1:
STORING INFORMATION

True/False Questions

Circle TRUE or FALSE for each of the following statements.

1. TRUE FALSE There is no limit in the capacity of short-term memory. (p. 168)

2. TRUE FALSE Visual and auditory memories are stored in different parts of the brain. (p. 170)

3. TRUE FALSE Your memory for terms in the text is an example of semantic memory. (p. 171)

4. TRUE FALSE Your left frontal lobe is activated when you recall episodic memories. (p. 171)

5. TRUE FALSE Habits are a type of memory. (p. 172)

6. TRUE FALSE Sensory memory holds information for 1 minute. (p. 167)

7. TRUE FALSE Working memory includes short-term memory. (p. 173)

8. TRUE FALSE Information must move into long-term memory before you become conscious of it. (p. 169)

9. TRUE FALSE Priming is a form of semantic memory. (p. 173)

10. TRUE FALSE People can become conscious of explicit memory, but not of implicit memory. (p. 171)

Multiple-Choice Questions

For each question, circle the letter of the best answer.

1. Jonah has learned how to remember more and more information by grouping it together. For example, when he needs to remember his computer password, Jonah thinks "nineteen sixty-seven" instead of "one-nine-six-seven." This shows that Jonah has _____. (p. 169)
    a. improved his ability to retrieve information
    b. improved his ability to chunk information
    c. used state-dependent retrieval
    d. used interactive images

2.   A fleeting memory that fades almost immediately after the stimulus has passed is best described as a(n) _____ memory. (p. 167)
   a.   flashbulb
   b.   short-term
   c.   sensory
   d.   long-term

3.   Carl forgot to bring the written list of grocery items to the store, and when he arrived home, he found that he had remembered the first five items, but few of the others, demonstrating the _____ effect. (p. 170)
   a.   primacy
   b.   Ebbinghaus
   c.   recency
   d.   reversal

4.   The primacy effect provides evidence for _____ memory. (p. 170)
   a.   iconic
   b.   short-term
   c.   echoic
   d.   long-term

5.   Working memory is somewhat like an expanded version of _____ memory. (p. 173)
   a.   sensory
   b.   recency
   c.   short-term
   d.   long-term

6.   The easiest modality-specific memory for *most* people to recall is a _____ memory. (p. 170)
   a.   visual
   b.   olfactory
   c.   verbal
   d.   short-term

7.   The meanings of words are part of your_____ memory. (p. 171)
   a.   implicit
   b.   semantic
   c.   long-term
   d.   sensory

8.   Conditioned responses and habits are _____ memories. (p. 172)
   a.   modality-specific
   b.   episodic
   c.   semantic
   d.   implicit

9.   Adrienne and Rob are fighting. She says, "You aren't listening to me," after which he says, "Sure, I am. You just said …" and repeats her previous sentence verbatim. Rob is probably able to do this because he is holding that information in his _____ memory. (p. 168)
      a.   iconic
      b.   echoic
      c.   semantic
      d.   working

10.   Six-year-old Michelle has just finished watching the movie *Bambi* when her mother tells her to write a thank-you letter to her grandparents. Michelle accidentally writes "Dear Grandma and Grandpa" as "Deer Grandma and Grandpa." This is probably because _____. (p. 173)
      a.   she has amnesia
      b.   she doesn't yet know how to spell "dear"
      c.   she has been primed for the word "deer"
      d.   the word "deer" is still in her long-term memory

PRACTICE TEST #2:
ENCODING AND RETRIEVING INFORMATION FROM MEMORY

Multiple-Choice Questions

For each question, circle the letter of the best answer.

1. According to the concept of dual codes, _____ are easy to remember because they can be encoded _____. (p. 177)
    a. words; semantically and episodically
    b. pictures; visually and verbally
    c. words; visually and verbally
    d. pictures; semantically and episodically

2. When trying to encode the names of her new students each semester, Professor Keely will have heightened activity in her _____. (p. 178)
    a. frontal lobes
    b. right temporal lobe
    c. occipital lobes
    d. left temporal lobe

3. Something will be remembered better if it has been stored _____ rather than _____. (p. 178)
    a. explicitly; implicitly
    b. dynamically; structurally
    c. implicitly; explicitly
    d. structurally; dynamically

4. *Depth of processing* refers to the number and complexity of _____ used to process something. (p. 178)
    a. connections to other information
    b. retrieval cues
    c. operations
    d. forms of encoding

5. Which of the following study techniques demonstrates the greatest depth of processing? (p. 178)
    a. Reading the textbook
    b. Recopying your notes
    c. Thinking of examples for key ideas
    d. Reading your notes aloud to a friend

6. To study for the GREs, Sandra took many practice tests that were similar in content and format, utilizing the concept of _____ to help her remember the material. (p. 179)
   a. chunking
   b. transfer appropriate processing
   c. primacy effect
   d. long-term potentiation

7. Learning without intention is called _____ learning. (p. 179)
   a. unintentional
   b. imaginal
   c. incidental
   d. inherent

8. During emotionally charged events, activity in the _____ influences the hippocampus, which in turn enhances memory. (p. 181)
   a. frontal lobe
   b. amygdala
   c. occipital lobe
   d. reticular activating system

9. Multiple-choice tests require _____ rather than _____. (p. 181)
   a. recognition; recall
   b. implicit memory; explicit memory
   c. recall; recognition
   d. explicit memory; implicit memory

10. Elaborative encoding involves _____. (p. 179)
    a. converting random numbers to track times
    b. repeating information over and over again
    c. connecting new information with what is already known
    d. trying hard to learn something

11. The advantage of converting a memory into a structural form is that it _____. (p. 178)
    a. no longer needs to be continually activated
    b. is particularly vivid
    c. can be retrieved at will
    d. is stored in the hippocampus

12. Which of the following statements about flashbulb memories is FALSE? (p. 181)
    a. Flashbulb memories are particularly vivid.
    b. People are usually very confident of their flashbulb memories.
    c. Flashbulb memories involve greater activation of the amygdala.
    d. All Americans have flashbulb memories for the same events.

13. Suppose that you are studying for your next psychology exam. Which of the following factors will be most influential in whether you can remember the material later? (p. 179)
    a. How hard you studied for your exam
    b. How much you wanted to do well
    c. How much you organized new information into your existing knowledge
    d. How emotionally charged the information was

14. Elaborative encoding will improve your _____ because it organizes and integrates information into what you already know. (p. 179)
    a. depth of processing
    b. breadth of processing
    c. reality monitoring
    d. dynamic memory

15. Alexa is given the following list of words to remember: rape, murder, burglary, book, arson, kidnapping, terrorism. Which word(s) would you think that Alexa would be most likely to forget? (p. 180)
    a. Rape
    b. Burglary
    c. Book
    d. Arson

PRACTICE TEST #3:
WHEN MEMORY GOES WRONG

True/False Questions

Circle TRUE or FALSE for each of the following statements.

1. TRUE   FALSE   We do not always remember what actually happens to us. (p. 184)

2. TRUE   FALSE   Most people will discount their own false memories when told that they are false. (p. 185)

3. TRUE   FALSE   Some false memories are easier to create than others. (p. 185)

4. TRUE   FALSE   Misleading questions can interfere with real memories. (p. 185)

5. TRUE   FALSE   The recall of false memories activates different areas of the brain than does the recall of actual memories. (p. 185)

6. TRUE   FALSE   Reality monitoring can help us to distinguish false from actual memories. (p. 186)

7. TRUE   FALSE   The decay theory of forgetting proposes that connections between neurons are lost over time. (p. 187)

8. TRUE   FALSE   Retroactive interference disrupts memory for things that are learned later. (p. 188)

9. TRUE   FALSE   Penfield's studies showed that people retain all memories forever. (p. 187)

10. TRUE   FALSE   Infantile amnesia is common. (p. 188)

Multiple-Choice Questions

For each question, circle the letter of the best answer.

1. To be able to distinguish real from imagined stimuli, individuals should use _____ when encoding information. (p. 186)
    a. state-dependent retrieval
    b. consolidation
    c. rehearsal
    d. reality monitoring

2.	Evidence for decay theory comes from _____. (p. 187)
	a.	studies of sea slugs showing that neural connections are lost over time
	b.	Penfield's studies, in which he stimulated parts of the brain during brain surgery
	c.	studies showing that retrieval cues can accidentally trigger the wrong memory
	d.	studies showing that some memories are never encoded

3.	Interference can occur because _____. (pp. 187-188)
	a.	the brain has limited capacity to store information
	b.	we don't want to remember certain events
	c.	we are distracted by extraneous factors when encoding information
	d.	retrieval cues for various memories are often similar

4.	_____ amnesia disrupts previous memories but doesn't prevent the learning of new facts. (p. 188)
	a.	Episodic
	b.	Anterograde
	c.	Retrograde
	d.	Semantic

5.	Anterograde amnesia affects all _____ memories. (p. 188)
	a.	implicit
	b.	false
	c.	explicit
	d.	source

6.	Hypnosis _____. (p. 193)
	a.	almost always enhances memory *and* confidence in recollections
	b.	usually enhances memory but not confidence in recollections
	c.	usually enhances confidence in recollections but not actual memories
	d.	enhances neither memory not confidence in recollections

7.	Schacter suggests that the reason for repressed memories of abuse is that _____. (p. 190)
	a.	therapists implant false memories
	b.	it is as if the person were "someone else" during the abuse and, thus, has few retrieval cues for accessing the memory until later
	c.	everyone experiences infantile amnesia
	d.	people who repress memories are more suggestible in general than other people

8.	Martha is unable to form new memories, but can remember her past perfectly. Martha probably has _____. (p. 188)
	a.	Alzheimer's disease
	b.	anterograde amnesia
	c.	retrograde amnesia
	d.	damage to her amygdala

9.   Which of the following memory techniques was discovered by the ancient Greek orator Simonides? (p. 191)
   a.   Interactive images
   b.   Method of loci
   c.   Pegword system
   d.   Hierarchical organization

10.   In the mnemonic technique involving a list of rhymes, such as *"One is a bun,"* the bun is the _____. (p. 191)
   a.   interactive image
   b.   pegword
   c.   initialism
   d.   loci

11.   Most people remember that *FBI* stands for Federal Bureau of Investigation because FBI is a(n) _____. (p. 191)
   a.   pegword
   b.   initialism
   c.   modality-specific memory
   d.   acronym

12.   In order to remember Dr. Oakley's name, Maureen imagines Dr. Oakley swinging from an oak tree. Which mnemonic device is Maureen using? (p. 190)
   a.   Method of loci
   b.   Forming a story
   c.   Interactive images
   d.   Hierarchical organization

13.   Mnemonic devices _____. (p. 190)
   a.   give people short-cuts for remembering information, so that the information does not waste a lot of space in working memory
   b.   provide an effort-free way to remember material
   c.   provide a visual way to remember information
   d.   help people make connections between information to-be-remembered and what they already know

14.   In most cases, hypnosis has the effect of _____. (p. 193)
   a.   improving people's confidence in their memories
   b.   improving the accuracy of people's memories
   c.   improving the quantity of people's memories
   d.   decreasing the vividness of people's memories

15.   Which of the following is NOT part of Fisher's method for interviewing, which is frequently used by detectives? (p. 192)
   a.   Focus on the task at hand.
   b.   Mentally reinstate the environment in which the information was learned.
   c.   If you can't remember immediately, it is gone and you should just give up.
   d.   Try to think of characteristics of the information you are trying to remember.

COMPREHENSIVE PRACTICE TEST

True/False Questions

Circle TRUE or FALSE for each of the following statements.

1.   TRUE   FALSE   Sensory memory happens automatically, without effort. (p. 167)

2.   TRUE   FALSE   Information in short-term memory can last for up to a day. (p. 168)

3.   TRUE   FALSE   Incidental learning can be as effective as intentional learning. (p. 179)

4.   TRUE   FALSE   Flashbulb memories are more emotionally charged than other memories. (p. 181)

5.   TRUE   FALSE   Misleading questions can lead to false memories. (p. 185)

6.   TRUE   FALSE   The interference theory has been largely supported by evidence. (p. 187)

7.   TRUE   FALSE   Anterograde amnesia leaves consolidated memories intact. (p. 188)

8.   TRUE   FALSE   The most effective mnemonic device is the use of interactive images. (p. 190)

9.   TRUE   FALSE   Memories are initially stored in long-term memory in a dynamic form. (p. 178)

10. TRUE   FALSE   Improved memory for the first few items in a set is called the recency effect. (p. 170)

Multiple-Choice Questions

For each question, circle the letter of the best answer.

1.   The type of memory that holds information for the shortest period of time is _____ memory. (p. 167)
   a.   short-term
   b.   sensory
   c.   long-term
   d.   working

2.	The visual form of sensory memory is called _____ memory. (p. 167)
	a.	iconic
	b.	working
	c.	echoic
	d.	sensory

3.	You can hold information in short-term memory by _____. (p. 169)
	a.	consolidation
	b.	priming
	c.	rehearsal
	d.	overlearning

4.	Suppose that you have been in Dr. Bolen's class for a whole semester. One day, your study partner remarks what blue eyes Dr. Bolen has. The fact that you never noticed this before is evidence that you have experienced _____. (p. 177)
	a.	amnesia
	b.	retrieval failure
	c.	storage failure
	d.	encoding failure

5.	Verbal and visual memories are *explicit* if the words or images _____. (p. 171)
	a.	can be called to mind
	b.	have been processed through working memory
	c.	are integrated in a coherent fashion
	d.	are autobiographical

6.	A *habit* is a type of _____ memory. (p. 172)
	a.	explicit
	b.	episodic
	c.	implicit
	d.	semantic

7.	Suppose that your professor includes some of the questions from this Grade Aid on her exams. You find that you can answer those questions more quickly than the test questions you haven't seen before. This is an example of _____. (p. 173)
	a.	repetition priming
	b.	recall
	c.	long-term memory
	d.	explicit memory

8.	Portions of the _____ lobes are particularly active when people encode new information. (p. 178)
	a.	occipital
	b.	frontal
	c.	temporal
	d.	parietal

9. Taking the practice tests in this Grade Aid will help you on your exams in your psychology class, particularly if the exams are multiple-choice. This is because of _____. (p. 179)
   a.   associative priming
   b.   elaborative encoding
   c.   repetition priming
   d.   transfer appropriate processing

10. Students who audit a class—take it without earning credit—often do not take notes or study, but learn nonetheless. In fact, they often learn as much as students who *try* to learn. This result reflects _____. (p. 179)
    a.   unintentional learning
    b.   transfer appropriate processing
    c.   incidental learning
    d.   associative priming

11. An unusually vivid and accurate memory of a dramatic event is called a _____. (p. 181)
    a.   flashbulb memory
    b.   declarative memory
    c.   flashlight memory
    d.   semantic memory

12. Improved memory for emotionally charged events can be attributed to _____. (p. 181)
    a.   an increase in people's confidence for these memories
    b.   increased activity in the amygdala
    c.   increased activity in the hypothalamus
    d.   people trying harder to learn this information

13. Most of us suffer from _____ amnesia, which prevents us from remembering our early childhood experiences. (p. 188)
    a.   retroactive
    b.   anterograde
    c.   infantile
    d.   repressed

14. Perhaps the most controversial issue in memory research today is whether or not _____. (p. 189)
    a.   flashbulb memories are accurate
    b.   information we forget is actually still in memory somewhere
    c.   repressed memories exist
    d.   false memories can be constructed

15. "ROY G BIV" is a name many people use to remember the seven colors of the rainbow. This use of letters that spell out a name is an example of a(n) _____. (p. 191)
    a. association
    b. method of loci
    c. pegword
    d. initialism

16. Suppose that your psychology class is held at noon each day, which is your preferred time to eat lunch. According to the effect called state-dependent retrieval, you will perform best on a test given _____. (p. 183)
    a. at noon
    b. just after lunch
    c. after you have completed the Grade Aid assignments
    d. after studying with a study partner

17. When you remember information without using it repetitively, the information has been stored in a _____ form. (p. 178)
    a. visual
    b. structural
    c. dynamic
    d. verbal

18. Episodic and semantic memories are _____. (p. 171)
    a. explicit
    b. implicit
    c. procedural
    d. autobiographical

19. After being in a car accident in which her head hit the windshield, Carly was no longer able to form new memories. Carly was probably suffering from _____. (p. 188)
    a. retroactive interference
    b. source amnesia
    c. anterograde amnesia
    d. retrograde amnesia

20. Working memory is different from short-term memory in that it _____. (p. 174)
    a. uses different neural patterns
    b. includes processes, as well as stores
    c. is more affected by genetics than short-term memory
    d. all of the above are differences between the two

Essay Questions

Answer each of the questions in the space provided.

1. Is short-term memory really different from long-term memory? _____

   _____

   _____

   _____

   _____

   _____

   _____

   _____

   _____

2. How is a habit also a memory? _____

   _____

   _____

   _____

   _____

   _____

   _____

3. "I understood everything you said. I just don't understand why I didn't do better on the test!" This is something college professors hear all the time. Why *don't* students remember all of the class material when taking an exam? _____

   _____

   _____

   _____

   _____

   _____

   _____

   _____

   _____

   _____

   _____

4. Are repressed memories real? _____

   _____

   _____

   _____

   _____

   _____

   _____

   _____

   _____

   _____

5.   On page 180, the text states that "it barely matters how much or how hard you *try* to learn
        something; what matters is how well you integrate and organize the material." What
        implications does this statement have for your academic success? Have you ever tried hard
        to remember something but found that you couldn't? Was the inability to recall due to
        faulty integration and organization? Did reading this chapter help you to recognize ways in
        which you could possibly enhance your own learning and memory? How?

        _____
        _____
        _____
        _____
        _____
        _____
        _____
        _____
        _____
        _____
        _____
        _____
        _____

6.   What implications do false memories have for eyewitness testimony? Should eyewitness
        testimony be allowed in court? What precautions should be taken in allowing eyewitness
        testimony? _____

        _____
        _____
        _____
        _____
        _____
        _____
        _____
        _____
        _____
        _____

7.   Imagine that you are a judge hearing a case involving a woman who alleges her father abused
        her when she was 2 years old. She has recently remembered the event, while undergoing
        psychotherapy. What questions would you want to ask the woman and her therapist?
        Would you allow the repressed memory evidence to be presented in the courtroom? Why or
        why not? _____

        _____
        _____
        _____
        _____
        _____
        _____
        _____
        _____
        _____

8.   People will often say, "I have a bad *memory*." Knowing what you do know, about how many different kinds of memories there are, why is this probably an inaccurate statement? Explain._____

_____

_____

_____

_____

_____

_____

9.   Why do you forget information that you need (such as information needed for exams)?

_____

_____

_____

_____

_____

_____

_____

_____

10.   What is the difference between short-term memory and working memory?

_____

_____

_____

_____

_____

_____

_____

_____

_____

When You Are Finished...Puzzle It Out

Across

4. Unit of memory
7. Discovered by Simonides
8. Amnesia that disrupts previous information
9. Unusually vivid and accurate memory
12. Matching encoded input to stored
14. Mental representations
15. Memory that is lost if inactive
17. Amnesia for childhood events
18. Established the forgetting curve

Puzzle created with Puzzlemaker at DiscoverySchool.com.

Down

1. Better memory for first few items in set
2. Also called declarative memory
3. Memories of general facts
5. Form of broad encoding
6. Theory that memory degrades over time
7. Devices that improve memory
8. Repeating information over and over
10. Learning without trying
11. Stimuli that help people remember
13. Visual sensory memory
16. Also called procedural memories

Chapter 6
Language, Thinking and Intelligence: What Humans Do Best

Before You Read . . .

When and how did you learn to speak? Why is your best friend a Spanish major, yet you can't roll your *r*'s? Language has many components, including sounds, word meanings, grammar, and implied meanings. Each of these components contributes to our abilities to produce and understand language. This chapter explores these and other topics related to language.

Moving from language to thought, the chapter next covers the foundations of thought before turning to problem solving, logic, and reasoning. After reading this chapter, maybe you'll be a more logical and effective problem solver!

Finally, this chapter presents an overview of intelligence and IQ, or intelligence quotient, which is a measurement of intelligence. Have you ever taken an IQ test? What did those results mean, exactly? The definition of intelligence continues to be debated, but generally it is considered to be "the ability to solve problems well and to understand and learn complex materials." However, some researchers have introduced new concepts of intelligence, including emotional intelligence and multiple intelligences.

You will learn what makes some people smart. Do smarter people have bigger heads, faster processing abilities, better memories, or just better DNA? Clearly, genetics play a role in intelligence, but so does the environment. Both factors also play a role in determining the intelligence and functioning level of people who are mentally retarded, gifted, or creative.

Chapter Objectives

After reading this chapter, you should be able to:

♦   Name the essential characteristics of all languages.

♦   Explain how first and second languages are learned and used.

♦   Discuss the relationship between language and thought.

♦   Describe how we think with mental images.

♦   Explain the idea of concepts and the different levels of concepts.

- Describe the methods used to solve problems.

- Discuss obstacles to problem solving.

- Define and discuss logical thinking.

- Compare and contrast different theories of intelligence.

- Identify and explain how intelligence is measured.

- Describe what IQ tests are, how they are scored, and what they say about a person's future.

- Discuss what makes people intelligent.

- Describe research on group differences in intelligence.

- Explain and summarize research on mental retardation and giftedness.

- Define creativity and explain why some people are more creative than others.

As You Read. . .Term Identification

Make flashcards using the following terms as you go. Use the definitions in the margins of this chapter for help. If you write the definitions in your own words, though, you will remember them better!

Affirming the consequent
Algorithm
Availability heuristic
Base-rate rule
Basic level
Category
Concept
Confirmation bias
Creativity
Crystallized intelligence
Deductive reasoning
Down syndrome
Emotional intelligence
Factor analysis
Fetal alcohol syndrome
Fluid intelligence
Functional fixedness
g
Gifted
Heuristic

Inductive reasoning
Intelligence
Intelligence quotient (IQ)
Language comprehension
Language production
Linguistic relativity hypothesis
Logic
Mental images
Mental set
Mentally retarded
Microenvironment
Morpheme
Norming
Phoneme
Phonology
Pragmatics
Primary mental abilities
Problem
Prodigies
Propositional representation

Prototype
Representation problem
Representativeness heuristic
s
Schema
Semantics
Standardized sample

Strategy
Syntax
Test bias
Theory of multiple intelligences
Typicality
Weschler Adult Intelligence Scale (WAIS)

As You Read. . . Questions and Exercises

Language: More Than Meets the Ear

The Essentials: What Makes Language Language?

What is the difference between **language production** and **language comprehension**?

_____

_____

_____

_____

Language is best understood as having four aspects: **phonology**, **syntax**, **semantics**, and **pragmatics**. Indicate below which aspect is illustrated in each example.

Example	Aspect of Language
Grammar produces this aspect of language	
Represented by morphemes	
Helps us to understand jokes and metaphors	
The difference between "cat" and bat"	
Can't program a computer to do this (at least, so far!)	
A sentence needs a noun and a verb phrase	
The difference between "read" and "reading"	
The basic building blocks of speech	

In the following sentence, identify a **phoneme**, a **morpheme**, the **semantic meaning** of the words, and the **pragmatic meaning** of the entire sentence.

"People in glass houses should not throw stones."

Phoneme: _____

Morpheme: _____

Semantic meaning: _____

Pragmatic meaning: _____

How many **morphemes** are in the word "redefined"? What are they? What do they mean?

_____
_____
_____
_____
_____

Write a sentence that has meaning, but is **syntactically incorrect**: _____

_____

Write a sentence that is **syntactically correct**, but has no meaning. _____

_____

Suppose that you were a lawyer, questioning a child witness. How could you use your knowledge of children's skills in pragmatics to obtain the best testimony? _____

_____
_____
_____

How are each of the **hemispheres** involved in **pragmatics**?

Left Hemisphere	Right Hemisphere

Explain the roles of the left and right hemispheres in language.

♦ **Left:** _____
_____
_____

♦ **Right:** _____
_____
_____

Bilingualism: A Window of Opportunity?

Have you taken a course in a foreign language in high school or college? What aspects of the **language** were the hardest to learn? The **vocabulary**? The **grammar**? **Reading** or **writing**? Given what you have learned in this chapter, explain why you may (or may not) have had difficulty learning a **second language**. _____
_____
_____
_____
_____
_____
_____
_____

Looking at Levels

Explain why—at the three levels—**language** is uniquely *human*. Draw arrows to show how factors at these levels may interact in creating language.

The Brain	The Person	The Group

TRY PRACTICE TEST #1 NOW!
GOOD LUCK!

Thinking: Understanding the World and Guiding Behavior

Words: Inner Speech and Spoken Thoughts

What are the three problems with asserting that **thinking** is just talking to yourself?

♦ _____

♦ _____

♦ _____

What is the evidence that **language** shapes **thought**?

♦ _____
_____
_____

♦ _____
_____
_____

♦ _____
_____
_____

What is the evidence that **language** does not shape **thought**?_____
_____
_____
_____

Mental Imagery: Perception Without Sensation

In your own words, describe the three properties of **mental space**:

♦ _____

♦ _____

♦ _____

Try the exercises for testing the properties of mental space described in the text. Does your experience demonstrate the three properties? _____
_____

How can we explain the following characteristics about **visual images**:

♦   **Spatial extent:** _____
_____
_____

♦   **Limits on spatial extent:** _____
_____
_____

♦   **Grain:** _____
_____
_____

Concepts: Neither Images nor Words

How are **concepts** different from words or images? For each of the following items, indicate whether you think of a word, an image, or neither (a concept):

Item	Word/Image/Concept
Book	
Anger	
Freedom	
Hunger	
Automobile	
Excitement	

Why was Aristotle's definition of the features of a **concept** (necessary and sufficient) inaccurate? For the following **concepts**, see if you can come up with **necessary and sufficient features:**

Concept	Necessary Feature	Sufficient Feature
Bird		
Friend		
Depression		
Hunger		

Name a **prototype** and a **non-prototype** to illustrate each of the following **concepts:**

Concept	Prototype	Non-prototype
Bird		
Mammal		
Furniture		
Fruit		

For the following concepts at the **basic level**, describe one related **concept** that is more **general** and one that is more **specific**.

Concept	More General	More Specific
Apple		
Car		
House		
Angry		
Computer		

For the following **schemas**, list one **necessary** and one **optional aspect.**

Schema	Necessary Aspect	Optional Aspect
Classroom		
Parent		
Airplane		
Beverage		
Tree		

How does the **brain** store **concepts**? _____
_____
_____

How to Solve Problems: More Than Inspiration

What difficulties can arise during the **representation** of a problem that can make it difficult to solve the problem? _____
_____
_____
_____

Name one instance in which you use an **algorithm,** and describe how you use it.
_____
_____
_____

Name one instance in which you use a **heuristic,** and describe how you use it.
_____
_____
_____

Can you remember any time you have used **analogical reasoning** to solve a problem? If so, describe. _____
_____
_____
_____

Name and briefly describe five things that you can do to overcome obstacles to **problem solving**:

◆ _____
  _____

◆ _____
  _____

◆ _____
  _____

◆ _____
  _____

◆ _____
  _____

GO SURFING ...

... at one of the following sites and try some of the **logic** puzzles there:
◆   http://www.thakur.demon.nl/
◆   http://einstein.et.tudelft.nl/~arlet/puzzles/logic.html
◆   http://puzzles.karplus.org/

What **obstacles** did you face? How did you overcome them? (Or did you?) _____
_____
_____
_____

Logic, Reasoning, and Decision Making

Identify the type of reasoning, **deductive** or **inductive**, in the following situations:

Situation	Type of Reasoning
In her new town, Susan met three people, all of whom were rude to her. She therefore assumed that all people in the new town would be rude.	
All aliens have an antenna. An antenna allows aliens to communicate with the mothership. All aliens can communicate with the mothership.	
Frank bought a car that turned out to be a lemon. He told his friends not to buy a car from that dealer, as all of the cars on the lot were sure to be lemons.	
When the barometric pressure drops, it rains. When it rains, the plants grow. When the barometric pressure drops, the plants grow.	

Identify the type of error, **affirming the consequent** or **confirmation bias** in each example:

Situation	Error
All babies are bald. Jim is bald. Jim must be a baby!	
Lara is convinced that she is psychic because yesterday she picked up the phone to call a friend just as her friend called her!	
Ignoring her dissatisfaction, poor coworker relationships, and demanding boss, Paula convinced herself that she loved her job because she was well-paid.	
If it rains today, people will carry umbrellas. People are carrying umbrellas, so it must be raining!	

People do not always use the **rules of logic**, but instead sometimes rely on sets of heuristics. These can result in wrong conclusions. Define each of the following **heuristics**, and explain how it may result in errors.

Heuristic	Definition	How May It Result in Errors?
Representativeness		
Availability		

Identify what type of **logical error** is made in each of the following situations: **representativeness heuristic** or **availability heuristic**.

Situation	Error
Vince's neighbor is a quiet, reserved unmarried woman. When asked to guess whether she is a nurse or a librarian, Vince guesses that she must be a librarian.	
More people are victims of homicide than die of stomach cancer every year.	

What is the evidence that **emotions** can facilitate **decision making**? _____

_____

_____

_____

_____

_____

_____

Looking at Levels

How could doctors use an analysis of pain at the three levels (and their interactions) to provide better patient care? Discuss. _____

_____

_____

_____

_____

_____

_____

TRY PRACTICE TEST #2 NOW!
GOOD LUCK!

Intelligence:
Is There More Than One Way To Be Smart?

Measuring Intelligence: What is IQ?

Who is the smartest person you know? Describe him or her. _____
_____
_____
_____

What makes that person so **intelligent**?_____
_____
_____
_____
_____

Based on the above, what is your definition of **intelligence**?_____
_____
_____
_____
_____

Who started **intelligence tests** and why?_____
_____
_____
_____
_____

What was **Wechsler**'s major complaint about the **Stanford-Binet Test of Intelligence**? How did
he design his IQ tests to overcome this limitation?_____
_____
_____

How were **IQ tests** originally scored? What was the problem with that method?_____
_____
_____
_____
_____

How are **intelligence tests** scored now? Why?_____
_____
_____
_____
_____

Name and describe a test or measurement that is not **reliable**. _____

_____

_____

_____

_____

Name and describe a test or measurement that is not **valid** for a certain purpose. _____

_____

_____

_____

_____

Draw a **normal curve** below.
-      Indicate the mean and mark off standard deviations.
-      In a different color ink, indicate the range of IQ scores of typical college students.

If **IQ** and **job success** are positively correlated, why can't we say that intelligence leads to success or that it causes one to be successful? _____

_____

_____

_____

_____

Intelligence: One Ability or Many?

Which theory of **intelligence** is most similar to yours? _____

_____

_____

_____

_____

Which theory of **intelligence** is most different from yours? _____

_____

_____

_____

_____

GO SURFING ...

... at the following sites and take the IQ tests there:
♦   http://www.iqtest.com/ (traditional psychometric test)
♦   http://www.utne.com/interact/test_iq.html (emotional intelligence test)
♦   http://www.acsu.buffalo.edu/~rom2/center/new_page_2.htm (multiple intelligences test)

What were your scores on these tests?_____
_____

Which test score do you think best represents your **intelligence**? Why? _____
_____
_____
_____
_____

What other variables might have influenced your score, besides your **intelligence**? _____
_____
_____
_____
_____

In the **normal curve** you drew (on the previous page), mark an X indicating where you fall, using the best score from the tests you took above.

In your own words, what are **fluid** and **crystallized intelligence**?

♦   **Fluid:** _____
_____
_____

♦   **Crystallized:** _____
_____
_____

Why do you think **fluid intelligence** tends to diminish as one ages, but **crystallized intelligence** does not? _____
_____
_____
_____

Do you think that people can improve their **crystallized** and/or **fluid intelligence**? If so, how?

_____
_____
_____
_____

Name three types of careers in which you think **crystallized intelligence** would be vital. Briefly explain why it would be so important in each.

♦   _____
       _____
       _____

♦   _____
       _____
       _____

♦   _____
       _____
       _____

Name three careers in which you think **fluid intelligence** would be vital. Briefly explain why it would be so important in each.

♦   _____
       _____
       _____

♦   _____
       _____
       _____

♦   _____
       _____
       _____

Do you think most of your school tests measure **fluid** or **crystallized intelligence** better? _____

_____
_____
_____
_____

Imagine that you are a social studies teacher and are trying to teach students about the Revolutionary War. How could you teach this so that students with each of the following kinds of intelligence could best grasp the material?

♦ **Linguistic:** _____
_____
_____

♦ **Spatial:** _____
_____
_____

♦ **Musical:** _____
_____
_____

♦ **Logical-mathematical:** _____
_____
_____

♦ **Bodily-kinesthetic:** _____
_____
_____

♦ **Intrapersonal:** _____
_____
_____

♦ **Interpersonal:** _____
_____
_____

♦ **Naturalist:** _____
_____
_____

♦ **Existential:** _____
_____
_____

Do you agree that **Gardner's theory** is about **intelligence** (or do you agree with his critics, who claim that some of these are talents, not intelligences)? Explain. _____
_____
_____
_____
_____

Write a question that would test each of the following types of intelligence (from **Sternberg's theory**.

♦ **Analytic:** _____
_____
_____

♦ **Practical:** _____
_____
_____

♦ **Creative:** _____
_____
_____

Can you think of someone who may or may not be highly **intelligent** (using a traditional definition), but who is very **emotionally intelligent**? Describe him or her. How successful has this person been? Why? _____
_____
_____
_____

After having taken **intelligence tests**, how do you feel about using such tests for school placement?
_____
_____
_____
_____

Suppose that parents had their child take an **IQ test** for the purpose of determining whether the child should be placed in a gifted and talented class. Analyze the effects of this decision at each of the three levels.

♦ **Level of the Brain:** _____
_____
_____

♦ **Level of the Person:** _____
_____
_____

♦ **Level of the Group:** _____
_____
_____

Looking at Levels

List some of the factors at the **three levels** that may affect a person's performance on an **intelligence test**. Draw arrows to indicate the interactions between events at the different levels.

The Brain	The Person	The Group

TRY PRACTICE TEST #3 NOW!
GOOD LUCK!

What Makes Us Smart: Nature and Nurture

In each pair of people below, circle those who would have more similar **IQs**:

Fraternal twins raised together	vs.	Identical twins reared apart
Child and adoptive mother	vs.	Child and biological mother
Fraternal twins raised apart	vs.	Child and biological mother
Siblings raised apart	vs.	Siblings raised together
Child and adoptive mother	vs.	Siblings raised apart
Fraternal twins raised together	vs.	Siblings raised together

The usual estimate of the **heritability** of intelligence is .50. What does this mean? _____
_____
_____
_____
_____

What are the four problems with interpreting **heritability scores**? Explain.

◆ _____
_____
_____

- ◆ _____
    _____
    _____
    _____

- ◆ _____
    _____
    _____
    _____

- ◆ _____
    _____
    _____
    _____

Group Differences in Intelligence

Why don't heritability estimates tell us anything about **group differences** in intelligence?_____
_____
_____
_____
_____
_____
_____

Discuss four possible reasons for the finding that White Americans have an average IQ that is 10-15 points higher than that of African Americans.

- ◆ _____
    _____
    _____

- ◆ _____
    _____
    _____

- ◆ _____
    _____
    _____

- ◆ _____
    _____
    _____

GO SURFING ...

... at http://www.highiqsociety.org/ and take the **Culture-Fair IQ test** there.

How was this test different than the **traditional IQ test** you took earlier? (Or, was it?) _____
_____
_____
_____
_____

Do you think this test was **culture-fair**? Why or why not? _____
_____
_____
_____
_____

How do men and women's intellectual strengths differ?_____
_____
_____
_____
_____

What is the evidence that these differences are **biologically determined**? _____
_____
_____
_____
_____

What is the evidence that these differences are **environmentally determined**?_____
_____
_____
_____
_____

Some research findings indicate that biology affects **gender differences** in intelligence; other findings indicate that the environment affects these differences. How can both sets of research findings be accurate? Explain._____
_____
_____
_____

Diversity in Intelligence

What are the three criteria for **mental retardation**?

♦ _____

♦ _____

♦ _____

Return to the **normal curve** you drew earlier. In a different colored ink, mark the borderline IQ for mental retardation.

Have you ever known anyone with **mental retardation**? If so, describe his or her level of functioning. _____
_____
_____
_____

Suppose that you had a child with **Down syndrome**. What could you do to maximize his or her functioning? _____
_____
_____
_____
_____

What does it mean to be "**gifted**"? _____
_____
_____
_____
_____

What are some possible "prices" of **giftedness**? _____
_____
_____
_____

Creative Smarts

What are the two types of thinking that lead to **creativity**? Name and briefly describe each type.

♦ _____

♦ _____

Now, give yourself exactly 2 minutes to think of as many uses for a paper clip as you can. List them here:

Now, divide the total number of uses by two. The answer is your **creativity** score: _____
(The average score is four; eight is a very high score.)

Do you think this test is a good measure of **creativity**? Why or why not? _____
_____
_____
_____
_____

Here is a checklist of some of the special abilities and characteristics that **creative** people appear to have. Check all of the abilities that you think you have.

_____   1.   the ability to generate many solutions
_____   2.   the ability to choose among solutions well
_____   3.   the ability to keep options open
_____   4.   the ability to keep from making snap decisions about the likely outcome of
                     an effort
_____   5.   the ability to see problems from multiple vantage points
_____   6.   the ability to be flexible
_____   7.   the ability to reorganize information
_____   8.   the ability to think in terms of analogies
_____   9.   high intelligence
_____   10.   wide interests
_____   11.   not liking traditional dogmas
_____   12.   high self-esteem
_____   13.   fondness for hard work
_____   14.   high motivation and persistence
_____   15.   being driven to create

Do you think of yourself as **creative**? Why or why not? _____

_____

_____

_____

_____

What environmental factors do you think contributed to your **creativity**?_____

_____

_____

_____

_____

Looking at Levels

Explain the factors at each of the three levels that influence **creativity**. Draw arrows to show how these factors may interact.

The Brain	The Person	The Group

TRY PRACTICE TEST #4 NOW!
GOOD LUCK!

After You Read . . . Thinking Back

1. How might being left-handed rather than right-handed influence language acquisition and disruption (following brain damage, for example)?_____

    _____

    _____

    _____

    _____

2. How do you think myelination of different brain parts (discussed in Chapter 2) affects individuals' language and thinking?_____

    _____

    _____

    _____

    _____

3. How do you think the shift from behaviorism to cognitive psychology (as discussed in Chapter 1) influenced the study of thinking? _____

    _____

    _____

    _____

    _____

    _____

4. Do you think that there are particular difficulties with the research methodology used to study thinking, as opposed to some other topics in psychology? _____

    _____

    _____

    _____

    _____

    _____

5. The importance of imagery was demonstrated in Tolman and Honzik's study of cognitive maps (described in Chapter 4). What did these researchers find?

    _____

    _____

    _____

    _____

    _____

    _____

6. This chapter discusses some of the obstacles in problem solving. What steps of the information processing theory (presented in Chapter 6) do these obstacles represent?_____

_____
_____
_____
_____
_____

7. What type of studies are adoption studies (e.g., experiments, correlational studies, quasi-experiments)? What are the advantages and disadvantages of this type of study? How are these reflected in adoption studies on intelligence? _____

_____
_____
_____
_____
_____

8. Do you think that people with high IQs differ from people with low IQs in terms of learning? If so, in what type of learning (classical, operant, social, or cognitive)? How? What evidence supports your opinion? _____

_____
_____
_____
_____
_____

After You Read . . . Practice Tests

PRACTICE TEST #1:
LANGUAGE

True/False Questions

Circle TRUE or FALSE for each of the following statements.

1.   TRUE   FALSE   Semantics refers to the meaning of a sentence. (p. 202)

2.   TRUE   FALSE   Pragmatics involves being able to read the underlying meaning of a sentence. (p. 204)

3.   TRUE   FALSE   Different languages use different numbers of phonemes. (p. 201)

4.   TRUE   FALSE   English uses approximately 45 phonemes. (p. 201)

5.   TRUE   FALSE   People store propositions, rather than the literal meanings of sentences. (p. 203)

Multiple-Choice Questions

For each question, circle the letter of the best answer.

1.   The basic building blocks of speech sounds are called _____. (p. 201)
   a.   vowels
   b.   phonemes
   c.   consonants
   d.   pragmemes

2.   In comparison to the English language, French _____. (p. 201)
   a.   is more difficult to speak
   b.   has fewer phonemes
   c.   is more "cultured"
   d.   doesn't stress syllables

3.   The smallest unit of meaning in a language is represented by a _____. (p. 202)
   a.   phoneme
   b.   word
   c.   morpheme
   d.   syllable

4.   The *implied* meaning of an utterance is called _____. (p. 204)
       a.   pragmatics
       b.   syntax
       c.   semantics
       d.   morphology

5.   Patients with damage to the right hemisphere cannot understand _____.
       (p. 204)
       a.   verbs
       b.   questions
       c.   sentences
       d.   jokes

6.   The ability to understand language is called _____. (p. 201)
       a.   language comprehension
       b.   language production
       c.   phonology
       d.   semantics

7.   The word "redialed" has _____ morphemes. (p. 202)
       a.   1
       b.   2
       c.   3
       d.   4

8.   Saying "car the drive" would violate rules of _____. (p. 202)
       a.   phonology
       b.   syntax
       c.   semantics
       d.   pragmatics

9.   How do humans and chimps differ with regard to language? (p. 206)
       a.   Only humans can string symbols together to make sentences.
       b.   Only humans spontaneously create new statements.
       c.   Only humans can learn sign language.
       d.   Only humans are motivated to use language.

10.   Under which circumstance will Jeff be more likely to learn a second language? (p. 205)
       a.   If his parents are native speakers of the second language
       b.   If he has an advanced formal education
       c.   If he is older than 15 when he starts learning the language
       d.   If he has a high IQ

PRACTICE TEST #2:
THINKING

True/False Questions
Circle TRUE or FALSE for each of the following statements.

1.   TRUE   FALSE   Language and images are the only means by which we think. (p. 211)

2.   TRUE   FALSE   Thinking is just "talking to oneself." (p. 208)

3.   TRUE   FALSE   The most common form of mental imagery is visual. (p. 209)

4.   TRUE   FALSE   The Dani, who have only two words for color ("light" and "dark"), do not perceive different shades of color. (p. 208)

5.   TRUE   FALSE   The written structure of a language may affect how people think. (p. 209)

Fill-in-the-Blank Questions
Fill in each blank with a word from the word bank.

WORD BANK	
algorithm analogy heuristic	representation strategies

The first step to solving any problem is figuring out how to approach it; this challenge is called the

_____ problem. There are two _____, or approaches to solving

problems. The first is a(n) _____, a methodical, step-by-step approach that often

results in the right answer but is slow and laborious. The second approach, using a(n) _____

_____, is quicker but more prone to error. Another way to solve problems is to use a(n)

_____, comparing features of the novel problem to a problem you have already solved.

(pp. 215-216)

Multiple-Choice Questions

For each question, circle the letter of the best answer.

1.   According to _____, thinking is shaped by the particular language we speak. (p. 208)
   a.   the language acquisition device
   b.   the linguistic relativity hypothesis
   c.   the critical period theory
   d.   John B. Watson

2.   The most common form of mental imagery is _____. (p. 209)
   a.   auditory
   b.   olfactory
   c.   visual
   d.   somatosensory

3.   The reason that it takes longer to mentally scan the walls of a big room than to mentally scan the walls of a small room is because of the _____ of mental space. (p. 209)
   a.   grain
   b.   limited size
   c.   spatial extent
   d.   topographical organization

4.   Which of the following is the best prototype of a chair? (p. 213)
   a.   Bar stool
   b.   Rocking chair
   c.   Dining-room chair
   d.   Lawn chair

5.   Which of the following words is most likely to be at the basic level of concepts? (p. 214)
   a.   Furniture
   b.   Chair
   c.   Easy chair
   d.   Household items

6.   Which of the following is the least likely to be included in the schema for an elementary-school classroom? (p. 214)
   a.   Books
   b.   Student desks
   c.   Blackboard
   d.   Carpet

7.   The brain appears to organize concepts into two general classes: _____.
      (p. 214)
      a.   familiar and unfamiliar things
      b.   living things and manufactured objects
      c.   colored and noncolored objects
      d.   things and people

8.   Which of the following would be most difficult to visualize? (p. 211)
      a.   A close relative's face
      b.   A chocolate-chip cookie
      c.   Love
      d.   A clock

9.   The relationship between concepts, words, and images is that _____. (p. 211)
      a.   they are the same thing
      b.   words and images are different types of concepts
      c.   words and images are methods of expressing concepts
      d.   a & b

10.   If you want to be 100% certain that you get the correct answer to a math problem, you
      should use a(n) _____. (p. 216)
      a.   analogy
      b.   heuristic
      c.   algorithm
      d.   strategy

11.   The representation problem involves determining _____. (p. 215)
      a.   how to best visualize the problem
      b.   how to best formulate the nature of the problem
      c.   how to determine the criteria for a good decision
      d.   what type of strategy to use

12.   If you want to have an answer quickly, you should probably use a(n) _____.
      (p. 216)
      a.   insight
      b.   heuristic
      c.   strategy
      d.   algorithm

13.   If you get stuck solving a problem, which of the following might be helpful to try? (p. 217)
      a.   Walk away from the problem for awhile.
      b.   Be willing to consider other possible outcomes.
      c.   Don't forget what the problem is.
      d.   All of the above will be helpful

14.	The process of applying the principles of correct reasoning to reach a decision or evaluate the truth of a claim is called _____. (p. 218)
	a.	deductive reasoning
	b.	affirming the consequent
	c.	inductive reasoning
	d.	logic

15.	Which of the following does NOT matter in logic? (p. 218)
	a.	Content
	b.	Conclusion
	c.	Premises
	d.	Form

16.	People often make the error of _____ by assuming that a specific cause is present because a particular result has occurred. (p. 218)
	a.	deductive reasoning
	b.	affirming the consequent
	c.	inductive reasoning
	d.	affirming the premises

17.	Jeremy *really* wants to buy a new Corvette, so he attends a Corvette Lovers Convention and asks the Corvette owners there if they are happy with their cars. Jeremy is making the error of _____. (p. 218)
	a.	affirming the consequent
	b.	using the confirmation bias
	c.	denying the premise
	d.	buying an expensive car

18.	Reasoning that moves from a particular case to a generalization is called _____. (p. 218)
	a.	deductive reasoning
	b.	affirming the consequent
	c.	inductive reasoning
	d.	narrowing the stimulus field

19.	The _____ heuristic assumes that the more similar something is to a prototype stored in memory, the more likely it is that the entity belongs to the category of the prototype. (p. 219)
	a.	inductive
	b.	availability
	c.	deductive
	d.	representativeness

20. The _____ might explain why people tend to remember airplane crashes, but not car crashes. (p. 220)
    a.   prototype hypothesis
    b.   availability heuristic
    c.   planning fallacy
    d.   representativeness heuristic

PRACTICE TEST #3:
INTELLIGENCE

Matching Questions
Match each of the following theorists with the appropriate type of intelligence.

_____	1.	Spearman (p. 227)	a.	Emotional intelligence
_____	2.	Thurstone (p. 228)	b.	Analytic, practical, and creative intelligence
_____	3.	Cattell and Horn (p. 228)	c.	g and s
_____	4.	Gardner (p. 229)	d.	Primary mental abilities
_____	5.	Sternberg (p. 231)	e.	Crystallized and fluid intelligence
_____	6.	Goleman (p. 232)	f.	Multiple intelligences

Multiple-Choice Questions
For each question, circle the letter of the best answer.

1. The first intelligence test was devised to identify _____. (p. 224)
    a. military recruits who would make suitable officers
    b. immigrants who might "water down" the gene pool
    c. children in French schools who might need extra help
    d. gifted children who might contribute in a positive way to society

2. The most widely used intelligence tests in the United States today are the _____. (p. 224)
    a. Stanford-Binet scales
    b. Terman scales
    c. Wechsler scales
    d. Kaufman scales

3. A mean IQ score is _____. (p. 226)
    a. 10
    b. 20
    c. 50
    d. 100

4. Tests that are _____ yield consistent scores over time. (p. 226)
   a. reliable
   b. valid
   c. normed
   d. standardized

5. Which of the following are correlated with high intelligence? (p. 227)
   a. High GPAs
   b. Job success
   c. Stable marriages
   d. All of the above

6. Becoming an expert in an area boosts one's _____ intelligence. (p. 228)
   a. crystallized
   b. fluid
   c. verbal
   d. nonverbal

7. As people age, their _____ intelligence tends to diminish. (p. 228)
   a. verbal
   b. nonverbal
   c. crystallized
   d. fluid

8. When faced with a novel situation, it would be best to have _____ intelligence. (p. 228)
   a. crystallized
   b. fluid
   c. native
   d. acquired

9. Almost always, IQ scores for a whole population fall along a(n) _____. (p. 226)
   a. normal curve
   b. abnormal curve
   c. skewed distribution
   d. standard deviation

10. According to Sternberg and his colleagues, measures of _____ intelligence are the best predictors of how well someone will do on the job. (p. 231)
    a. standard
    b. analytic
    c. interpersonal
    d. practical

11. People with high emotional intelligence _____. (p. 232)
    a.   are self-motivating
    b.   understand their own emotions
    c.   recognize others' emotions
    d.   All of the above are true about such people.

12. Which statistical technique is used to uncover similar groups of attributes? (p. 228)
    a.   Factor analysis
    b.   Correlation
    c.   Norming
    d.   Calculating means

13. Sarah Hughes, 2002 Olympic gold-medal winner in figure skating, is probably high on which of Gardner's nine forms of intelligence? (p. 230)
    a.   Intrapersonal
    b.   Interpersonal
    c.   Naturalist
    d.   Bodily-kinesthetic

14. In the original Binet intelligence test, a bright child was one whose mental age was _____ his chronological age. (p. 224)
    a.   lower than
    b.   the same as
    c.   higher than
    d.   comparable to

15. Because the subtest scores on intelligence tests are all positively correlated, but to different degrees, Spearman argued that intelligence involves _____. (pp. 227-228)
    a.   the g factor
    b.   the a factor
    c.   the s factors
    d.   both a and c

PRACTICE TEST #4:
WHAT MAKES US SMART?

True/False Questions
Circle TRUE or FALSE for each of the following statements.

1.   TRUE   FALSE   Men are smarter than women. (p. 242)

2.   TRUE   FALSE   Women have better verbal skills than men. (p. 242)

3.   TRUE   FALSE   Evolutionary explanations for gender differences in IQ have received tremendous support. (p. 242)

4.   TRUE   FALSE   A woman's spatial ability depends on her monthly cycle of hormone levels. (p. 242)

5.   TRUE   FALSE   Some studies show a positive correlation between amount of testosterone and spatial ability. (p. 242)

6.   TRUE   FALSE   Men are worse at spatial tasks in the fall. (p. 242)

7.   TRUE   FALSE   People with mental retardation have IQs lower than 70 (p. 243)

8.   TRUE   FALSE   Creativity is highly heritable. (p. 245)

9.   TRUE   FALSE   Creative individuals tend to have high IQs. (p. 245)

10.   TRUE   FALSE   Prodigies have high IQs in all domains. (pp. 244-245)

Multiple-Choice Questions
For each question, circle the letter of the best answer.

1.   Males tend to be better than females at tasks requiring _____. (p. 242)
      a.   crystallized intelligence
      b.   fluid intelligence
      c.   verbal reasoning
      d.   spatial reasoning

2.   Better spatial ability appears to be related to _____. (p. 242)
      a.   excess testosterone (the more the better)
      b.   less testosterone (the less the better)
      c.   average amounts of testosterone (not too much or too little)
      d.   fluctuating amounts of testosterone throughout the day

3.   Approximately _____ of the variation in IQ is due to inherited characteristics. (p. 236)
        a.   10%
        b.   25%
        c.   50%
        d.   75%

4.   The environment you create by your presence is called the _____. (p. 238)
        a.   self-environment
        b.   microenvironment
        c.   minienvironment
        d.   microcosm

5.   As people age, genetic influences _____. (p. 239)
        a.   become more apparent
        b.   become less apparent
        c.   interact more with the environment
        d.   are more objective

6.   Which of the following findings suggest(s) that the environment has an influence on intelligence? (p. 238)
        a.   Biologically unrelated siblings show no IQ correlations as adults.
        b.   More enriched environments can raise IQ scores.
        c.   Identical twins have more similar IQs than fraternal twins.
        d.   All of the above

7.   According to the text, the high correlations between the IQ scores of identical twins separated at birth _____. (p. 237)
        a.   is clear evidence that IQ is largely heritable
        b.   needs to be interpreted cautiously
        c.   is clear evidence that IQ is largely environmental
        d.   suggests that intelligence is influenced by both heredity and the environment

8.   People with an IQ score of _____ or lower are traditionally considered to be mentally retarded. (p. 243)
        a.   100
        b.   80
        c.   70
        d.   50

9.   The most common form of mental retardation is _____. (p. 243)
        a.   Williams syndrome
        b.   Down syndrome
        c.   fetal alcohol syndrome
        d.   autism

10.   The prevalence of mild mental retardation appears to _____. (p. 243)
        a.   be increasing
        b.   be decreasing
        c.   be holding steady
        d.   vary from year to year

COMPREHENSIVE PRACTICE TEST

True-False Questions

Circle TRUE or FALSE for each of the following statements.

1. TRUE   FALSE   Because a dog whines when hungry, it is using language. (p. 201)

2. TRUE   FALSE   It is relatively easy to learn the grammar of a second language as an adult. (p. 205)

3. TRUE   FALSE   A kiwi fruit is a good prototype of "fruit." (p. 213)

4. TRUE   FALSE   The most accurate problem-solving method is the algorithm. (p. 216)

5. TRUE   FALSE   Emotion always hurts problem-solving abilities. (p. 221)

6. TRUE   FALSE   Visual imagery relies on many of the same brain parts that are used in visual perception. (p. 210)

7. TRUE   FALSE   Heritability can explain group differences in intelligence. (p. 239)

8. TRUE   FALSE   IQ scores predict job prestige. (p. 227)

9. TRUE   FALSE   Wechsler believed that there was too much emphasis on math skills on IQ tests. (p. 224)

10. TRUE   FALSE   Men score higher than women on emotional intelligence tests. (p. 233)

Multiple-Choice Questions

For each question, circle the letter of the best answer.

1. "Sandwich ate boy all the" is an example of incorrect _____. (p. 202)
    a. morphology
    b. syntax
    c. phonology
    d. logic

2.	Jane asked her 2-year-old son, "Could you hand me the salt?" He replied, "Yes,"	clearly not understanding the _____ of her statement. (p. 204)
	a.	morphology
	b.	pragmatics
	c.	phonology
	d.	syntax

3.	Which of the following aspects of a second language is generally easiest to learn? (p. 205)
	a.	Grammar
	b.	Sound patterns
	c.	Vocabulary
	d.	All would be equally difficult to learn.

4.	People consistently name objects at the _____ level. (p. 214)
	a.	prototypical
	b.	conceptual
	c.	ordinary
	d.	basic

5.	Maria can't find the rice in the store, and doesn't know where to look, so she starts in the first aisle and looks on all shelves before moving to the next. Maria is using a(n) _____ to find the rice. (p. 216)
	a.	heuristic
	b.	function
	c.	algorithm
	d.	representation

6.	The quickest way to solve a problem is often by using a(n) _____. (p. 216)
	a.	algorithm
	b.	prototype
	c.	heuristic
	d.	schema

7.	When people seek information that will confirm a rule but do not seek information that might refute it, they are _____. (p. 218)
	a.	denying the inevitable
	b.	deciding the alternative
	c.	affirming the consequent
	d.	using the confirmation bias

8.	The ability to understand metaphor depends on _____. (p. 204)
	a.	semantics
	b.	pragmatics
	c.	syntax
	d.	morphology

9. Intuition is _____. (p. 221)
   a. a myth; it doesn't exist
   b. based on implicit memories
   c. based in the medial frontal cortex
   d. both B and C

10. One night, John goes to a bar. He meets a really nice woman whose name is Susan Smith. They exchange phone numbers, but he loses her number before he gets home. An algorithm for solving this problem would be _____. (p. 216)
   a. to call every Smith in the phone book and ask to speak with "Susan," until he reaches her
   b. to go to the same bar next week and hope that she shows up again
   c. to go to the same bar next week and ask patrons if they know Susan Smith's phone number
   d. to wait for her to call him

11. If you are stuck solving a problem, which of the following might help you come up with the answer? (p. 217)
   a. Make sure you really understand the problem.
   b. Walk away from the problem for awhile.
   c. See if you can come up with multiple ways of solving the problem.
   d. All of the above might help.

12. Gigerenzer says that people fail to use the base-rate rule because _____. (p. 220)
   a. they do not have the required cognitive illusion
   b. they have trouble understanding descriptions of probabilities
   c. they cannot apply the rule in unfamiliar situations
   d. it is a heuristic and people prefer to use algorithms

13. Jeannie is in her 70s. She finds that whereas she can reason about familiar situations well, she has trouble solving new types of problems. Jeannie has good _____ intelligence but poor _____ intelligence. (p. 228)
   a. crystallized; fluid
   b. fluid; crystallized
   c. analytical; practical
   d. practical; analytical

14. Which of the following is NOT one of Gardner's forms of multiple intelligence? (pp. 229-230)
   a. Intrapersonal
   b. Emotional
   c. Bodily-kinesthetic
   d. Logical-mathematical

15. Mikhail was his high school's valedictorian and had perfect SAT scores. However, he has a great deal of trouble in college because he can't seem to figure out the registration process or how to manage the campus buses. In terms of Sternberg's theory of multiple intelligences, Mikhail has great _____ but is lacking in _____ intelligence. (p. 231)
    a.   analytic; creative
    b.   analytic; practical
    c.   practical; analytic
    d.   practical; creative

16. Although Anjuli did not have the highest GPA of the students applying for the job of peer advisor, she was hired because her interview went so well. The interviewer felt that she had good insight into her own strengths and weaknesses, as well as those of other people. Anjuli probably has a high level of _____ intelligence. (p. 232)
    a.   practical
    b.   existential
    c.   emotional
    d.   analytical

17. The reason within-group differences cannot be generalized to between-group differences is that _____. (p. 240)
    a.   within-group differences are larger
    b.   within-group differences are smaller
    c.   the individuals within a group may be influenced by different factors
    d.   the groups may be affected by different factors overall

18. As environmental factors have gotten more similar, the average IQ difference between African Americans and White Americans _____. (p. 241)
    a.   has remained the same
    b.   has actually widened
    c.   has gotten smaller
    d.   is still produced by biased testing

19. To be considered retarded, someone must have an IQ below _____; to be considered gifted, someone must have an IQ above _____. (pp. 243-244)
    a.   60; 150
    b.   70; 120
    c.   60; 135
    d.   70; 135

20. Creative people are _____. (p. 245)
    a.   more flexible in their thinking
    b.   motivated by extrinsic rewards
    c.   less likely to be hardworking
    d.   focused on one interest

Essay Questions

Answer each of the following questions in the space provided.

1.   Is thought simply talking to oneself? Why or why not? _____
_____
_____
_____
_____
_____
_____

2.   Researchers state that true language must have phonology, syntax, semantics, and pragmatics. Do you agree? Is this how you defined language before having read this chapter? Have your thoughts about the communication of other species (e.g., dolphins and apes) changed after reading this chapter? What is the difference between language and communication?_____
_____
_____
_____
_____
_____
_____
_____

3.   Do people reason logically? _____
_____
_____
_____
_____
_____
_____

4.   Consider children raised in Spanish-speaking homes in the United States. Frequently, they are not exposed to English until they go to school, and then they often act as interpreters for their parents and grandparents (at doctors' offices and other places). The parents in these homes often insist on maintaining their cultural background and resist learning and teaching English to their children. Given what you have learned about bilingualism, do you agree or disagree with these parents? _____
_____
_____
_____
_____
_____
_____
_____
_____

5. You may know someone who you believe "has no common sense." What is meant by this phrase? How would you define "common sense"? Is it related to problem solving or logical thinking? Do people with "no common sense" make more errors of logic and reasoning?

    _____
    _____
    _____
    _____
    _____
    _____

6. Why do people make errors of logic and reasoning? Would some real-life decisions be better made by a computer? Consider the Challenger disaster, the decision to enter into conflict with another country, and the decisions to marry, divorce, or have children. Which types of situations would best be handled by an emotionless but accurate computer decision-making program? _____

    _____
    _____
    _____
    _____
    _____
    _____

7. Discuss the pros and cons of using heuristics and algorithms. Under what circumstances would you want to use each strategy?_____

    _____
    _____
    _____
    _____
    _____
    _____

8. If you were designing your own test of intelligence, what would it look like? Explain.

    _____
    _____
    _____
    _____
    _____
    _____
    _____
    _____
    _____
    _____
    _____
    _____
    _____
    _____

9. Is intelligence a single characteristic or a complex set of characteristics?

_____
_____
_____
_____
_____
_____
_____
_____
_____

10. Clinical psychologists are sometimes asked to test children to assess their intelligence level, for placement in gifted programs. Often, they are asked to test the children after the children failed to meet the cutoff for the program based on their performance on a similar test in school. What would you say to a parent who approached a psychologist, asking that his or her child be re-tested?

_____
_____
_____
_____
_____
_____
_____
_____
_____
_____

11. Which of Gardner's types of intelligence are emphasized, rewarded, and nurtured in our U.S. culture? Why? Do you feel that American schools should do more to nurture the other types of intelligence? Which ones? Why?_____

_____
_____
_____
_____
_____
_____
_____
_____

12. Do you think it would be possible to "boost" intelligence? If so, which types? Explain.

_____
_____
_____
_____
_____
_____
_____
_____

13.   How do the environment and genetics contribute to intelligence? _____
       _____
       _____
       _____
       _____
       _____
       _____

14.   How can we interpret group differences in IQ? _____
       _____
       _____
       _____
       _____
       _____
       _____

15.   If you were asked to develop a culture-fair test of intelligence, what types of items would you
       include? Why? Could you develop a test that is culture fair not only for all races and
       socioeconomic groups in the United States, but also for people of other cultures (even in
       underdeveloped countries)? _____
       _____
       _____
       _____
       _____
       _____
       _____

16.   Do you believe that IQ tests measure how smart you are? Explain. _____
       _____
       _____
       _____
       _____
       _____

17.   Do you think that intelligence needs to be measured at all? Why or why not? _____
       _____
       _____
       _____
       _____
       _____
       _____
       _____

18.   If you could have only crystallized or fluid intelligence, but not both, which one would you choose? Why?_____

_____

_____

_____

_____

_____

_____

_____

_____

19.   Compare and contrast the methodologies used by Thurstone (and other psychometric researchers) and those used by Gardner. _____

_____

_____

_____

_____

_____

_____

20.   What are the characteristics of a creative individual? Discuss._____

_____

_____

_____

_____

_____

When You Are Finished . . . Puzzle It Out

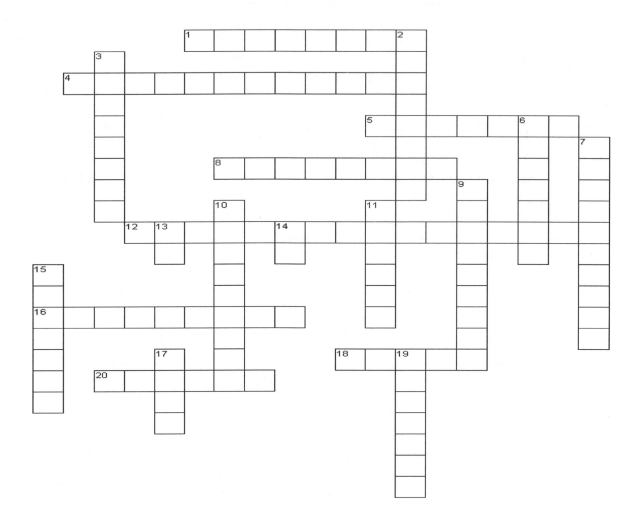

Across

1. Humans can produce 100 of these
4. Most common type of mental retardation
5. Child with immense talent in certain areas
8. Possible reason for group differences in intelligence
12. Environment created by person's own presence
16. Rule of thumb
18. French physician who developed first intelligence test
20. Representations based on stored information

Puzzle created with Puzzlemaker at DiscoverySchool.com.

Down

2. Believed in *g* and *s*
3. Smallest unit of meaning in a language
6. Developed theory of multiple intelligences
7. The ability to make something new
9. Fixed way of viewing the kind of solution required
10. Most typical example of a category
11. People with IQs of at least 135
13. Measure of intelligence
14. Ability to understand and regulate emotion
15. Set of concepts about a situation
17. Most used intelligence test
19. Setting mean and SD for a scale

Chapter 7
Emotion and Motivation: Feeling and Striving

Before You Read . . .

How are you feeling right now: Happy? Excited? Bored? Angry? Why do you feel that way? In this chapter, you will gain an overview of emotion, ranging from basic emotions to more complex ones. You will also learn several theories of the causes of emotion and explore the evidence that supports or refutes them. Of special interest will be the role of cognition in emotion. Two particular emotions, fear and happiness, are explored in detail. Cultural norms, body language, and lie detection are part of the story.

The chapter then moves to motivation, the needs and wants of humans and animals. The concepts of drives and incentives (being pushed and pulled toward certain events) are explained, as are the different needs of people. The needs for achievement and cognition are explained in greater detail. Lastly, the motivations behind eating and sex are discussed. Overeating and sexual orientation are covered in some detail.

Chapter Objectives

After reading this chapter, you will be able to:

♦   Name the basic emotions.

♦   Understand what causes emotion.

♦   Explain how culture affects our emotional lives.

♦   Name the sources of motivation.

♦   Explain the differences between needs and wants and how culture affects them.

♦   Describe the human sexual response cycle.

♦   Understand what determines whether we are attracted to the same or opposite sex.

As You Read . . . Term Identification

Make flashcards using the following terms as you go. Use the definitions in the margins of this chapter for help. If you write the definitions in your own words, though, you will remember them better!

Androgens
Basic emotions
Bisexual
Collectivist culture
Deprived reward
Display rules
Drives
Emotions
Estrogens
Facial feedback hypothesis
Heterosexual
Homeostasis
Homosexual
Incentives

Individualist culture
Instincts
Insulin
Learned helplessness
Metabolism
Misattribution of arousal
Motivation
Needs
Need for achievement
Nondeprived reward
Polygraph
Set point
Sexual response cycle (SRC)
Wants

As You Read . . . Questions and Exercises

Emotion: I Feel, Therefore I Am

Types of Emotions: What Can You Feel?

Before reading this section, list below the various *distinct* emotions you believe individuals have.

_____
_____
_____
_____

What did **Ekman** and **Friesen** (1971) find when they showed Caucasian facial expressions of emotion to members of a New Guinea tribe?_____
_____
_____
_____
_____
_____
_____
_____

What are the six **basic emotions** as outlined by Ekman (1984)?

- ♦ _____
- ♦ _____
- ♦ _____
- ♦ _____
- ♦ _____
- ♦ _____

Does your list of emotions differ at all from Ekman's? How so? _____
_____
_____

Define **approach** and **withdrawal emotions**. What parts of the brain do these emotions activate?

Approach: _____
_____

Withdrawal: _____
_____

What Causes Emotions?

Complete the following paragraph, which contrasts the various theories of emotion.

The earliest theory of emotion, put forth by _____ and _____ argued that emotions arise *after* your body reacts – that different emotions cause different sets of bodily reactions. In 1929, Cannon and Bard argued that _____ and _____ occur in tandem, arising at the same time. In other words, arousal is arousal! The _____ theory, on the other hand, holds that we interpret situations differently, which gives rise to different emotions. But Joseph LeDoux (1996) argued that interpretation takes place only for some emotions such as _____, not for other emotions, such as _____, since these emotions arise from different parts of the brain.

Since the leading **theories of emotion** have been posited, evidence has been found to cast doubt on their veracity. For each of the theories below, list some evidence that serves to refute it.

Theory	Evidence to refute
James-Lange	
Cannon-Bard	
Cognitive	

What is the **facial feedback hypothesis**? How can you use this in your daily life? _____

_____

_____

_____

What are the four important research findings about **fear** that researchers have discovered?

♦   _____

       _____

       _____

♦   _____

       _____

       _____

♦   _____

       _____

       _____

♦   _____

       _____

       _____

How do these four findings about **fear** support the following theories?

Theory	Support
James-Lange	
Cannon-Bard	
Cognitive	
LeDoux	

List the factors involved in **happiness** below.

At the Level of the Group:

♦ _____

♦ _____

At the Level of the Person:

♦ _____

♦ _____

♦ _____

♦ _____

At the Level of the Brain:

♦ _____

♦ _____

Expressing Emotion: Letting It All Hang Out?

For the following situations, describe the **display rules** that apply.

Situation	Display Rules
A bar	
A funeral	
A classroom	
Thanksgiving dinner at home	
A football game	

Name some of the factors that make some people better able to read **nonverbal communication** than others:

◆ _____

◆ _____

◆ _____

Can people **control their emotions**? Why is such control important? _____

_____

_____

_____

_____

_____

_____

GO SURFING ...

... at the following sites and take one of the road rage tests there:

- ◆   http://webhome.idirect.com/~kehamilt/rage.htm
- ◆   http://www.aaafoundation.org/quizzes/index.cfm?button=aggressive
- ◆   http://www.werner.com/home.cfm?page=roadRage.cfm
- ◆   http://www.roadrageiq.org/home.asp

What do these tests say about you? Do you **"let it all hang out"** on the road?_____
_____
_____
_____

If so, what are some ways that you could try to control your **road rage** in the future?_____
_____
_____
_____

Looking at Levels

People with antisocial personality disorder, by definition, feel no remorse for crimes they commit. What effect would this characteristic have on the use of **lie detector tests** with these individuals?
_____
_____
_____
_____
_____
_____
_____
_____
_____
_____

TRY PRACTICE TEST #1 NOW!
GOOD LUCK!

Motivation and Reward: Feeling Good

Getting Motivated: Sources and Theories of Motivation

Describe the focus of each of the following **theories of motivation**:

Theory	Focus
Instinct theory	
Evolutionary theory	
Drive theory	
Arousal theory	

What is the **drive** that motivates you to:

♦   Drink alcohol? _____

♦   Go to a party? _____

♦   Eat chocolate? _____

♦   Study for a test? _____

What is **homeostasis**? How do you maintain homeostasis?

_____

_____

_____

_____

_____

_____

_____

Graph and explain the **Yerkes-Dodson law**.

_____

_____

_____

_____

GO SURFING ...

...to discover how much arousal you need in your life. Complete the Sensation Seeking Scale at http://www.bbc.co.uk/science/humanbody/mind/sensation/.

What do the results of this scale say about your need for arousal? How do you see this need in your everyday life? How can you modify your life to meet the level of your need for arousal?

_____

_____

_____

_____

_____

_____

Which of the following are **drive-related motivations**, and which are **incentive-related**?

Sex	drive-related	**OR**	incentive-related
Hunger	drive-related	**OR**	incentive-related
Wanting Praise	drive-related	**OR**	incentive-related
Making Money	drive-related	**OR**	incentive-related
Thirst	drive-related	**OR**	incentive-related

What is the difference between **needs** and **wants**? _____
_____
_____
_____
_____

What are some of your **needs**?_____
_____
_____

What are some of your **wants**? _____
_____
_____

GO SURFING ...

... to discover what the following scales say about your motivations:

♦   **Work and Family Orientation Questionnaire**
     http://www.rrcc-online.com/~psych/WorknFamQuest.htm
♦   **Desirability of Control Scale**
     http://www.rrcc-online.com/~psych/DesConScale.htm
♦   **Entrepreneur Test**
     http://www.liraz.com/webquiz.htm

Based on the results of these tests, what do you think **motivates** you? What doesn't? _____
_____
_____

The following is a list of **needs** as proposed by researchers. Given your results on the surveys above, rank-order these needs in terms of importance to you (i.e., 1 indicates the need that is most important to you):

The need to be competent   _____

The need to be autonomous   _____

The need to have social approval   _____

The need to be dominant   _____

The need for affiliation   _____

The need to be powerful   _____

The need for closure   _____

The need to understand   _____

The need to maintain self-esteem   _____

The need to find the world benevolent   _____

The need for achievement

Are you surprised by the priorities established by this list? _____
_____
_____
_____
_____

How can you use knowledge of your **motivations** in everyday life?_____
_____
_____
_____
_____

List the seven needs outlined by **Maslow**, from lowest to highest:

◆ _____

◆ _____

◆ _____

◆ _____

◆ _____

◆ _____

◆ _____

What evidence do we have that casts doubt on **Maslow's theory**? _____

_____

_____

_____

_____

_____

_____

How do **individualist** and **collectivist** cultures differ? _____

_____

_____

_____

How do people from these two types of cultures differ with regard to **motivation**? _____

_____

_____

_____

_____

Do you know anyone from a **collectivist** culture? Does this person exemplify the research findings? How? _____

_____

_____

_____

Looking at Levels

How can **learned helplessness** explain why a woman would stay with her abusive husband, at the **three different levels of analysis**? Draw arrows to indicate how these events may interact.

The Brain	The Person	The Group

Can you think of situations in which a person might experience **learned helplessness**? Describe.

_____

_____

_____

TRY PRACTICE TEST #2 NOW!
GOOD LUCK!

Hunger and Sex: Two Important Motivations

Eating Behavior: The Hungry Mind in the Hungry Body

There are two distinct brain systems involved in eating:

♦ **One system leads you to feel a need to eat.**
  This feeling arises when your brain senses that the blood level of one of two types of food molecules is too low:

  ♦ _____ or

  ♦ _____ .

♦ **The other system leads you to feel full.**
  This feeling arises because of signals sent by the _____ in the _____ to the _____ of the brain.

What role does the **ventromedial hypothalamus** play in eating behaviors? _____
_____
_____

What role does prior experience play in **eating behaviors**?_____
_____
_____

What effect does each of the following factors have on the size and/or timing of your **appetite**?

Factor	Effect
Appetizer effects	
Opioids	
Changes in flavor, texture, color, shape of food	
Presence of other people	
Insulin	
Memory	
The clock/time of day	

Overeating: When Enough Is Not Enough

Using the words **set point** and **metabolism** explain why dieting can lead to eventual increases in weight rather than decreases. _____

_____

_____

_____

_____

GO SURFING ...

... to discover your current and ideal body mass index. Visit one of the following sites:

♦ **National Heart, Lung and Blood Institute**
   http://nhlbisupport.com/bmi/bmicalc.htm

♦ **Total Health Dynamics**
   http://www.totalhealthdynamics.com/bodymass.htm

The maximum recommended BMI is 24.9. What is your BMI? _____

Use the charts on the websites to calculate how many pounds you would have to gain or lose to reach a BMI of 24.9. How many? _____

What is the best way that you could gain or lose this weight? _____

_____

_____

_____

_____

What is the evidence for a genetic factor in **obesity**?

♦ _____

♦ _____

♦ _____

♦ _____

♦ _____

What are the possible environmental reasons for **obesity**?

♦ _____

♦ _____

♦ _____

♦ _____

The **range-of-reaction theory** has been used to reconcile findings on the genetic and hereditary nature of obesity. Explain. _____
_____
_____
_____
_____
_____
_____

Is your weight similar to your parents' weights? Why do you think this is? _____
_____
_____
_____

Sexual Behavior: A Many-Splendored Thing

Would you volunteer to be in a **study of sexual behavior**? Why or why not? _____
_____
_____
_____

How are **volunteers in sexual behavior studies** different from nonvolunteers? _____
_____
_____
_____

What do these differences mean for the **validity** of the studies? _____
_____
_____
_____

Fill in the boxes below with the stages of the **sexual response cycle**.

```
┌──────────┐      ┌──────────┐      ┌──────────┐
│          │  →   │          │  →   │          │
│          │      │          │      │          │
└──────────┘      └──────────┘      └──────────┘
                                          │
                                          ↓
                                    ┌──────────┐
                                    │          │
                                    │          │
                                    └──────────┘
                                          │
                                          ↓
                                    ┌──────────┐
                                    │          │
                                    │          │
                                    └──────────┘
                                          │
                                          ↓
                                    ┌──────────┐
                                    │          │
                                    │          │
                                    └──────────┘
```

Hormones are controlled by the _____, which in turn is controlled by the
_____. Hormones **are** secreted into the bloodstream by the
_____ .

Testosterone is one male hormone. The male hormones, _____, have the
following effects:

♦   _____

♦   _____

Female hormones, or _____, cause many characteristics including:

♦   _____

♦   _____

What type of **hormone(s)** do you have in your body?_____
_____

Women's **sex hormones** change over the course of their menstrual cycles. This change has the following effects:

- _____
  _____

- _____
  _____

- _____
  _____

- _____
  _____

Describe the different **motives** that people have for having sex, using the two dimensions described by Cooper and colleagues. _____
_____
_____
_____

Evolutionary theory suggests that men should be more interested in short-term sexual relationships and less particular about mates; females, who are typically very invested in nurturing and raising children, should have opposite preferences. Does research support this idea? Why or why not?
_____
_____
_____
_____
_____
_____

Sexual Orientation: More Than a Choice

What is the evidence that **sexual orientation** has a biological basis?

- _____
  _____
  _____

- _____
  _____
  _____

♦ _____
  _____
  _____

What evidence is there that the environment may play a role in **sexual orientation**?

♦ _____
  _____
  _____
  _____

♦ _____
  _____
  _____
  _____

Looking at Levels

Describe why, at **the levels of the brain, the person, and the group**, homophobic men might be **sexually aroused** by homosexual films. Draw arrows to indicate how events at the different levels may interact.

The Brain	The Person	The Group

TRY PRACTICE TEST #3 NOW!
GOOD LUCK!

After You Read . . . Thinking Back

1. In Chapter 3, you learned about how people sense and perceive. How do you think people's emotions affect what they sense and perceive?_____
_____
_____
_____
_____

2. How is classical conditioning involved in emotions? _____
_____
_____
_____
_____

3. How does emotion affect memory? _____
_____
_____
_____
_____

4. Does memory also affect emotion? If so, how?_____
_____
_____
_____
_____

5. Is there a relationship between IQ and motivation? If so, what types of motivation are involved? _____
_____
_____
_____
_____

6. How is learning involved in motivation? _____
_____
_____
_____
_____

7. What other aspects of emotions, besides control of them, are involved in emotional intelligence? _____
_____
_____
_____
_____

After You Read . . . Practice Tests

PRACTICE TEST #1:
EMOTION

True/False Questions
Circle TRUE or FALSE for each of the following statements.

1.   TRUE   FALSE   Money can buy happiness. (p. 261)

2.   TRUE   FALSE   The strongest emotion is happiness. (p. 261)

3.   TRUE   FALSE   Westerners focus on external evaluation as a source
                             of happiness more than people from China. (pp. 261-262)

4.   TRUE   FALSE   Married people are happier than unmarried people. (p. 262)

5.   TRUE   FALSE   In Western countries, assertive people are happier than
                             unassertive people. (p. 262)

6.   TRUE   FALSE   Surprise is one of the six basic emotions. (p. 255)

7.   TRUE   FALSE   It is impossible to hate and love someone at the same time.
                             (p. 256)

8.   TRUE   FALSE   Once you learn to fear an object, you may always fear it.
                             (p. 261)

9.   TRUE   FALSE   The amygdala responds only to negative emotions. (p. 261)

10. TRUE   FALSE   Emotions can be associated with single brain parts, although
                             the parts differ for each emotion. (p. 261)

Multiple-Choice Questions
For each question, circle the letter of the best answer.

1.   Which of the following is NOT a basic emotion, according to Ekman? (p. 255)
     a.   Love
     b.   Happiness
     c.   Fear
     d.   Surprise

2.   People with more activation in their left frontal lobe tend to be _____ in comparison to people with more activation in their right frontal lobe. (p. 256)
    a.   more guilt-ridden
    b.   more negative generally
    c.   more likely to have intense episodes of rage
    d.   happier

3.   According to James and Lange, _____. (p. 257)
    a.   bodily reactions cause emotions to arise
    b.   emotions happen first, causing us to act in certain ways
    c.   bodily reactions and emotions occur simultaneously
    d.   we *think* about the situation before we experience emotions

4.   The Cannon-Bard theory of emotion holds that _____. (p. 257)
    a.   bodily reactions cause emotions to arise
    b.   emotions happen first, causing us to act in certain ways
    c.   bodily reactions and emotions occur simultaneously
    d.   we *think* about the situation before we experience emotions

5.   LeDoux argued that _____. (p. 258)
    a.   bodily reactions cause emotions to arise
    b.   emotions happen first, causing us to act in certain ways
    c.   cognition always precedes the experience of emotion
    d.   cognition precedes some emotions, but not all

6.   The fact that many emotions are accompanied by distinct patterns of physiological arousal casts doubt on the _____ theory of emotion. (p. 259)
    a.   James-Lange
    b.   cognitive
    c.   Cannon-Bard
    d.   LeDoux

7.   According to the facial feedback hypothesis, people who walk around with frowns on their faces _____. (p. 259)
    a.   make others feel unhappy
    b.   are *making* themselves unhappy
    c.   are clinically depressed
    d.   are more stressed than others

8.   Westerners focus on _____ when asked about the sources of happiness. (p. 262)
    a.   money and prestige
    b.   achievement and internal evaluation
    c.   interpersonal interactions
    d.   intelligence and external evaluation

9.   Which of the following Americans is most likely to be happy? (p. 262)
    a.   Martha, who is married
    b.   Paul, who is poor
    c.   Nancy, who is nonassertive
    d.   Ollie, who is overweight

10.   Which of the following statements about gender differences in emotional expression is FALSE? (p. 263)
    a.   Women are more expressive than men.
    b.   Men are more expansive than women.
    c.   Women can register nonverbal signs of happiness better than men.
    d.   Women can register nonverbal signs of anger better than men.

PRACTICE TEST #2:
MOTIVATION AND REWARD

Multiple-Choice Questions

For each question, circle the letter of the best answer.

1. A(n) _____ is an inherited tendency to produce organized and unalterable responses to particular stimuli. (p. 267)
    a. insight
    b. motive
    c. inclination
    d. instinct

2. Which of the following could not be easily explained by Maslow's theory? (p. 272)
    a. The fact that Stephania harbored Jews during World War II, despite the enormous risk to herself
    b. The fact that 16-year-old Chris spent more time trying to fit into the high school scene than learning his lessons
    c. The fact that Jean divorced her emotionally abusive husband, despite their many similar intellectual interests and the fact that he stimulated her mentally
    d. The fact that Irving, who lived in the inner city, joined a gang to feel protected, even though he knew he was jeopardizing his future

3. The process of maintaining a steady physiological state is called _____. (p. 267)
    a. drive maintenance
    b. heterostasis
    c. homeostasis
    d. motive maintenance

4. The Yerkes-Dodson law states that _____. (p. 268)
    a. we perform best when we are at an intermediate level of arousal
    b. we perform best when we are at a high level of arousal
    c. we perform best when we are at a low level of arousal
    d. the optimal level of arousal for performance depends upon the individual

5. After her long run, Georgina is parched and swigs down a bottle of Gatorade. Georgina's behavior is being driven by a(n) _____. (p. 269)
    a. want
    b. nondeprived reward
    c. need
    d. intrinsic motivation

6. According to Maslow, which of the following needs must be met first? (p. 271)
   a. A need to feel appreciated by others
   b. A need to be all that you can be
   c. A need to understand the world
   d. A need for harmony and order

7. People who have a high need for achievement attribute their successes to _____, and their failures to _____. (p. 271)
   a. good luck; bad luck
   b. personal characteristics; environmental circumstances
   c. outside circumstances; bad luck
   d. personal characteristics; personal characteristics

8. According to Hall and Nougaim (1968), the longer a need is satisfied _____. (p. 272)
   a. the more important it becomes
   b. the more we want other things
   c. the less important it becomes
   d. the less we want other things

9. What is one negative effect of being raised in an individualist culture? (p. 272)
   a. People in individualist cultures have lower needs for achievement than people in collectivist cultures.
   b. People in individualist cultures have greater needs for dominance than people in collectivist cultures.
   c. People in individualist cultures don't live as long as people in collectivist cultures.
   d. People in individualist cultures don't like themselves as much as people in collectivist cultures.

10. Learned helplessness may lower the levels of _____ in the brain. (pp. 272-273)
    a. dopamine
    b. serotonin
    c. GABA
    d. endorphins

11. Ben had previously learned, through classical conditioning, that the MSG in Chinese food makes him sick. Therefore, he always ordered his Chinese food without MSG. After being in a car accident, however, Ben appears to have forgotten this association. Ben probably damaged his _____. (p. 269)
    a. brainstem
    b. frontal lobes
    c. parietal lobes
    d. cerebellum

12. Which of the following is NOT a criticism of Maslow's theory? (p. 272)
    a. There is not much evidence that needs are organized in a hierarchy.
    b. The importance of needs seems to differ across cultures.
    c. This theory can't explain why people do dangerous things to save others.
    d. It is impossible to meet all of these needs and become a self-actualized person.

13. Leanne likes to bungee jump and sky-dive. Leanne is probably highly motivated by a need _____. (p. 268)
    a. for cognition
    b. for arousal
    c. to be unique
    d. for achievement

14. When a person is not deprived, the pleasure of a nondeprived reward comes primarily from _____. (p. 269)
    a. the brainstem
    b. dopamine
    c. serotonin
    d. the hypothalamus

15. Seligman found that when dogs were put in a cage in which they received shocks and from which they could not escape, the dogs _____. (pp. 272-273)
    a. eventually gave up trying to escape, even when they could have escaped
    b. eventually died
    c. always associated cages with shocks
    d. became aggressive

PRACTICE TEST #3:
HUNGER AND SEX

True/False Questions

Circle TRUE or FALSE for each of the following statements.

1. TRUE   FALSE   Obese people have weaker personalities than trim people. (p. 277)

2. TRUE   FALSE   Obesity is defined as being 30% above ideal body weight. (p. 277)

3. TRUE   FALSE   Insulin increases the level of food molecules in the blood. (p. 276)

4. TRUE   FALSE   Feeling full depends on the level of food molecules in the blood. (p. 275)

5. TRUE   FALSE   A person's set point can be changed by her environment, activities, or emotional states. (p. 277)

6. TRUE   FALSE   Researchers found that Hispanic American women were more open about sex than African-American women. (p. 279)

7. TRUE   FALSE   Men stay aroused longer than women during sex. (p. 279)

8. TRUE   FALSE   Many women can have multiple orgasms. (p. 279)

9. TRUE   FALSE   If a man is worried about it, penis size *does* matter. (p. 279)

10. TRUE   FALSE   Bisexual men tend to become heterosexual over time. (p. 282)

11. TRUE   FALSE   Programs to train homosexuals to be heterosexual have failed. (p. 282)

12. TRUE   FALSE   A small part of the hypothalamus is larger in homosexual men than in heterosexual men. (p. 283)

13. TRUE   FALSE   There may be different biological bases for male and female homosexuality. (p. 283)

14. TRUE   FALSE   Homosexuality may be inherited on the X chromosome. (p. 283)

15. TRUE   FALSE   The environment plays no role in homosexuality. (p. 284)

Multiple-Choice Questions

For each question, circle the letter of the best answer.

1. When you first begin eating food that tastes good, _____ is (are) released. (p. 275)
    a. opioids
    b. protein molecules
    c. glucose
    d. serotonin

2. Even the thought of food can cause the pancreas to secrete _____, which may lead to feelings of hunger. (p. 276)
    a. serotonin
    b. dopamine
    c. insulin
    d. opioids

3. The best method of losing weight is to _____. (p. 277)
    a. eat fewer fats
    b. exercise
    c. eat fewer carbohydrates
    d. sleep

4. Almost _____ of Americans are obese. (p. 277)
    a. one fourth
    b. one half
    c. one third
    d. two thirds

5. Which of the following is NOT one of Rozin's (1986, 1996) findings? (p. 276)
    a. Once a food came into contact with something unpleasant, most people kept away from the food.
    b. People believe that "you are what you eat."
    c. Long-lasting taste aversions are formed through classical conditioning.
    d. Many people incorrectly believe that fat and salt are harmful even at trace levels.

6. According to psychodynamic theorists, people are obese because _____. (p. 278)
    a. they are storing fat for leaner times
    b. they have cognitive distortions that make them believe that they are more attractive when heavy
    c. they overeat when stressed, as a defense mechanism
    d. they have learned to associate food and love

7. Which situation typically leads people to eat more? (pp. 277-278)
   a. Being alone
   b. Being full
   c. After having a first taste of a good food
   d. Being stressed

8. The second stage of the sexual response cycle is _____. (p. 279)
   a. orgasm
   b. plateau
   c. excitement
   d. resolution

9. Which of the following was NOT a conclusion of Masters and Johnson? (p. 279)
   a. Men and women follow the same stages of the sexual response cycle.
   b. Women are aroused more slowly than men.
   c. Women can have multiple orgasms, but men cannot.
   d. Women are more likely to have homosexual encounters than men.

10. Hormones _____ affect our physical characteristics and _____ affect our thoughts and behaviors. (p. 280)
    a. directly; directly
    b. indirectly; indirectly
    c. directly; indirectly
    d. indirectly; directly

11. Homosexuality is probably the result, at least in part, of _____. (p. 283)
    a. inadequate parenting
    b. childhood sexual abuse
    c. extreme fear of the opposite sex
    d. a biological predisposition

12. Men have predominately _____. (p. 280)
    a. androgens
    b. estrogens
    c. testosterone
    d. androgens and estrogens

13. Oxytocin is released _____. (p. 281)
    a. by the hypothalamus
    b. after orgasm
    c. in the early stages of the sexual response cycle
    d. only after menopause

14. Matt has sexual intercourse frequently with casual partners. According to evolutionary theory, this is probably because _____. (p. 281)
    a.   Matt is less particular than most women are about his mates, since he will invest less than women do in nurturing and raising children
    b.   Matt's friends are also having the same types of relationships
    c.   like most men, Matt does not want to be in a long-term stable relationship
    d.   Matt is trying to prove his heterosexuality to himself

15. When homophobic men were exposed to homosexual male videos, they _____. (p. 284)
    a.   vomit
    b.   became violent
    c.   were aroused
    d.   changed their sexual orientation

COMPREHENSIVE PRACTICE TEST

True/False Questions

Circle TRUE or FALSE for each of the following statements.

1. TRUE   FALSE   Incentives draw a person toward a goal, in anticipation of a reward. (p. 268)

2. TRUE   FALSE   "Putting on a happy face" can make one feel happier. (p. 259)

3. TRUE   FALSE   People who are married are happier than people who are not. (p. 262)

4. TRUE   FALSE   Women can register nonverbal signs of anger better than men can. (p. 263)

5. TRUE   FALSE   It is impossible to voluntarily dampen emotional responses. (p. 264)

6. TRUE   FALSE   Chinese children are better able to detect basic emotions than Australian children are. (p. 263)

7. TRUE   FALSE   The best way to change your balance of energy input and output is to eat less. (p. 277)

8. TRUE   FALSE   Sexual orientation is a choice. (p. 282)

9. TRUE   FALSE   There are no environmental factors involved in sexual orientation. (p. 284)

10. TRUE   FALSE   Programs designed to train homosexuals to be heterosexual have not been successful. (p. 282)

Multiple-Choice Questions

For each question, circle the letter of the best answer.

1. The Fore in the New Guinea tribe who were interviewed by Ekman and Friesen in 1971 had the most difficulty distinguishing _____. (p. 255)
   a. fear from surprise
   b. anger from sadness
   c. joy from happiness
   d. disgust from shame

2.   In general, the _____ tends to be more active when people experience approach emotions such as love and happiness. (p. 256)
      a.   right frontal lobe
      b.   ventromedial hypothalamus
      c.   left frontal lobe
      d.   lateral hypothalamus

3.   Cannon's criticism of the James-Lange theory of emotion was that
      _____. (p. 257-258)
      a.   people with spinal cord injuries still report feeling emotions
      b.   people can experience both withdrawal and approach emotions at the same time
      c.   behavior clearly comes before the experience of emotion.
      d.   emotions are instantaneous, but it takes seconds for the body to become aroused

4.   At least 20 muscles in your face are used for _____. (p. 259)
      a.   chewing
      b.   forming facial expressions
      c.   talking
      d.   breathing

5.   The failure to interpret signs of bodily arousal correctly, leading to the experience of inappropriate emotions, is called _____. (p. 260)
      a.   misattribution of arousal
      b.   misinterpretation of signals
      c.   misattribution of emotion
      d.   misinterpretation of emotion

6.   People with damage to the amygdala _____. (p. 261)
      a.   cannot feel happiness
      b.   cannot recognize fear or anger in others
      c.   feel emotions more intensely than others do
      d.   are emotionally "dead" to all feelings

7.   Paul was once in an airplane accident. Though everyone on the plane survived, Paul remains afraid of flying to this day. The reason for this is probably that _____. (p. 261)
      a.   Paul thinks about this incident too much
      b.   Paul has an anxiety disorder
      c.   Paul has acquired a classically conditioned response, which continues even after extinction
      d.   Paul has sustained brain damage to his cerebellum

8. Much of Freud's theory relied on the assumption that people's urges are
   _____. (p. 267)
   a.   instinctual
   b.   need-motivated
   c.   homeostatic
   d.   related to an aversion to pain

9. Drives _____ and incentives _____. (pp. 267-268)
   a.   pull; push
   b.   approach; withdraw
   c.   push; pull
   d.   withdraw; approach

10. A meta-analysis revealed that needs for achievement that are _____ are most
    predictive of actual success. (p. 271)
    a.   extrinsic
    b.   implicit
    c.   intrinsic
    d.   explicit

11. The *appetizer effect* arises when _____ are released. (p. 275)
    a.   opioids
    b.   insulin molecules
    c.   neurotransmitters
    d.   fatty acids

12. Overeating may cause one's set point to _____. (p. 277)
    a.   become higher
    b.   fluctuate widely
    c.   become lower
    d.   None of the above; set point is stable.

13. Which of the following does NOT describe participants who are willing to complete sex
    surveys? (p. 279)
    a.   They have had more sexual experience that people not willing to participate.
    b.   They are more inclined to seek out sensation and excitement than people not willing
         to participate.
    c.   They are less socially conforming than people not willing to participate.
    d.   They are more extroverted and outgoing than people not willing to participate.

14. Hormones produce their effects _____. (p. 280)
    a.   because they are released into the bloodstream
    b.   by triggering receptors on neurons and other types of cells
    c.   because they lead people to want to act in certain ways
    d.   for all of the above reasons

15. Studies of bisexual men have shown that many of them tend to become _____ over time. (p. 282)
    a. more heterosexually inclined
    b. less interested in sex
    c. more homosexually inclined
    d. more interested in sex

16. Which of the following is an example of a deprived reward? (p. 269)
    a. Drinking a big bottle of water after exercising hard
    b. Eating a piece of chocolate cake for your birthday
    c. Working hard to win your parents' praise, which is rarely given
    d. Bungee-jumping because you have been working hard at a boring job for months

17. Roberta has just been in a heated argument with her supervisor. Afterwards, Roberta is very upset and walks the hallways of her office building crying. Roberta is violating the _____ that are common in most U.S. offices. (p. 262)
    a. intrinsic motivation
    b. display rules
    c. nonverbal communication patterns
    d. instincts

18. The difficulties associated with studying sexuality include _____. (p. 279)
    a. a lack of statistical measures to analyze such data
    b. the fact that people may lie about sexual matters
    c. the impossibility of using observational measures
    d. a lack of potential research questions on the topic

19. Which of the following would be most likely to be predicted by an evolutionary psychologist? (p. 282)
    a. Men are more interested in short-term sexual encounters than women.
    b. Women are more upset than men at the idea of their mate being sexually involved with someone else.
    c. Men and women are equally interested in having a long-term stable relationship.
    d. Men and women value similar characteristics in potential mates.

20. Which of the following statements supports the idea that obesity may be inherited? (p. 278)
    a. Obese people tend to eat more when stressed.
    b. Exercise can raise a person's set point.
    c. If one identical twin is obese, the other one probably is too.
    d. If a person overeats for a long period of time, the number of fat cells in his body will probably increase.

Essay Questions

Answer the following questions in the space provided.

1. What evidence do we have that the James-Lange theory of emotion is incorrect? _____
    _____
    _____
    _____
    _____
    _____
    _____
    _____
    _____
    _____

2. Why are some people generally happy and others aren't? _____
    _____
    _____
    _____
    _____
    _____
    _____
    _____
    _____
    _____

3. What role might the Yerkes-Dodson law play in your performance on an exam?
    _____
    _____
    _____
    _____
    _____
    _____

4. If putting on a happy face can make one have a rosier outlook on life, do you think that
    putting on a sad face can make one have a negative view of life? Think of people you know
    who are "happy-go-lucky" and others who are always "down-in-the-mouth." How much of
    their attitude might be attributed to their facial expressions? _____
    _____
    _____
    _____
    _____
    _____
    _____
    _____
    _____
    _____
    _____

5.	Why might people from cultures where the expression of emotions is downplayed be better able to read others' emotional expressions? Do you think that emotionally expressive individuals are less sensitive to others' emotional cues? Why or why not?

_____

_____

_____

_____

_____

_____

_____

_____

_____

_____

6.	What factors might lead individuals to have different hierarchies of motives? Think of your own hierarchy of motives. Is it similar to your parents'? To your siblings'? Have your parents or peers encouraged or discouraged certain motives? What role has your culture played? Have your motives changed over time? Why? How do you suspect they will change in the future? _____

_____

_____

_____

_____

_____

_____

_____

_____

_____

_____

_____

7.	Consider a perplexing phenomenon observed in the United States. On the one hand, Americans appear to be increasingly weight-oriented: There are many diet pills on the market, numerous dieting books, a plethora of health clubs, etc. On the other hand, this is a very overweight culture: Americans love to "super-size" everything! Why the inconsistency? Are there two types of people: those who diet and those who super-size? Do you think the motives of health-conscious people are different from the motives of less healthy individuals? Why? _____

_____

_____

_____

_____

_____

_____

_____

_____

8. Homosexuality was once classified as a psychological disorder, but was removed from the classification manual after a poll of the American Psychiatric Association's members in 1973. What does this tell you about how mental disorders are defined? What factors do you think led to the removal of homosexuality from the classification manual?

_____
_____
_____
_____
_____
_____
_____

9. How does culture influence the emotions that people feel and how they display them?

_____
_____
_____
_____
_____
_____
_____
_____

10. Develop your own comprehensive theory of motivation. _____

_____
_____
_____
_____
_____
_____
_____
_____
_____
_____
_____

When You Are Finished . . . Puzzle It Out

Across

4. Person attracted to both sexes
5. Commonly known as a lie detector
6. Turns goals into incentives
8. Male hormones
11. Maintaining a steady state
16. Highest of Maslow's levels
18. Being 20% above ideal weight
19. Discovered the basic emotions
20. Arises from lack of a requirement

Puzzle created with Puzzlemaker at DiscoverySchool.com.

Down

1. Emotions that are generally positive
2. Internal imbalance pushing toward a goal
3. Rules about showing emotions
7. Proposed a hierarchy of motivation
9. Hormone that stimulates fat storage
10. Female hormones
12. Body weight easiest to maintain
13. A draw toward a goal
14. Proposed most accepted emotion theory
15. Number of basic emotions
17. Fore confused this with surprise

Chapter 8
Personality: Vive la Difference!

Before You Read ...

Are you the same person when with your parents as you are when with your best friend? How are you the same or different? In this chapter, you will learn about personality, including how and why it changes. You will also learn about how different types of personalities can be described and how personality is measured.

In addition, you will apply the three levels of analysis to personality. As you will see, personality has its roots in genetics, but is also affected by a variety of individual characteristics. You will learn how psychodynamic theorists, humanistic psychologists, and cognitive psychologists view personality. Finally, you will review some of the environmental factors that may affect personality, including birth order, peer influences, and culture.

Chapter Objectives

After reading this chapter, you should be able to:

♦   Define personality, and describe the roles of traits and situations in personality.

♦   Identify the number of dimensions in different models of personality.

♦   Describe the different ways that personality can be measured and the pros and cons of each of these methods.

♦   Describe the role of genetics in personality.

♦   Explain and critique Freud's view of personality, including the three parts of personality, the stages of development, and the defense mechanisms.

♦   Summarize the humanistic theory of personality.

♦   Discuss the cognitive view of personality.

♦   Discuss the role of family, peers, birth order, gender, and culture on personality.

As You Read . . . Term Identification

Make flashcards using the following terms as you go. Use the definitions in the margins of this chapter for help. If you write the definitions in your own words, though, you will remember them better!

Activity
Big Five
Castration anxiety
Defense mechanism
Ego
Emotionality
Expectancies
Id
Impulsivity
Interactionism
Locus of control
Minnesota Multiphasic Personality Inventory-
    2 (MMPI-2)
Neurosis
Personality

Personality inventory
Personality trait
Projective test
Psychological determinism
Psychosexual stages
Repression
Rorschach test
Self-actualization
Self-efficacy
Situationism
Sociability
Social desirability
Superego
Temperament
Unconditional positive regard

As You Read . . . Questions and Exercises

What Is Personality?

Personality is a _____ set of characteristics that people display _____ and _____ and that distinguish individuals from each other.

Personality: Traits or Situations?

Personality traits are consistent characteristics exhibited in different situations. Name some of your characteristics that you think are consistent:

◆ _____

◆ _____

◆ _____

◆ _____

◆ _____

Some theorists say that personality is largely determined by **situations**. Think of a characteristic that you display in some situations, but not in others. Explain. What determines whether or not you display this characteristic? _____

_____

_____

_____

_____

_____

_____

_____

Interactionism is a synthesis of the traditional trait view and **situationism**. There are two major ways that individuals can affect their situations. Provide an example of each of these ways from your own life.

1.   **People choose their situations.**

_____

_____

_____

_____

2.   **People find opportunities to create their environments.**

_____

_____

_____

_____

Factors of Personality: The Big Five? Three? More?

GO SURFING ...

... to learn more about your personality. Take a web version of the **NEO-PI-R**, which is used to measure the **Big Five**. It is online at:
*   http://www.outofservice.com/bigfive/
*   http://cac.psu.edu/~j5j/test/ipipneo1.htm

How did you score on each of the following five **superfactors**?

*   **Extraversion:** _____

*   **Neuroticism:** _____

♦ **Agreeableness:** _____

♦ **Conscientiousness:** _____

♦ **Openness:** _____

List some of the **traits** that contribute to each of the **superfactors**.

♦ **Extraversion:** _____
_____

♦ **Neuroticism:** _____
_____

♦ **Agreeableness:** _____
_____

♦ **Conscientiousness:** _____
_____

♦ **Openness:** _____
_____

Now, read these traits to a friend and ask how he/she thinks you would score on each **superfactor**. Write his/her predictions below:

♦ **Extraversion:** _____

♦ **Neuroticism:** _____

♦ **Agreeableness:** _____

♦ **Conscientiousness:** _____

♦ **Openness:** _____

How did your friend's observations compare with your results? Why do you think he/she was so accurate (or inaccurate)? _____
_____
_____
_____
_____
_____

Below are listed of the five **superfactors** of the **Five-Factor Model** and **Eysenck**'s three personality dimensions. Draw lines between the superfactors and dimensions that are similar to each other.

<u>**Five-Factor Model**</u>   <u>**Eysenck's Three Dimensions**</u>

Extraversion   Extraversion

Neuroticism   Neuroticism

Agreeableness   Psychoticism

Conscientiousness

Openness

Name two problems with the **superfactors** approach to personality:

◆ _____
  _____

◆ _____
  _____

Measuring Personality: Is Grumpy Really Grumpy?

List the pros and cons of using **self-report measures** (like personality inventories) to measure personality.

Pros	Cons

Do you think that personality can be revealed through people's interpretations of inkblots, as in the **Rorschach test**? Why or why not?_____
_____
_____

Looking at Levels

Consider again the results of the personality test you took online. How do factors at the **three levels** affect your personality, as reflected by this test? What evidence do you have that genetic factors are at play in your personality? How might these genetic factors have affected personal characteristics (such as your thoughts) and group-level factors? List the evidence for factors at each level below. Draw arrows indicating how the factors may interact.

The Brain	The Person	The Group

TRY PRACTICE TEST #1 NOW!
GOOD LUCK!

The Brain: The Personality Organ

Eysenck's Theory

In the table below, indicate whether each behavior or quality described would be indicative of arousal in the areas of the brain associated with **extraversion**, **neuroticism**, or **psychoticism**.

Description	Extraversion	Neuroticism	Psychoticism
Has many phobias			
Criminality			
Bungee-jumping			
Schizophrenia			
Is easily saddened			
Likes loud parties			

Temperament: Waxing Hot or Cold

CALL...

... a parent or someone who knew you when you were young. Ask him/her to describe what you were like at age 3. Write his/her comments below. Be sure to ask specifically about the following dimensions:

♦ **Your vigor** (intensity of activity):_____

_____

♦ **Your tempo** (speed of activity): _____

_____

♦ **Your sociability** (preference of being with others):_____

_____

♦ **Your emotionality** (inclination to be aroused in emotional situations):

_____

_____

♦ **Your impulsivity** (propensity to respond to stimuli immediately):_____

_____

♦ **Other observations**: _____

_____

_____

_____

How are these dimensions of temperament similar to the **Big Five superfactors** of personality?

_____
_____
_____
_____
_____
_____

Compare the above observations of your temperament at age 3 with the results from the online personality test you took earlier and with your friend's rating of your personality. How similar or dissimilar are they? _____

_____
_____
_____

What reasons can you think of for these similarities and/or dissimilarities?_____

_____

_____

_____

Longitudinal studies have found correlations between children's temperaments at age 3 and their personalities at age 18. Is this true of you? Why or why not? _____

_____

_____

_____

GO SURFING ...

... to find out whether you are high or low in **sensation seeking**. Online tests can be found at:
+ http://www.bbc.co.uk/science/humanbody/mind/sensation/
+ http://www.dushkin.com/connectext/psy/ch09/survey9.mhtml

Are you high or low in **sensation seeking**?_____

Do these tests suggest that you like or don't like to take physical risks? _____

_____

_____

How accurate are the test results: Do you or don't you like to take physical risks?

_____

_____

There is evidence that **sensation seeking** is genetic. Do any of your biological relatives share your tendency to seek or avoid risks? Discuss. _____

_____

_____

_____

What does **MISTRA** stand for? What is it? _____

_____

_____

_____

MISTRA has found substantial **heritability** for two of the **Big Five superfactors**:

♦ _____

♦ _____

In general, MISTRA and other studies have found that families do not play a large role in personality. However, there are several critiques of **twin studies** that may compromise this finding. Describe two of them:

♦ _____
_____

♦ _____
_____

What is the difference between **shared** and **nonshared environmental influences**? Give an example of each from your own life. _____
_____
_____
_____

Looking at Levels

List the factors at each of the **three levels** that contribute to shyness. Draw arrows between the factors to show how they might interact.

The Brain	The Person	The Group

Imagine an extraverted person growing up in a culture where reserved behavior is the **norm**. How would an extroverted person do in such a situation? Consider what parents might do to shape an extraverted child's behavior in a socially reserved culture. _____
_____
_____
_____

TRY PRACTICE TEST #2 NOW!
GOOD LUCK!

The Person: Beliefs and Behaviors

Freud's Theory: The Dynamic Personality

According to Freud, in what part of your **consciousness** would the following information or feelings be found?

Information/Feeling	Part of Consciousness
Your favorite color	
Feelings of aggression toward your teacher	
What you did on your last birthday	
Sexual feelings for your parent	
The name of your roommate	
Your mother's maiden name	

According to Freud, which part of your **personality** would be responsible for the following behaviors?

Behavior	Part of Personality
Delaying gratification	
Feeling guilty	
Balancing reality and needs	
Eating a gallon of ice cream	
Deciding something is morally wrong	
Screaming when you're angry	

Describe the **developmental tasks** and **consequences of fixation** (if any) for each of the following psychosocial stages of development:

Stage	Developmental Task	Consequence of Fixation
Oral		
Anal		
Phallic		
Latency		
Genital		

Describe the **Oedipal** and **Electra complexes** as explained by psychodynamic theory. _____

_____

_____

_____

_____

_____

_____

_____

_____

_____

_____

_____

_____

_____

Give an example from your own life of each of the **common defense mechanisms** listed below.

Defense Mechanism	Example
Denial	
Intellectualization	
Projection	
Rationalization	
Reaction formation	
Repression	
Sublimation	
Undoing	

For each of the following theorists, describe the unique contribution to the understanding of **personality development**:

Theorist	Contribution
Carl Jung	
Alfred Adler	
Karen Horney	

Name three criticisms of the **psychodynamic theory** of personality development.

♦ _____
_____

♦ _____
_____
_____

♦ _____
_____

Name three aspects of **psychodynamic theory** that have been supported by research.

♦ _____
_____

♦ _____
_____
_____

♦ _____
_____

Humanistic Psychology

As opposed to psychodynamic theorists, humanistic theorists focus on the positive aspects of the individual. They say people have a drive toward **self-actualization**, which is _____
_____
_____

Do you know anyone you believe is **self-actualized**? Describe this person. What characteristics does this person have that makes you think this person is self-actualized? (If you don't know anyone who is self-actualized, just summarize the characteristics of a self-actualized person here.)

_____
_____
_____
_____
_____

What are the criticisms of the **humanistic theory** of personality? _____
_____
_____
_____

The Cognitive View of Personality: You Are What You Expect

Consider how you felt about your performance on your last exam. Using the following terms, describe how you interpreted your success (or failure), and how it will affect how you study for your next exam.

Term	My Interpretation
Locus of control	
Self-efficacy	

Looking at Levels

Suppose that a friend asks you to go on a blind date with her cousin, "a really _nice_ person." Consider the **levels of the brain, the person, and the group**. How might events at each of these levels affect your behavior during the date? Draw arrows to indicate how these events might interact.

The Brain	The Person	The Group

TRY PRACTICE TEST #3 NOW!
GOOD LUCK!

The World: Social Influences on Personality

Birth Order: Are You Number One?

Think of a family you know with at least three children (e.g., your own, one of your parent's, a friend's, etc.). In the table below, describe the first-born, middle-born, and later-born children. Then, describe **Sulloway's findings** on the personalities of children with these different birth orders.

Birth Order	Your Example	Sulloway's Findings
First-born		
Middle-born(s)		
Last-born		

Peer Relationships: Personality Developed by Peer Pressure

According to **Judith Harris**, what are the only two ways in which parents can influence a child's personality and social behavior?

♦ _____

♦ _____

Harris asserts that **peers**, not parents, most influence children's personality and social behavior. This assumes that all children in the same family experience the same environment. What are the problems with this assumption?

♦ _____

♦ _____

♦ _____

Do you have siblings? If so, how did your environment differ from theirs? Describe. _____

_____

_____

Gender Differences in Personality: Nature and Nurture

For each of the following **personality traits**, indicate with a checkmark in the appropriate column whether men or women have consistently displayed the trait *more*, or there have been inconsistent findings (or men and women don't differ on the trait).

Trait	More in Women	More in Men	Inconsistent/ No Difference
Social anxiety			
Locus of control			
Impulsiveness			
Reflectiveness			
Social connectedness			
Individuality and autonomy			
Empathy			
Nurturing			
Assessing emotion			
Spotting deception			
Neuroticism			
Anger			
Aggression			
Assertiveness			

Describe how each of the following theories or factors explains sex differences in personality.

Theory/Factor	Explanation
Biological theory	
Social role theory	
Expectancy effects	
Cultural factors	

Culture and Personality

List the differences between **individualist** and **collectivist** cultures.

Individualist cultures are more . . .	Collectivist cultures are more . . .

Looking at Levels

How might individuals respond to emotional films when in the presence of a person of the same sex or a person of the opposite sex? Analyze the responses at the **levels of the brain, the person, and the world**. Draw arrows to indicate how events at the different levels might interact.

The Brain	The Person	The Group

TRY PRACTICE TEST #4 NOW!
GOOD LUCK!

After You Read . . . Thinking Back

1.   This chapter did not specifically consider the behaviorist perspective on personality. Based on what you learned about behaviorism in Chapters 1 and 6, can you speculate as to how behaviorists might think about personality? _____

_____

_____

_____

2.   Can you think of any ways to overcome the difficulties associated with response biases that are present in self-report methodologies, such as the NEO-PI-R? _____

_____

_____

_____

3.   How have the validity and reliability of some of the personality measures (such as the NEO-PI-R) been established? Why is this important?_____

_____

_____

_____

4.   In Chapter 4, you learned about top-down and bottom-up processing. Which theory of personality best represents top-down processing? Explain. _____

_____

_____

_____

5.   Which theory of personality best represents bottom-up processing? Explain.

_____

_____

_____

6.   In previous chapters, you read about evolutionary theory. What is the evolutionary theory of gender differences in personality? What are some of the criticisms of this evolutionary theory? _____

_____

_____

_____

7.   Do you think there is any relationship between intelligence (in Chapter 6) and personality? Why or why not? _____

_____

_____

_____

After You Read . . . Practice Tests

PRACTICE TEST #1:
WHAT IS PERSONALITY?

Multiple-Choice Questions

For each question, circle the letter of the best answer.

1. Greg is very conscientious about his job; however, he is frequently behind in his studying. Which of the following does Greg's behavior best exemplify? (p. 293)
    a.   The personality trait of neuroticism
    b.   Situationism
    c.   Interactionism
    d.   The personality trait of consciousness

2. The term "central traits" refers to _____. (p. 293)
    a.   Eysenck's three personality dimensions
    b.   the Big Five superfactors
    c.   the personality traits that affect a wide variety of behavior
    d.   extraversion and neuroticism, because these are found in most models of personality

3. Personality dimensions and superfactors _____. (p. 297)
    a.   help people to understand what causes behavior
    b.   predict behavior
    c.   help us to understand personality better
    d.   are very reliable

4. Which of the following is more predictive of behavior? (p. 295)
    a.   Personality traits
    b.   Superfactors
    c.   Personality dimensions
    d.   Personality inventories

5. What is the value of defining a personality trait narrowly? (p. 295)
    a.   It can be applied to more situations.
    b.   It is more accurate in predicting behavior.
    c.   It provides more information about a person.
    d.   All of the above are true.

6.   Which of the following is NOT one of the Big Five superfactors? (p. 296)
        a.   Openness
        b.   Neuroticism
        c.   Intellect
        d.   Extraversion

7.   Both _____ and _____ are on almost all lists of personality traits, suggesting that they are fundamental dimensions of personality. (p. 296)
        a.   neuroticism; agreeableness
        b.   neuroticism; extraversion
        c.   extraversion; agreeableness
        d.   conscientiousness; extraversion

8.   People who score high on Eysenck's dimension of psychoticism may be more likely than others to _____. (p. 296)
        a.   be alcoholics
        b.   be extraverted
        c.   be neurotic
        d.   all of the above

9.   The most common method of personality assessment is _____. (p. 297)
        a.   personality inventories
        b.   observations
        c.   interviews
        d.   projective tests

10.   Miguel is completing a self-report measure of personality. He checks "strongly agree" to an item that reads "I like to take risks." Then, fifty items later, he checks "strongly agree" to an item that reads "I am not a very risky person." This response pattern is called _____. (p. 298)
        a.   acquiescence
        b.   social desirability
        c.   ambiguity
        d.   novelty seeking

11.   Although she has four siblings, Judith assumes almost all of the responsibility for caring for her elderly and ailing mother. Judith probably scores high on which superfactor? (p. 296)
        a.   Conscientiousness
        b.   Extraversion
        c.   Agreeableness
        d.   Openness

12.   The MMPI-2 is a(n) _____. (p. 298)
        a.   observational method of assessing personality
        b.   structured interview for assessing psychopathology
        c.   projective test of personality
        d.   paper-and-pencil personality inventory to assess psychopathology

13.	Projective tests of personality are so named because _____. (p. 298)
	a.	stimuli are projected onto the ceiling
	b.	the examinee "projects" his or her personality when imposing structure onto ambiguous stimuli
	c.	the examiner "projects" his or her knowledge of the examinee onto the assessment answers
	d.	aggression is projected by the stimuli

14.	People who have schizophrenia are likely to score high on _____. (p. 296)
	a.	extraversion
	b.	neuroticism
	c.	psychotism
	d.	openness

15.	Which of the five superfactors is NOT represented in Eysenck's model? (p. 296)
	a.	Extraversion
	b.	Neuroticism
	c.	Psychoticism
	d.	Openness

16.	You would expect someone with an acquiescent response style to _____. (p. 298)
	a.	complete an entire survey, no matter how long it is
	b.	answer "yes" or "agree" to most questions on a survey
	c.	answer "no" or "disagree" to most questions on a survey
	d.	leave survey questions blank if he or she doesn't agree with them

17.	How are personality inventories commonly used? (p. 297)
	a.	To assess mental illness
	b.	To assess how personality traits relate to other personal characteristics
	c.	To assess how personality relates to job performance
	d.	For all of the above

18.	The TAT and the Rorschach tests are similar in that they both _____. (pp. 298-299)
	a.	ask respondents to make sense of ambiguous stimuli
	b.	use inkblots
	c.	are based on the Five-Factor Model
	d.	are based on Jungian theory

19.	Which statistical technique was used to reveal superfactors? (p. 295)
	a.	Correlations
	b.	Standard deviations
	c.	Factor analysis
	d.	Means

20.   People with a particular gene that produces a type of dopamine receptor tend to be more _____. (p. 300)
    a.   depressed.
    b.   introverted.
    c.   novelty-seeking.
    d.   conforming.

PRACTICE TEST #2:
THE BRAIN

Multiple-Choice Questions

For each question, circle the letter of the best answer.

1. Which of the following personality dimensions is most likely to predict criminality, according to Eysenck? (p. 303)
    a.   Extraversion
    b.   Introversion
    c.   Neurotocism
    d.   Psychoticism

2. According to Eysenck, how are introverts and extraverts different? (p. 302)
    a.   Introverts enjoy people and social stimulation more.
    b.   Extraverts have difficulty learning to refrain from certain behaviors.
    c.   Extraverts are more arousable than introverts.
    d.   It takes more stimulation to arouse extraverts.

3. Being high on the dimension of psychoticism may result from _____.
    (p. 303)
    a.   underarousal of the autonomic and central nervous systems
    b.   an overproduction of cells that produce dopamine
    c.   an overactive amygdala
    d.   drug use

4. According to Eysenck, the foundation of personality (at the base of the personality hierarchy) consists of _____. (p. 301)
    a.   personality traits
    b.   personality dimensions
    c.   superfactors
    d.   stimulus-response associations

5. Mike has been in three car accidents, all caused by his tendency to speed. Mike is probably high on which of Eysenck's dimensions? (p. 302)
    a.   Sensation-seeking
    b.   Extraversion
    c.   Psychoticism
    d.   Neuroticism

6.   Monica was working as a bank teller when the bank was robbed. Although she was not physically injured at the time, she now finds that she cannot go into banks without shaking and sweating. Based on Eysenck's theory, which of the following is most true of Monica? (p. 302)
    a.   She is an extravert.
    b.   She is an introvert.
    c.   She has a neurotic nervous system.
    d.   She is high on psychoticism.

7.   Which of the following personality dimensions is most likely to involve increased sensitivity of the amygdala? (p. 302)
    a.   Extraversion
    b.   Introversion
    c.   Neuroticism
    d.   Psychoticism

8.   Introverts are more likely than extraverts to _____. (p. 302)
    a.   like parties
    b.   be underaroused and thus, seek greater stimulation
    c.   take drugs
    d.   be sensitive to punishment

9.   Which of the following is NOT a temperament, according to Buss and Plomin? (p. 303)
    a.   Activity
    b.   Sociability
    c.   Emotionality
    d.   Neuroticism

10.   Which of the following is true of temperament? (p. 303)
    a.   It is completely inherited.
    b.   It is not related to adulthood personality.
    c.   It refers to innate inclinations to engage in a certain style of behavior.
    d.   It does not appear until age 3.

11.   At 18 months old, Alexa loves to play with her friends and her brother. She screams when she is left alone. Which of the following of Eysenck's personality dimensions do these behaviors probably reflect? (p. 303)
    a.   Sensation-seeking
    b.   Extraversion
    c.   Neuroticism
    d.   Activity

12. Angelo prefers to play outside on the monkey bars or go biking than doing more sedate activities, like reading. He would probably be characterized as high on which of the following temperament dimensions? (p. 303)
   a. Activity
   b. Sociability
   c. Emotionality
   d. Impulsivity

13. The MISTRA study found that _____. (p. 304)
   a. there is little heritability for any of the personality dimensions
   b. almost all of the Big Five superfactors are inherited
   c. there is high heritability for extraversion and neuroticism
   d. there is high heritability for psychoticism and openness to experience

14. The MISTRA study found that the family environment contributed to _____. (p. 305)
   a. social closeness
   b. psychoticism
   c. extraversion
   d. negative emotionality

15. Which of the following is not a criticism of twin studies? (p. 305)
   a. Adoptive and natural homes are often very similar.
   b. Some twins who are reared apart spent their early months or years in the same household.
   c. Adoption studies do not find correlations as high as those from twin studies.
   d. Adoptive parents are very similar to their adoptive children.

16. What is the best way of explaining the roles of genes and the environment in personality? (pp. 304-306)
   a. Personality is completely inherited.
   b. Personality is attributable to the environment.
   c. For extraverts, personality is inherited, but for introverts, it is the product of the environment.
   d. Genetics and the environment are part of a single system that determines personality.

17. Which of the following is not generally a large contributor to personality traits? (p. 306)
   a. Family environment
   b. Genes
   c. Personal experience
   d. Nonshared environmental influences

18. Children who are shy _____. (pp. 306-307)
   a. have sympathetic nervous systems that are more easily aroused
   b. are so self-conscious that they analyze their behavior after every social interaction
   c. can be helped by supportive parents
   d. All of the above are true of shy children.

19. Jim loves to sky-dive, bungee-jump, and ski. He is probably high in _____.
(p. 303)
    a. sensation seeking
    b. psychoticism
    c. extraversion
    d. emotionality

20. Many aspects of the family environment are not shared because _____.
(p. 306)
    a. children create microenvironments based on their temperaments
    b. children may be different in their susceptibility to environmental forces
    c. parents may interact differently with each of their children
    d. of all of the above

PRACTICE TEST #3:
THE PERSON

Multiple-Choice Questions

For each question, circle the letter of the best answer.

1. The view that all behavior has an underlying psychological cause is called
    _____. (p. 308)
    a. psychological determinism
    b. the pleasure principle
    c. the reality principle
    d. psychodynamic theory

2. Material that can be brought into awareness but that a person is not conscious of is held in
    _____. (p. 308)
    a. the id
    b. the ego
    c. the conscious
    d. the preconscious

3. The ego ideal is _____. (p. 309)
    a. the underlying principle of the ego
    b. the ultimate standard of what a person should be
    c. held in the conscious
    d. the result of a fixation

4. The superego is responsible for _____. (p. 309)
    a. a sense of right and wrong
    b. expressing sexual and aggressive impulses
    c. seeking pleasure
    d. protecting the self from anxiety

5. Arrested development, caused by fixation at an earlier stage of psychosexual development,
    could create _____, according to Freud. (p. 309)
    a. neurosis
    b. depression
    c. psychosis
    d. aggression

6. For both boys and girls in the phallic stage, an intense feeling of dislike is initially directed
    toward the _____. (p. 310)
    a. mother
    b. same-sex parent
    c. father
    d. opposite-sex parent

7.   A person who smokes probably became fixated in the _____. (p. 310)
       a.   anal stage
       b.   latency stage
       c.   oral stage
       d.   genital stage

8.   One of the most important defense mechanisms is _____, a process that occurs
       when the unconscious prevents threatening thoughts, impulses, and memories from entering
       consciousness. (p. 311)
       a.   regression
       b.   denial
       c.   repression
       d.   sublimation

9.   According to Jung, we share common ideas and memories with all other humans through
       our _____. (p. 313)
       a.   ego ideal
       b.   subconscious
       c.   preconscious
       d.   collective unconscious

10.   Adler believed that _____ important in forming one's personality. (p. 313)
       a.   sexual and aggressive feelings were
       b.   feelings of inferiority were
       c.   the collective unconscious was
       d.   relationships with others were

11.   Horney emphasized the importance of _____ in forming
       personality. (p. 313)
       a.   sexual and aggressive feelings
       b.   feelings of inferiority
       c.   the collective unconscious
       d.   early parent-child interactions

12.   Horney suggested that little girls experience _____. (p. 313)
       a.   penis envy
       b.   the Oedipus complex
       c.   the Electra complex
       d.   privilege envy

13.   Which of the following statements is true of humanistic psychologists? (p. 313)
       a.   They focus on the positive aspects of the individual.
       b.   They try to solve cultural, rather than personal, problems.
       c.   They believe that actions have underlying, unconscious meanings.
       d.   They believe that the drive to self-actualization is learned.

14. When Corey, age 4, misbehaves, his mother tells him, "I love you, but I do not like this behavior." This response is in accord with _____ theory. (p. 314)
    a. Freud's psychosexual
    b. Maslow's humanistic
    c. Bandura's cognitive
    d. Rogers' humanistic

15. In the previous question, Corey's mother's statement is designed to meet the child's needs for _____. (p. 314)
    a. peak experiences
    b. locus of control
    c. conditions of worth
    d. unconditional positive regard

16. Which of the following terms refers to the sense of being able to produce the behaviors that one would like to? (p. 315)
    a. Locus of control
    b. Self-efficacy
    c. Extraversion
    d. Expectancies

17. When Betsy fails a math test, she blames herself and vows to try harder next time. Betsy probably has _____. (p. 315)
    a. low self-regulation
    b. an internal locus of control
    c. an external locus of control
    d. low self-efficacy

18. According to Freud, during the latency period, a girl _____. (p. 311)
    a. begins identifying with the same-sex parent
    b. experiences penis envy
    c. is preoccupied with toilet training
    d. represses sexual urges

19. Which of the following is NOT a criticism of Freud's theory? (p. 313)
    a. It was based only on upper-middle-class and upper-class individuals.
    b. Research has disproved the idea that the unconscious affects memory.
    c. It can explain anything.
    d. It is a product of his time period, which was very different from our own.

20. Lawson tells his mother, Marie, that he loves her and wants to marry her. According to Freud, Lawson is probably in the _____ stage. (pp. 310-311)
    a. oral
    b. anal
    c. phallic
    d. genital

PRACTICE TEST #4:
THE WORLD

True/False Questions

Circle TRUE or FALSE for each of the following statements.

1.   TRUE   FALSE   Sulloway found that first-born children tend to be less open to new experiences. (p. 318)

2.   TRUE   FALSE   Sulloway found that first-born children are less supportive of parental authority. (p. 318)

3.   TRUE   FALSE   Salmon found that middle-born children were less close to their families. (p. 318)

4.   TRUE   FALSE   Harris says that one of the few ways that parents influence children is through their values. (p. 319)

5.   TRUE   FALSE   Women are generally more socially anxious than men. (p. 320)

6.   TRUE   FALSE   The five factors have not been found in non-American cultures. (p. 321)

7.   TRUE   FALSE   The personality differences within each sex are greater than the personality differences between the sexes. (p. 320)

8.   TRUE   FALSE   People in collectivist cultures are more likely to define themselves in relation to others than are people in individualistic cultures. (p. 321)

9.   TRUE   FALSE   Men are generally more neurotic than women. (p. 320)

10.   TRUE   FALSE   People's personalities remain the same when they switch from a collectivist to an individualistic culture. (p. 322)

Multiple-Choice Questions

For each question, circle the letter of the best answer.

1.   Sulloway found that first-born children tend to be less _____ than younger siblings. (p. 318)
   - a.   sociable
   - b.   open to new experiences
   - c.   driven toward success
   - d.   neurotic

2. In Sulloway's research, "only" children were found to be similar to _____ children in their personalities. (p. 318)
   a. first-born
   b. both first-born and later-born
   c. later-born
   d. middle-born

3. Salmon found that in comparison to first-born and later-born children, middle-born children are _____. (p. 318)
   a. more extroverted
   b. more achievement-motivated
   c. less close to their families
   d. more depressed and anxious

4. According to Harris, the most influential determinant of children's personality and social behavior is their _____. (p. 319)
   a. mothers
   b. siblings
   c. fathers
   d. peers

5. According to Harris, parents can influence their children's personalities by _____. (p. 319)
   a. choosing where they live and go to school
   b. modeling appropriate behaviors
   c. monitoring the amount of television they watch
   d. maintaining open lines of communication

6. In general, personality differences between females and males are _____. (p. 320)
   a. pretty significant.
   b. evident only in early childhood.
   c. not very great.
   d. more evident as people mature.

7. Women tend to score higher on _____ than men do. (p. 320)
   a. social anxiety
   b. impulsiveness
   c. locus of control
   d. social connectedness

8. Men score lower on _____ than women do. (p. 320)
   a. neuroticism
   b. aggression
   c. anger
   d. assertiveness

9.   It is difficult to compare personalities across cultures because _____.
      (p. 321)
      a.   some personality concepts don't translate very well
      b.   personality measures are not available in other languages
      c.   ethical considerations prevent us from making comparisons
      d.   people in other cultures do not like to be compared to people in our culture

10.   Which of the following statements about collectivist cultures is FALSE? (pp. 321-322)
      a.   Collectivist cultures tend to value group needs more than individual needs.
      b.   People from collectivist cultures tend to see the self in relation to specific situations
            and contexts.
      c.   Collectivist cultures value personal freedom, equality, and enjoyment.
      d.   Collectivist cultures exert considerable social control over individuals.

COMPREHENSIVE PRACTICE TEST

True/False Questions

Circle TRUE or FALSE for each of the following statements.

1. TRUE   FALSE   Traits are relatively good predictors of behavior. (p. 295)

2. TRUE   FALSE   Like McCrae and Costa, Eysenck also found five superfactors. (p. 296)

3. TRUE   FALSE   Psychodynamic theorists believe that people have an innate drive to self-actualize. (p. 314)

4. TRUE   FALSE   Extraverts are less arousable than introverts. (p. 302)

5. TRUE   FALSE   Temperament at age 3 is correlated with personality at age 18. (p. 303)

6. TRUE   FALSE   The ego is the home of the conscience. (p. 309)

7. TRUE   FALSE   Freud developed his theory by studying college students. (p. 312)

8. TRUE   FALSE   First-born children are generally more rebellious than later-born children. (p. 318)

9. TRUE   FALSE   People with low self-efficacy are more likely to give up early than those with high self-efficacy. (p. 316)

10. TRUE   FALSE   People from collectivist cultures tend to be value personal freedom more than people from individualistic cultures do. (p. 321)

Multiple-Choice Questions

For each question, circle the letter of the best answer.

1. What conclusion have researchers drawn about the consistency of people's personality traits? (p. 294)
    a.   Most people display consistent levels of all of the important personality traits.
    b.   Everyone is consistent on some traits, but the particular traits on which people display consistency differ across individuals.
    c.   People are mostly inconsistent in their display of major personality traits.
    d.   Personality traits have proven so difficult to measure that it is impossible to conclude anything about their consistency.

2.   Researchers have found that children who cheat on a test will _____. (p. 294)
      a.   lie to their parents.
      b.   hurt others.
      c.   steal.
      d.   not necessarily do any of the above.

3.   A view of personality in which both traits and situations are believed to affect behavior,
      thoughts, and feelings is called _____. (p. 295)
      a.   reciprocal determinism
      b.   interactionism
      c.   biopsychosocialism
      d.   multiplicity

4.   Many factor analytic studies have revealed that traits can be reduced to _____
      superfactor(s). (p. 296)
      a.   1
      b.   4
      c.   5
      d.   6

5.   The traits of anxiety, hostility, depression, self-consciousness, impulsiveness, and
      vulnerability are considered to be included in the superfactor _____. (p. 296)
      a.   neuroticism
      b.   extraversion
      c.   psychoticism
      d.   openness

6.   Criminals are likely to score _____. (p. 296)
      a.   high on extraversion
      b.   high on neuroticism
      c.   low on agreeableness
      d.   high on psychoticism

7.   The superfactor _____ has no direct counterpart in Eysenck's model.
      (p. 296)
      a.   neuroticism
      b.   psychoticism
      c.   openness
      d.   extraversion

8.   Which of the following is NOT a criticism of projective tests? (p. 299)
      a.   The number of questions on them can lead the test-takers to become tired.
      b.   They have questionable reliability.
      c.   They have questionable validity.
      d.   The norms used to score these tests may not be representative.

9. A person who checks off "agree" on a personality inventory, regardless of the content of the statement, is said to have a(n) _____ response style. (p. 298)
   a. socially desirable
   b. acquiescent
   c. defensive
   d. accepting

10. The Thematic Personality Test is a(n) _____. (p. 299)
    a. objective personality measure
    b. unstructured interview
    c. projective personality measure
    d. personality inventory

11. People who score high on _____ are easily and intensely emotionally aroused and are more likely to experience conditioned emotional responses. (p. 302)
    a. extraversion
    b. psychoticism
    c. neuroticism
    d. openness

12. The temperament dimension of activity has two components: _____. (p. 303)
    a. vigor and tempo
    b. impulsivity and tempo
    c. vigor and impulsivity
    d. impulsivity and sociability

13. On which of the following superfactors are twins generally similar? (p. 304)
    a. Impulsivity
    b. Extraversion
    c. Openness
    d. Agreeableness

14. One of the criticisms of Freud's theory is that _____. (p. 312)
    a. later research indicates that the unconscious does not have a role in personality
    b. later research indicates that early experiences are unimportant in personality formation
    c. most of his patients were upper-middle-class or upper-class Victorian women
    d. his theory is too optimistic for modern times, when evil is rampant in the world

15. Which of the following is NOT a criticism of humanistic theories? (p. 314)
    a. They are overly focused on the level of the brain.
    b. They are difficult to test.
    c. They have received little empirical support.
    d. They have a more positive view of humankind than is reflected in our violent world.

16. Humanists believe that people have a tendency toward _____, an inborn motivation to achieve the highest emotional and intellectual potential. (p. 314)
    a. collective unconscious
    b. unconditional positive regard
    c. superiority striving
    d. self-actualization

17. Which of the following people is least likely to maintain close relationships with his or her family? (p. 318)
    a. Bart, the eldest of three children
    b. Lisa, the middle of three children
    c. Maggie, the last-born of three children
    d. None of them is likely to maintain close relationships.

18. Which of the following statements about gender differences in personality is FALSE? (p. 320)
    a. There are many gender differences, of large magnitude, in personality.
    b. There are more differences within each sex than between them.
    c. Women generally score higher on measures of social connectedness than do men.
    d. Men generally score higher on measures of aggression than do women.

19. Marge has an external locus of control. As a result, when she fails her psychology test, she is likely to _____. (p. 315)
    a. lower her expectancies in the future
    b. raise her expectancies in the future
    c. feel personally responsible for her failure
    d. attribute her failure to her stupidity

20. Collectivist cultures are more likely than individualist cultures to value _____. (p. 321)
    a. social order and humility
    b. equality
    c. personal freedom
    d. enjoyment

When You Are Finished . . . Puzzle It Out

Across

1. Personality test using inkblots
3. Tests with ambiguous stimuli
5. Developed client-centered therapy
6. Proposed hierarchy of needs
8. Said there are 16 personality factors
9. Most conscientious of children
11. Cultures emphasizing group needs
13. Freud's stage for from 3 to 6 years old
15. Source of control in life
16. Consistent personality characteristics
18. Pursuit of novelty
19. Number of superfactors

Down

2. "Yes" or "Agree" response style
4. Men score lower on this superfactor
7. Measure of genetic influence
10. Measures the Five-Factor Model
12. Lives by the pleasure principle
14. Said family influences on personality are small
17. Groupings of traits into more general traits
20. Proposed three personality dimensions

Puzzle created with Puzzlemaker at DiscoverySchool.com

Chapter 9
Psychology Over the Lifespan:
Growing Up, Growing Older, Growing Wiser

Before You Read . . .

Did your mother enjoy being pregnant with you? When did you start walking and talking? Are you the same person now as you were as a child? Will you be the same person in your 60s? How will you change?

This chapter presents an overview of human development, from conception to death. In the first section, you will learn about prenatal development, from the gametes that start it to the newborn infant. You will learn about both positive and negative events (teratogens) that can affect the developing fetus. You will also learn about the newborn, its perceptual abilities, reflexes, and even personality (temperament).

In childhood, we grow rapidly and undergo remarkable physical changes. You will learn about these, as well as about the qualitative and quantitative changes children experience in language and cognition. You will learn about Piaget's classical framework for understanding child development and the new areas of understanding developed by more modern researchers. You will also learn about adolescence and adulthood, including changes in the sense of self, morality, gender roles, and relationships.

Chapter Objectives

After reading this chapter, you should be able to:

♦   Describe how development progresses in the womb.

♦   Describe the capabilities of a newborn.

♦   Explain how the ability to control the body develops with age.

♦   Describe physical, cognitive, social, and emotional development during childhood and adolescence.

♦   Discuss whether or not adolescence is a time of emotional upheaval.

♦   Explain how aging affects physical abilities, perception, memory, and intelligence.

♦   Describe the course of social and emotional development during adulthood.

As You Read ... Term Identification

Make flashcards using the following terms as you go. Use the definitions in the margins of this chapter for help. If you write the definitions in your own words, though, you will remember them better!

Accommodation
Adolescence
Assimilation
Attachment
Child-directed speech
Concrete operation
Conservation
Critical period
Cross-sectional study
Egocentrism
Embryo
Fetus
Formal operation
Gender roles
Grammar

Longitudinal study
Maturation
Moral dilemmas
Object permanence
Overextension
Overregularization error
Psychosocial development
Puberty
Self-concept
Separation anxiety
Schema
Telegraphic speech
Teratogen
Underextension
Zygote

As You Read . . . Questions and Exercises

In the Beginning: From Conception to Birth

Prenatal Development: Nature and Nurture from the Start

How do **nature** and **nurture** interact during conception? Explain. _____
_____
_____
_____
_____

Why do siblings often turn out so differently? Discuss the different factors that ensure **human variety**:

♦ _____
_____
_____
_____
_____

♦ _____
_____
_____
_____
_____

GO SURFING …

… to see photographs of the developing **embryo**.
♦ http://www.visembryo.com/
♦ http://www.w-cpc.org/fetal.html
♦ http://anatomy.med.unsw.edu.au/CBL/Embryo/embryo.htm

Name the important developments at each of the following **prenatal stages**:

♦ **2 weeks:** _____
_____

♦ **8 weeks:** _____
_____

♦ **20 to 25 weeks:**_____
_____

♦ **28 weeks:** _____
_____

♦ **25 to 34 weeks:**_____
_____

Describe the effects of the following **teratogens** on developing babies:

Teratogen	Effect
Rubella in the embryonic period	
HIV	
Heroin/cocaine	
Environmental pollutants	
Excessive caffeine	
Tobacco smoke	
Maternal stress	

The Newborn: A Work in Progress

What is **temperament**? _____
_____
_____
_____
_____
_____

What is meant by a **temperament** inclined toward **approach**? What is meant by a **temperament** inclined toward **withdrawal**? _____
_____
_____
_____
_____
_____
_____

CALL ...

... your parents. Describe the different **temperament** types of infants. What type of **temperament** do they think you had as an infant? Why? _____

_____

_____

How is this type of temperament similar to your personality now? _____

_____

_____

How **stable** is temperament? _____

_____

_____

_____

How might the **environment** influence the **stability** of **temperament**?_____

_____

_____

_____

Looking at Levels

How does a baby learn emotional reactions through interactions with his/her mother? Discuss this at the **levels of the brain, the person, and the group**. Draw arrows to indicate how events at the different levels may interact.

The Brain	The Person	The Group

TRY PRACTICE TEST #1 NOW!
GOOD LUCK!

Infancy and Childhood: Taking Off

Physical and Motor Development: Getting Control

What type of **motor control** do infants gain first? After this? _____
_____
_____
_____

Does the **environment** play any role at all in the development of **motor control**? Explain.
_____
_____
_____
_____
_____

Perceptual and Cognitive Development: Extended Horizons

Describe the **visual abilities** of infants._____
_____
_____
_____
_____
_____
_____
_____
_____

Describe the **auditory abilities** of infants._____
_____
_____
_____
_____
_____
_____
_____
_____
_____

Describe **child-directed speech (CDS)**:

- ♦ _____

- ♦ _____

- ♦ _____

Give the age at which each of the following linguistic developments occur.

Age	Development
	Ignore distinctions among sounds from other languages
	Identify individual words
	Pay attention to different sound distinctions in different tasks
	Babbling
	Adultlike intonations
	Understand 50 words
	Speak 50 words

In what way are babies' language abilities more sophisticated than those of adults. _____
_____
_____
_____
_____

What is an **overextension**? _____
_____
_____

Give your own, unique example of an **overextension**._____
_____
_____

What is an **underextension**?_____
_____
_____

Give your own, unique example of an **underxtension**. _____
_____
_____

CALL ...

... your parents (or someone else who knew you when you were young). Ask them what your first sentence was. Did it have the typical characteristics of **telegraphic speech**? Explain._____

_____

_____

What are **overregularization errors**? _____

_____

_____

Give your own, unique example of an **overregularization error**. _____

_____

_____

GO SURFING ...

... at http://www.feralchildren.com/ to find out more about Victor, Genie, and other feral children.

Based on observations of feral children, some researchers argue that there is a **critical period** for learning language. What is a **critical period**? _____

_____

_____

Have you tried to learn a foreign language as an adult? Have you ever met a child who tried to learn a foreign language? How do those learning experiences compare? Does this comparison support the idea of a **critical period** for language development? Explain. _____

_____

_____

_____

_____

Explain the **habituation technique**. What does this technique tell us about infants?_____

_____
_____
_____
_____
_____
_____
_____
_____
_____

Several studies have shown that **infants** can store information as both **implicit** and **explicit memories**. Summarize this evidence.

Type of Memory	Evidence
Implicit	
Explicit	

How does **memory** change through **childhood**?_____

_____
_____
_____
_____
_____
_____

Complete the table below, indicating the **approximate age** of each stage of cognitive development and the **accomplishments** by the end of each. Use Piaget's theory, not the findings of more contemporary researchers.

Stage	Approximate Age	Accomplishments
Sensorimotor		
Preoperational		
Concrete operations		
Formal operations		

What are **schemas**, according to **Piaget**? _____

_____

_____

_____

_____

_____

What two processes does the child use to change his/her **schemas**?

♦ _____

_____

_____

♦ _____

_____

_____

How do **schemas** change as the child develops?

◆ _____
_____
_____

◆ _____
_____
_____

More contemporary researchers, using different research methodology, have suggested that **Piaget underestimated** the ages at which children achieve certain cognitive goals. Give two examples of recent research showing infants' earlier development of cognitive abilities.

◆ _____
_____
_____

◆ _____
_____
_____

How does **working memory** change with age? _____
_____
_____
_____

How might changes in **working memory** lead to changes such as those Piaget described? _____
_____
_____
_____

How is **Vygotsky**'s theory different from **Piaget**'s? _____
_____
_____
_____

How might **brain changes** affect children's information-processing abilities? _____
_____
_____
_____
_____

Social and Emotional Development: The Child in the World

Why does **separation anxiety** occur between the ages of 6 months and 2 years? _____
_____
_____
_____

Name the name of the **type of attachment** indicated by each of the following reactions of babies to the **Strange Situation**.

Reaction	Type of Attachment
Babies will leave mother, but are upset when mother leaves and are not comforted by a stranger. Babies calm down when mother returns.	
Babies stay close to mother and become angry when she leaves. When mother returns, babies are still angry and won't calm down easily.	
Babies don't care if mother is present or absent, and are easily comforted by a stranger.	
Babies become depressed and unresponsive, and show sudden spurts of emotion at the end of the *Strange Situation*.	

What **type of attachment** do you think you had as a baby? Support your answer. _____
_____
_____
_____
_____

GO SURFING ...

... to http://p034.psch.uic.edu/cgi-bin/crq.pl to see what **type of attachment** you currently have.

Describe your attachment style here. _____
_____
_____
_____
_____

Is this style consistent with your type of **attachment** as an infant? _____
_____
_____
_____
_____

What is **self-concept**?_____
_____
_____
_____
_____

At what age do children first exhibit a **self-concept**?_____
_____
_____
_____
_____

How would a child define him/herself at the following ages:

◆   **3 years old:**_____

◆   **8 years old:**_____

◆   **11 years old:**_____

Bobby just received too much money from the teller at the bank. What level of **moral development** is indicated by each of the possible thoughts Bobby might have, as indicated below.

Bobby's Thought	Level of Moral Development
"I could use this money to buy a bike, as long as I don't get caught!"	
"If I kept this money, my dad would think I'm a bad person."	
"It would be in the best interest of everyone who has an account at this bank if I give the money back."	
"Taking this money is the same thing as stealing, and stealing is wrong."	

Explain **Gilligan**'s criticisms of **Kohlberg**'s theory of **moral development**. _____
_____
_____
_____
_____

What has later work concluded about **Gilligan**'s criticisms? _____

_____

_____

_____

_____

Some researchers emphasize the difference between **moral reasoning** and **moral behavior**. What factors influence whether a child acts morally?

♦   _____

        _____

♦   _____

        _____

♦   _____

        _____

Looking at Levels

Describe **gender role development** at the three levels. Use arrows to indicate how these factors may interact.

The Brain	The Person	The Group

TRY PRACTICE TEST #2 NOW!
GOOD LUCK!

Adolescence: Between Two Worlds

Physical Development: In Puberty's Wake

Describe the **physical changes** that happen to boys and girls during **puberty**.

Changes to Boys	Changes to Girls

What is the **secular trend**? What has caused it?_____
_____
_____
_____
_____

Cognitive Development: Getting It All Together

How does thinking change during **adolescence**?

♦ _____

♦ _____

Think back to your adolescence. What were you interested in doing and reading? Were these preferences you had earlier in your life? How do they reflect changes in **thinking** during **adolescence**? _____
_____
_____
_____
_____

What are the possible reasons for the cognitive changes that occur in adolescence?

- ♦ _____
  _____
  _____
  _____

- ♦ _____
  _____
  _____
  _____

Think back to your adolescence. Do you remember using any **cognitive distortions**? How could this tendency be dangerous for teens? _____
_____
_____
_____
_____
_____
_____

What is an **imaginary audience**? Give a personal example of an experience with this phenomenon.
_____
_____
_____
_____

What is a **personal fable**? Give a personal example of such a fable. _____
_____
_____
_____
_____

Social and Emotional Development: New Rules, New Roles

What are the three **problems** that have been identified as "normal" during **adolescence**?

- ♦ _____
  _____

- ♦ _____
  _____

- ♦ _____
  _____

Did you experience any of these **problems** during **adolescence**? Discuss. _____

_____

_____

_____

_____

How do **biology** and **culture** interact during adolescence? _____

_____

_____

_____

_____

_____

Did you experience **"storm and stress"** during adolescence? Why or why not, do you think?

_____

_____

_____

_____

_____

What types of adolescent **life experiences** will positively affect later **intimate relationships**?

◆ _____

◆ _____

What types of negative **peer relationships** sometimes occur during adolescence?_____

_____

_____

_____

Did you experience **positive** or **negative peer relationships** during adolescence? Describe.

_____

_____

_____

_____

Looking at Levels

Consider the fact that only about half of pregnant teens choose to keep their babies. What factors do you think play a role in their decision, at the **levels of the brain, the person, and the group**. Draw arrows to indicate how events at the different levels may interact.

The Brain	The Person	The Group

TRY PRACTICE TEST #3 NOW!
GOOD LUCK!

Adulthood and Aging: The Continuously Changing Self

The Changing Body: What's Inevitable, What's Not

When do noticeable changes in the **body** begin to occur?_____

What are some of the inevitable **age-related changes** that are programmed into our **genes**?
_____
_____
_____
_____
_____

How can people minimize **age-related changes**? _____
_____
_____
_____
_____

Perception and Cognition in Adulthood: Taking the Good with the Bad

What is **terminal decline**? Why does it occur? _____

_____

_____

_____

_____

_____

_____

Describe the **age-related changes** in each of the following areas:

Area	Age-Related Changes
Vision	
Hearing	
Semantic memory	
Storage of new episodic memories	
Recall of specific episodic memories	
Working memory	
Crystallized intelligence	
Fluid intelligence	

Think of elderly people you know. Do they appear to have experienced **age-related changes** in any of the above areas? If so, which ones? How do you know? _____

_____

_____

_____

_____

_____

Why is it important to note what type of **research design** was used to study **intelligence** during adulthood?_____

_____

_____

_____

_____

_____

_____

Social and Emotional Development During Adulthood

What are the three **psychosocial stages** of adulthood (according to **Erikson**), and the goal at each stage?

Stage	Goal

Does **personality** remain relatively stable, or does it change, over the life-span? Do men and women differ in the stability of personality?_____

_____

_____

_____

_____

_____

Do people generally feel **happier** or **sadder** as they get older? Describe some emotional changes associated with aging._____

_____

_____

_____

Do **interpersonal relationships** tend to improve or weaken with age? Explain. _____

_____

_____

_____

CALL ...

... your grandparents or someone else of their generation. Interview these older adults about the following topics.

♦   Do they feel their personalities have changed? If so, how? _____
_____
_____
_____

♦   Do they feel happier or sadder than earlier in their lives? Why? _____
_____
_____
_____

♦   Are their interpersonal relationships weaker or stronger than earlier in their lives? In what ways? _____
_____
_____
_____

How do these answers match the research findings described in the text? _____
_____
_____
_____

Looking at Levels

Should elderly people be encouraged to engage in **mental workouts** to keep their minds sharp? What about the elderly person who does not wish to do so? What factors, at the **levels of the brain, the person, and the group**, may lead to diminished motivation for such tasks? Use arrows to indicate how these factors may interact.

The Brain	The Person	The Group

TRY PRACTICE TEST #4 NOW!
GOOD LUCK!

After You Read . . . Thinking Back

1. This chapter underscores a point made earlier: that memory is not a single entity, but is instead composed of multiple systems that develop at different rates. Discuss.

_____
_____
_____
_____
_____
_____

2. This chapter revisits an issue initially raised in Chapter 2: the nature-nurture debate. What are some of the ways that developmental theorists have thought about the interaction of nature and nurture? _____

_____
_____
_____
_____
_____
_____

3. Given that even young infants have been shown to be capable of learning, what does this say about the biological basis of learning? _____

_____
_____
_____
_____
_____
_____

4. Can you think of confounds that may influence research findings about age-related changes in intelligence? Explain. _____

_____
_____
_____
_____
_____
_____

5. Think back to Chapter 1, where you learned about research in psychology. Why is it particularly difficult to make causal statements in developmental studies? For example, why can't we say, "Age causes memory decline"? _____

_____
_____
_____
_____

After You Read . . . Practice Tests

PRACTICE TEST #1:
IN THE BEGINNING

Fill-in-the-Blank Questions
Fill in each blank with a word from the word bank.

WORD BANK	
egg	male
embryo	sperm
female	trimesters
fetus	zygote
gametes	

Life begins when the _____ from the woman meets the _____ from the man. These specialized sex cells are called _____, and when they join together, they form a zygote, a combination of cells with 23 pairs of chromosomes. If the sperm contributes an X chromosome, the offspring will be _____; if the sperm contributes a Y chromosome, the offspring will be _____. Development in the womb is divided into _____, three equal periods of time. The first period of time is divided into three stages: _____, _____, and _____. (p. 331-332)

True/False Questions
Circle TRUE or FALSE for each of the following statements.

1.   TRUE   FALSE   Male fetuses are more active than female fetuses. (p. 332)

2.   TRUE   FALSE   A fetus is sensitive to sound and light. (p. 332)

3.   TRUE   FALSE   By 10 weeks, a fetus can detect human speech. (p. 332)

4.   TRUE   FALSE   There is evidence that fetuses can learn. (p. 333)

5.   TRUE   FALSE   Drugs taken by the father cannot affect the developing fetus. (p. 333)

Multiple-Choice Questions

For each question, circle the letter of the best answer.

1. The fertilization of the egg by the sperm creates a cell called a(n) _____. (p. 331)
    a. zygote
    b. germinal cell
    c. ovum
    d. embryo

2. Which of the following depicts the order of prenatal development? (pp. 331-332)
    a. zygote → fetus → embryo
    b. embryo → zygote → fetus
    c. zygote → embryo → fetus
    d. zygote → embryo → fetus

3. Drugs taken and illnesses experienced by the mother during her pregnancy are called _____. (p. 333)
    a. teratogens
    b. alleles
    c. toxins
    d. gametes

4. Differences in temperament are apparent as early as _____. (p. 335)
    a. birth
    b. 1 month
    c. 1 week
    d. 2 months

5. Which of the following capabilities does the newborn have? (pp. 334-335)
    a. The ability to distinguish between women who bottle-feed and those who breastfeed
    b. The ability to suck
    c. The ability to learn through classical conditioning
    d. All of the above

6. What are the effects of teratogens? (p. 333)
    a. It depends on what organs are developing when the exposure to the teratogen occurs.
    b. They all affect the intellectual functioning of the developing child.
    c. They all affect behavior.
    d. They all cause emotional difficulties.

7. All cells in the human body contain 23 pairs of chromosomes, except the _____, which contain(s) _____ chromosomes. (p. 331)
    a. zygote; 11
    b. zygote; 23
    c. gametes; 23
    d. gametes; 11

8. What may happen to a fetus when a pregnant woman is stressed? (p. 334)
   a. The operation of genes guiding brain growth may slow down.
   b. The infant may have attentional difficulties later.
   c. The child may have unusual social behaviors later.
   d. All of the above may happen.

9. Throughout her pregnancy, Theresa watched reruns of *Friends* before going to bed. When her daughter was born, the infant probably _____. (p. 333)
   a. preferred the men's voices on the show to the father's voice
   b. preferred the women's voices on the show to her mother's voice
   c. preferred to listen to the *Friends* theme song rather than other songs she hadn't heard before
   d. disliked noise and preferred silence

10. Which of the following difficulties may prevent a sperm from reaching an egg? (p. 331)
    a. Uterine contractions move sperm the wrong way.
    b. Uterine contractions are weak.
    c. Uterine fluid does not have the right consistency for sperm to move.
    d. All of the above may prevent sperm and egg from meeting.

PRACTICE TEST #2:
INFANCY AND CHILDHOOD

True/False Questions
Circle TRUE or FALSE for each of the following statements.

1.   TRUE   FALSE   The working memory of young children is comparable to that of adults. (p. 347)

2.   TRUE   FALSE   Improvements in working memory over time probably have a biological basis. (pp. 347-348)

3.   TRUE   FALSE   Vygotsky emphasized the role of biological maturation in the cognitive development of children. (p. 348)

4.   TRUE   FALSE   Kohlberg's theory was based on Piaget's theory. (p. 351)

6.   TRUE   FALSE   Gilligan critiqued Kohlberg's work because it was based on studies of girls only. (p. 352)

Fill-in-the-Blank Questions
Fill in each blank with a word from the word bank.

WORD BANK	
Accommodation Assimilation	Schemas

Piaget believed that babies begin with simple, innate _____, mental

structures that organize perceptual input and connect it to the appropriate responses.

Schemas develop in two ways. Through the process of _____, infants use

existing schemas to take in new stimuli, and by the process of _____

_____, infants adjust their schemas to cope with novel situations that the original schemas can't

satisfy. (pp. 343-344)

Fill-in-the-Blank Questions

Fill in each blank with a word from the word bank.

WORD BANK	
cognitive	self-concept
formal operational period	three
personality traits	two

The term _____ refers to the beliefs, desires, values, and attributes

that define a person to him/herself. The development of self-concept in childhood

closely follows _____ development. By the age of _____,

virtually all children will recognize themselves in a mirror, although some researchers

argue that self-concept is present even earlier. By the age of _____, children begin to

appreciate that they have distinct psychological characteristics, but it is not until between ages 8 and

11 that children describe themselves in terms of _____. This ability to self-label

depends on reasoning abilities that develop during the _____. (p. 350)

Multiple-Choice Questions

For each question, circle the letter of the best answer.

1.   The development of physical control in an infant progresses in the sequence: (p. 338)
        a.   legs → arms → trunk → head.
        b.   head → trunk → arms → legs.
        c.   trunk → head → arms → legs.
        d.   head → trunk → legs → arms.

2.   When Jeri says that she is artistic and creative, she is expressing her _____.
        (p. 350)
        a.   self-concept
        b.   gender identity
        c.   attachment style
        d.   self-esteem

3. Mariah says, "I am kind and helpful." Mariah is probably _____. (p. 350)
    a.   3 years old
    b.   5 years old
    c.   6 years old
    d.   10 years old

4. A baby who puts everything in her mouth, even if it doesn't belong there, is _____, according to Piaget. (p. 344)
    a.   assimilating
    b.   scheming
    c.   accommodating
    d.   adjusting

5. The two key achievements of the sensorimotor period are _____. (p. 344)
    a.   conservation and logic
    b.   objective permanence and imitation
    c.   imitation and humor
    d.   hypothetical thinking and loss of egocentricity

6. Charlie said that it was wrong for his brother, Patrick, to take a cookie from the cookie jar because he would get spanked for it. Charlie is reasoning at a _____ level or morality. (p. 351)
    a.   formal operational
    b.   preconventional
    c.   conventional
    d.   postconventional

7. Studies on moral development that have followed Gilligan indicate that _____. (p. 352)
    a.   there are no fundamental differences in how men and women reason morally
    b.   both men and women use justice and caring perspectives
    c.   the type of reasoning people use depends on the dilemma they are given
    d.   All of the above are true

8. Eighteen-month-old Alicia screams whenever her mother leaves, but is easily soothed when her mother returns. What type of attachment does Alicia probably have to her mother? (p. 350)
    a.   Secure
    b.   Avoidant
    c.   Resistant
    d.   Disorganized/disoriented

9.   Harlow's findings indicate that _____. (p. 348)
    a.   parents' ability to feed their children is the primary reason why the children attach to them
    b.   the desire to be comforted is an innate characteristic of mammals
    c.   securely attached children usually don't go to daycare
    d.   attachment is dependent on the amount of time that children spend with their parents

10.   The habituation (or looking time) technique is used to study _____. (p. 339)
    a.   moral development
    b.   visual preferences in infancy
    c.   the heritability of personality
    d.   children's language development

PRACTICE TEST #3:
ADOLESCENCE

Multiple-Choice Questions
For each question, circle the letter for the best answer.

1. Puberty begins around ages _____ for girls and ages _____ for boys. (p. 354)
    a. 8-14; 9-15
    b. 12-14; 13-15
    c. 10-12; 12-16
    d. 7-10; 12-14

2. American girls typically stop growing at around age _____, while American boys typically grow until they are _____. (p. 355)
    a. 12; 13
    b. 16; 13
    c. 13; 16
    d. 14; 18

3. The major cognitive development of adolescence is _____. (p. 356)
    a. the attainment of concrete operations
    b. the development of a working memory
    c. the ability to reason abstractly
    d. the sense of personal responsibility

4. The frequency of parent-child conflict is greatest in _____ adolescence, and the intensity of conflict is greatest in _____ adolescence. (p. 347)
    a. early; middle
    b. early; late
    c. middle; early
    d. late; early

5. Approximately _____ of teens are seriously depressed by mid-adolescence. (p. 357)
    a. one tenth
    b. one third
    c. one fourth
    d. one half

6. Emotional mood swings in adolescents are likely due to _____. (p. 358)
    a. cultural stressors
    b. school pressures
    c. family stressors
    d. hormonal changes

7.   Which of the following is evidence of adolescent egocentrism? (p. 356)
    a.   The inability to take another person's perspective
    b.   The inability to believe the world exists outside of one's interaction with it
    c.   The belief that one is the actor and everyone else is the audience
    d.   The belief that everyone in one's community knows him/her

8.   Adolescents may engage in risky behavior because of _____.
    (pp. 356-357)
    a.   fluctuating hormones
    b.   a desire to "cheat death"
    c.   decreased parental monitoring
    d.   a perception of being immune to possible consequences

9.   The secular trend refers to the fact that _____. (p. 354)
    a.   puberty occurs earlier than it did in the past
    b.   the body grows from the limbs inward during adolescence
    c.   girls' growth spurts start earlier than do boys' growth spurts
    d.   there are cognitive changes that accompany adolescence

10. The greatest risk factors for teen pregnancy are _____. (p. 358)
    a.   being poor and lacking a clear career plan
    b.   being African American and from a lower socioeconomic group
    c.   lacking a clear sense of self and having low self-esteem
    d.   being from a broken family and having negative opinions of the opposite sex

PRACTICE TEST #4:
ADULTHOOD AND AGING

Multiple-Choice Questions

For each question, circle the letter of the best answer.

1.   Significant age-related cognitive changes occur by the age of _____. (p. 361)
      a.   20
      b.   30
      c.   40
      d.   50

2.   Aging most severely affects _____. (p. 361)
      a.   the occipital lobe
      b.   communication among neurons in the brain
      c.   brain functioning in the limbic system
      d.   the parietal and temporal lobes of the brain

3.   A clouding of the lens of the eye that occurs after the age of 65 is called
      _____. (p. 361)
      a.   cataracts
      b.   myopia
      c.   glaucoma
      d.   hyperopia

4.   Which of the following types of memory is most impaired in elderly people? (p. 362)
      a.   Visual memory
      b.   Storage of new episodic memories
      c.   Semantic memory
      d.   Recall of specific episodic memories

5.   Which of the following types of intelligence decline(s) after the age of 20? (p. 362)
      a.   Crystallized
      b.   Fluid
      c.   Both a and b
      d.   Neither a nor b

6.   Signs of aging may not result from inevitable processes, but instead from
      _____. (p. 360)
      a.   nutritional deficits
      b.   lack of exercise
      c.   lack of meaningful activities
      d.   all of the above

7.	According to Erikson, the second stage of psychosocial development in adulthood is
	_____. (p. 363)
	a.	generativity vs. self-absorption
	b.	integrity vs. despair
	c.	intimacy vs. isolation
	d.	identity vs. diffusion

8.	Costa and McCrae (1988) found age-related changes in personality in
	_____. (p. 364)
	a.	men, but not women
	b.	both men and women
	c.	women, but not men
	d.	neither men nor women

9.	Which of the following is NOT a typical change in perception during adulthood? (p. 361)
	a.	Difficulty perceiving contrasts
	b.	Difficulty in distinguishing sounds
	c.	Difficulty in shutting out background noise
	d.	Decrease in the glare perceived on surfaces

10.	To keep the brain functioning at a peak level, an elderly person is best advised to
	_____. (p. 366)
	a.	take a multivitamin every day
	b.	avoid drinking alcohol and taking drugs
	c.	engage in mentally stimulating tasks
	d.	do none of the above; age-related changes are inevitable

COMPREHENSIVE PRACTICE TEST

True/False Questions

Circle TRUE or FALSE for each of the following statements.

1.   TRUE   FALSE   The ovum is the largest cell in the human body. (p. 331)

2.   TRUE   FALSE   Deaf children do not babble. (p. 341)

3.   TRUE   FALSE   Some people never attain formal operational thought.
                             (p. 347)

4.   TRUE   FALSE   In general, Piaget seems to have underestimated the abilities
                             of infants. (p. 347)

5.   TRUE   FALSE   Piaget said that children cannot think logically until 12 years
                             of age. (p. 346)

6.   TRUE   FALSE   One third of adolescents are seriously depressed. (p. 357)

7.   TRUE   FALSE   Adults who are concerned with generativity are the most
                             optimistic adults. (p. 363)

8.   TRUE   FALSE   Crystallized intelligence declines during adulthood, while
                             fluid intelligence increases. (p. 362)

9.   TRUE   FALSE   People tend to expand their circle of friends throughout
                             adulthood. (p. 365)

10. TRUE   FALSE   Even 3-month-olds can form memories. (p. 343)

Multiple-Choice Questions

For each question, circle the letter of the best answer.

1.   Maleness is determined by the contribution of a(n) _____ sex chromosome by   the
     _____. (p. 331)
     a.   X; father
     b.   X; mother
     c.   Y; father
     d.   Y; mother

2.   In the first stage of the first trimester of prenatal development, the developing person is
     called the _____. (p. 331)
     a.   zygote
     b.   embryo
     c.   ovum
     d.   fetus

3.   Matthew's mother smoked during pregnancy. As a result, Matthew is at increased risk for
_____. (pp. 333-334)
   a.   attentional difficulties
   b.   having a small head
   c.   dying of SIDS
   d.   all of the above

4.   When Ben is given a cookie for the first time, he calls it a "cracker" because he is very
familiar with this term. This is an example of _____. (p. 341)
   a.   child-directed speech
   b.   an underextension
   c.   an overextension
   d.   an overregularization error

5.   Separation anxiety, or fear of being away from the primary caregiver, is typical from
_____. (p. 349)
   a.   birth to 8 months
   b.   6 months to 2 years
   c.   2 years to 3 years
   d.   3 years to 5 years

6.   In 2003, Dr. Lehman tests a group of 20-year-olds, a group of 40-year-olds, and a group of
60-year-olds on memory skills. This type of study is a(n) _____. (p. 362)
   a.   experiment
   b.   cross-sectional study
   c.   longitudinal study
   d.   time-lag design

7.   According to Piaget, when does a child begin fantasy play? (p. 345)
   a.   During the sensorimotor period
   b.   During the preoperational period
   c.   During the concrete operational period
   d.   At various times throughout development

8.   Vygotsky's theory emphasizes the role of _____ in the development of
children's cognitive abilities. (p. 348)
   a.   theory of mind
   b.   culture
   c.   working memory
   d.   biological changes

9.   The least common type of attachment among American babies is _____.
(p. 350)
   a.   avoidant
   b.   resistant
   c.   secure
   d.   disorganized/disoriented

10. Children at the _____ level of moral development behave in ways that focus on the rules that maintain social order. (p. 351)
   a.   preconventional
   b.   postconventional
   c.   conventional
   d.   formal operational

11. In Maccoby's view, _____ are the key to learning gender roles. (p. 353)
   a.   peer-group interactions
   b.   interactions with parents
   c.   interactions with siblings
   d.   hormonal influences

12. Abby spends two hours primping for a concert. She is convinced that everyone will notice how she looks, despite the fact that there will be 4,000 people at the concert. This is because Abby has _____. (p. 356)
   a.   an imaginary audience
   b.   a personal fable
   c.   post-conventional reasoning
   d.   depression

13. Menopause typically occurs between _____. (p. 360)
   a.   35 and 45
   b.   55 and 65
   c.   45 and 55
   d.   65 and 75

14. After the age of 50 or so, people have increased difficulty hearing _____. (p. 361)
   a.   low-frequency sounds
   b.   music
   c.   high frequency sounds
   d.   voices

15. As people age, _____ influences on general intelligence increase. (p. 362)
   a.   environmental
   b.   peer
   c.   genetic
   d.   academic

Essay Questions

Answer the following questions in the space provided.

1. If an infant is not exposed to language before a certain time, will she develop any language? How do we know this? _____

    _____
    _____
    _____
    _____
    _____
    _____
    _____

2. Was Piaget accurate in his description of cognitive development? _____

    _____
    _____
    _____
    _____
    _____
    _____
    _____

3. Is adolescence a period of "storm and stress"? _____

    _____
    _____
    _____
    _____
    _____
    _____

4. Do people exhibit age-related declines in memory? _____

    _____
    _____
    _____
    _____
    _____

5. Explain why it is so important for infants to learn to understand and produce language.

    _____
    _____
    _____
    _____
    _____

6. Researchers have recently uncovered almost all of the human genetic sequence. What benefits of having this knowledge do you foresee? What dangers may lie ahead? _____

_____
_____
_____
_____
_____
_____

7. After the age of 2, separation anxiety begins to diminish in young toddlers. Why do you think this happens? Why do you think that some children later develop a psychological disorder that causes them to fear separation from their parent(s), even though they have clearly developed object permanence? _____

_____
_____
_____
_____
_____
_____

8. Name and discuss three factors that contribute to moral behavior. _____

_____
_____
_____
_____
_____
_____

9. What was your adolescence like? Was there strife in your family? Did you experience more conflict with your mother or with your father? What was the source of the conflict? How is your relationship with both parents now? _____

_____
_____
_____
_____
_____
_____

10. How do people's relationships with their parents affect their other relationships during childhood, adolescence, and adulthood? _____

_____
_____
_____
_____
_____
_____

When You Are Finished . . . Puzzle It Out

Across
5. Emotional bond between parent and child
10. From puberty till end of teen years
12. Tests infant's depth perception
13. Rules for organizing words
15. He emphasized culture in development
16. Has been reduced by back-sleeping
18. Developed theory of attachment
19. Contained on the "rungs" of the chromosomes
20. Any chemical that can damage a fetus

Down
1. Developed theory of moral thinking
2. Piaget's period from 2 to 7 years
3. Developing baby from 8 weeks till birth
4. Faster-maturing gender
6. Looking-time technique
7. Automatic response to an event
8. Number of stages in Piaget's theory
9. "Motherese"
11. Mental structure for organizing events
14. A fertilized ovum
17. The startle reflex

Puzzle created with Puzzlemaker at DiscoverySchool.com.

Chapter 10
Stress, Health, and Coping:
Dealing With Life

Before You Read . . .

Do you feel stressed? If so, what does this feel like physically and emotionally? In this chapter, you will learn exactly what stress is, from its physiology to its sources. You will learn that stress is a subjective experience, and that certain qualities of situations (perceived controllability and predictability) make them more or less difficult to handle. You will also read about the different aspects of your life that might lead you to feel stressed, including internal conflicts, hassles, and feelings of anger.

Be careful—too much stress can take a toll on your health, as you'll read about in the second section. Immune dysfunction, cancer, heart disease, and sleep disturbances are all linked to stress. But at least there's something you can do about it. You *can* develop more effective coping strategies. You will learn about these strategies, as well as about the importance of social support and mind-body interventions, in the last section of this chapter. The roles of gender and culture in coping are covered as well.

Chapter Objectives

After reading this chapter, you should be able to:

♦   Define stress.

♦   Describe the physiology of stress.

♦   Name common sources of stress.

♦   Explain how stress affects health.

♦   Name and describe the different types of coping strategies.

♦   Describe how relationships affect stress and health.

♦   Explain mind-body interventions.

♦   Describe the roles of gender and culture in coping.

As You Read . . . Term Identification

Make flashcards using the following terms as you go. Use the definitions in the margins of this chapter for help. If you write the definitions in your own words, though, you will remember them better!

Activation-synthesis hypothesis
Acute stressor
Aggression
Alarm phase
Alcohol myopia
Amphetamines
Approach-approach conflict
Approach-avoidance conflict
Atherosclerosis
Avoidance-avoidance conflict
B cell
Blackout
Chronic stressor
Circadian rhythms
Coping
Crack
Depressant
Disinhibition
Emotion-focused coping
Enacted social support
Exhaustion phase
Flashback
General adaptation syndrome (GAS)
Glucocorticoids
Hallucinogen
Health psychology
Hostile attribution bias
Hostility
Hypnogogic sleep

Inhibitory conflict
Insomnia
Internal conflict
Latent content
Manifest content
Narcotic analgesics
Natural killer (NK) cell
Nocebo effect
Opiates
Perceived social support
Problem-focused coping
REM rebound
REM sleep
Resistance phase
Sleep
Sleep apnea
Social support
Stimulant
Stress
Stressor
Stress response
Substance abuse
Substance dependence
Suprachiasmatic nucleus (SCN)
T cell
Thought suppression
Tolerance
Withdrawal symptoms

As You Read . . . Questions and Exercises

What is Stress?

Stress: The Big Picture

Distinguish between **stress** and a **stressor**._____
_____
_____
_____
_____

Give an example of each of the following **stressors**.

◆   **An acute stressor:** _____

_____

◆   **A chronic stressor:** _____

_____

Provide an example from your life of each of the following types of **stressors**:

	Acute Stressor	Chronic Stressor
Physical Stressor		
Psychological Stressor		
Social Stressor		

The Biology of Stress

Describe what happens during each phase of the **General Adaptation Syndrome**:

Phase	Body's Response
Alarm	
Resistance	
Exhaustion	

How can **glucocorticoids** be both good and bad for our bodies? _____

_____

_____

_____

_____

Sources of Stress

Provide a personal example of a **stressor** in your life that might not be a **stressor** to someone else.

_____

_____

_____

_____

Distinguish between **primary appraisal** and **secondary appraisal**. _____

_____

_____

_____

_____

_____

Fill in the table below with examples of **stressors** that are either **controllable** or **uncontrollable** and **predictable** or **unpredictable**. Which stressors would be more stressful to you? Why?

Controll-ability / Predictability	Controllable	Uncontrollable
Predictable		
Unpredictable		

Under what circumstances is **predictability** unlikely to be helpful in dealing with a stressor?

_____

_____

_____

_____

_____

Identify the following situations as **approach-approach, approach-avoidance**, or **avoidance-avoidance conflicts**:

Situation	Type of Conflict
Two people you really like ask you out on a date for the same night.	
You have to take biology or chemistry, and you can't stand either one.	
You *love* the new Miata, but you can't really afford it.	
Only one graduate school accepted you, and you have nowhere else to go.	
Your mom offers you two tickets to the movies, but you have to take your sister.	
You can't decide between chocolate and vanilla ice cream.	

GO SURFING ...

... to find out how you would score on a **Life Events Stress Test**. You can find these tests at the following sites:

♦ http://www.stresstips.com/lifeevents.htm
♦ http://www.eap.com.au/stress_test.htm
♦ http://www.stress-help.co.uk/SRRS.htm
♦ http://www.success.net.au/stress_test.html

This type of test is no longer thought to be a good measure of **stress**. Why not? _____
_____
_____
_____

What are **daily hassles** and what are their negative effects on a person's functioning?
_____
_____
_____
_____
_____
_____

What are some of the **daily hassles** in your life that create **stress**? _____

_____

_____

_____

_____

As the manager of a company, what policies could you institute to reduce your employees' **stress**?

_____

_____

_____

_____

_____

GO SURFING ...

... to find out if you have a **Type A personality**. Short inventories are available at the following sites:

♦   http://itech.fgcu.edu/cgi-bin/lchallenges/survey/typea.html
♦   http://www.prenhall.com/whetten_dms/chap2_3.html
♦   http://attila.stevens-tech.edu/~rreilly/TYPE_A/TYPE_A.HTM

What did these surveys indicate about your personality type? _____

_____

Do you agree or disagree with the results? _____

_____

According to the text, what does current research say about the idea of a **Type A personality**?

_____

_____

_____

What does current research say about the health effects of **hostility**? _____

_____

_____

_____

Looking at Levels

How can **hostility** lead to illness, at the **levels of the brain, person, and the group**. Use arrows to indicate how factors at the different levels may interact.

The Brain	The Person	The Group

TRY PRACTICE TEST #1 NOW!
GOOD LUCK!

Stress, Disease, and Health

The Immune System: Catching Cold

How does stress harm the **immune system**? _____
_____
_____
_____
_____
_____
_____

What types of stressors are most likely to alter **immune functioning**? _____
_____
_____
_____
_____
_____
_____

Cancer

What are the two ways in which stress can affect the growth of cancerous cells?

♦ _____

♦ _____

What role does **perception of control** play in the progression of cancer? _____
_____
_____
_____
_____
_____
_____

Heart Disease

Describe the link between **stress** and **heart disease**. _____
_____
_____
_____
_____
_____

What role does depression play in **heart disease**? _____
_____
_____
_____
_____
_____

Sleep

How does **sleep** differ from normal consciousness? _____
_____
_____

Fill in the table below with the characteristics of the stages of sleep.

	Length of Stage (at Beginning and End of Night)	Physical Activity	Brain Activity
Non-REM stages			
Stage 1			
Stage 2			
Stages 3 and 4			
REM sleep			

How do **sleep patterns** change over the life-span?

♦ **Infancy:** _____
_____
_____
_____
_____

♦ **After age 40:** _____
_____
_____
_____

GO SURFING ...

... at the following sites and take the online sleep tests:

♦   http://www.powersleep.org/selftestb.htm

♦   http://quiz.ivillage.com/parentsoup/tests/sleepdep.htm?arrivalSA=1&arrival_freqCap=2

According to these tests, are you **sleep-deprived**?_____

Do you agree with the results of these tests? Why or why not? _____
_____
_____

How has **sleep deprivation** (either current or previous) affected you in each of the following **areas**?

♦   **Cognitive effects:** _____
      _____
      _____

♦   **Emotional effects:** _____
      _____
      _____

♦   **Physical effects:** _____
      _____
      _____

Sleep deprivation has been used by some governments as a method of torture. (For more information about this, visit the Human Rights Watch website at http://www.hrw.org/.) Based on this information, as well as studies with rats, if you were not allowed to sleep for a *protracted* length of time (e.g., 2 weeks), what effects could you expect in each of the following areas?

♦   **Cognitive effects:** _____
      _____
      _____

♦   **Emotional effects:** _____
      _____
      _____

♦   **Physical effects:** _____

_____

_____

Why is **sleep** so important? In your own words, summarize the following theories:

♦   **Restorative theory:** _____

_____

_____

♦   **Evolutionary theory:** _____

_____

_____

Keep a diary of your dreams for the next few days (or more). Summarize the **manifest content** of one of your dreams here:_____

_____

_____

_____

_____

_____

GO SURFING ...

… at one of the following "dream interpretation" sites. Use the dream dictionaries there to interpret your dreams.
♦   http://www.sleeps.com/dictionary/dictionary.html
(There are also other sites available; just search for them! Do *not* pay any money to have your dream interpreted online!)

Now, offer an explanation of the **latent content** of your dream, based on what you found at the sites above._____

_____

_____

_____

_____

_____

_____

How else could your **dream** be explained (besides using Freud's ideas of manifest and latent content)?_____

_____
_____
_____
_____
_____
_____
_____
_____

Which **dream theory** does Solms' research support? Explain. _____

_____
_____
_____
_____

Complete the following table, indicating how the **neurotransmitter** (NT) or **hormone** (H) levels change during sleep and the effects of these changes.

Chemical	Increase or Decrease?	Effects of Change
Acetylcholine (NT)		
Serotonin (NT)		
Norepinephrine (NT)		
Melatonin (H)		

Describe the timing of your **circadian rhythms**: Are you a **lark** or an **owl**? _____

_____
_____
_____

How do you deal with this timing in your everyday life?_____

_____
_____
_____
_____

Why are some people grouchy on Monday mornings? _____

_____
_____
_____
_____

What can they do to keep from being grouchy?_____
_____
_____
_____
_____

What are **circadian rhythms**? _____
_____
_____
_____
_____

What brain part is involved in regulating **circadian rhythms**? How? _____
_____
_____
_____
_____

For most people, what is the least energetic time of the day? Why?_____
_____
_____
_____
_____

GO SURFING …

… at the following site and take the online **sleep tests** there. (Follow the links at the bottom of the page.)
♦   http://www.nationalsleep.com/patient_selftest.asp

Does this site indicate that you may have a **sleep disorder**? If so, name and describe the disorder.
_____
_____
_____
_____

Do you agree with the results of this test? Why or why not?_____
_____
_____
_____
_____

Can you think of factors that may influence such test results? _____

_____

_____

_____

_____

Looking at Levels

Amanda is embarrassed when her husband, Robin, tells her that she snores. Robin urges Amanda to see the doctor, but she refuses. Because he cannot sleep in the bedroom when she snores, Robin sleeps on the couch in the living room. After 2 months of this, both partners are very grumpy. Finally, Robin issues an ultimatum: Amanda must seek help, or he will move out and get his own apartment. Describe the factors at each of the three levels that have contributed to this situation. Draw arrows to indicate how the factors may have interacted.

The Brain	The Person	The Group

GO SURFING ...

... at the following site and take the online Sleep IQ test to test your knowledge of sleep:

♦   http://www.sleepfoundation.org/nsaw/sleepiq99i.html

How did you do?_____

_____

_____

TRY PRACTICE TEST #2 NOW!
GOOD LUCK!

Strategies for Coping

Coping Strategies: Approaches and Tactics

Check the appropriate column to indicate whether each of the following coping responses is **problem-focused** or **emotion-focused**.

Coping response	Emotion-focused	Problem-focused
"I refuse to feel bad about this grade – everyone else got a bad grade too!"		
"This is a bad grade. I better buckle down and study harder for the next exam."		
"This is a bad grade. I think I'll go and talk to the teacher about how I can do better."		
Joan calls her mother and talks for hours on end about her boss, her husband, and her kids – they're driving her crazy!		

Define each of the following **coping strategies**, and describe a situation in which you have tried it.

Coping Strategy	Definition	Example
Problem-Focused Strategies		
Active coping		
Planning		
Instrumental social support		
Suppression of competing activities		
Restraint coping		
Emotion-Focused Strategies		
Emotional social support		

Coping Strategy	Definition	Example
Venting emotions		
Positive reinterpretation/growth		
Behavioral disengagement		
Mental disengagement		

Did you notice if you have a preference for certain **coping strategies** over others? If so, which ones? Why? Are these known to be effective coping strategies?_____
_____
_____
_____
_____
_____

Do you ever use **thought suppression** to try to cope with stress? _____

According to research, is this an effective technique? Why or why not? _____
_____
_____
_____
_____
_____

Name the factors at each of the following levels that may lead to **aggression**.

Personal Factors	Environmental Factors

Do you know anyone who is **aggressive**? Which of the factors above—personal or environmental—might explain that person's aggressive behavior? _____

_____

_____

_____

_____

Are men or women more **aggressive**? Explain. _____

_____

_____

GO SURFING ...

... at the following sites to determine your self-esteem and narcissism:
♦   http://discoveryhealth.queendom.com/self_esteem_abridged_access.html
♦   http://www.psych-net.org/test/narc-test.html

What do the tests say? Do you have high self-esteem? Are you high in narcissism? _____

_____

_____

How are self-esteem and narcissism related to **aggression**? _____

_____

_____

_____

_____

Given your test results, do you think you have a propensity to act **aggressively**? Why or why not?

_____

_____

_____

_____

GO SURFING ...

... at the following sites to see if you have any substance dependencies:

♦ http://www.alcoholscreening.org/screening/index.asp
♦ http://www.efn.org/~pfarmer/

Do these tests reveal that have problems with **substance abuse**? _____
_____
_____
_____
_____

Do you agree with these results? Why or why not?_____
_____
_____
_____

If you do have a problem, do you abuse substances *chronically*? In other words, do you have a **substance dependence**?_____
_____
_____
_____

The two most important symptoms of substance dependence are tolerance and withdrawal. In your own words, define those terms here:

♦ **Tolerance** = _____
_____
_____

♦ **Withdrawal** = _____
_____
_____

Why is alcohol characterized as a **depressant**?_____
_____
_____

Complete the following table, indicating the physical effects of **alcohol** at different dosages.

Dosage	Physical Effects
Low doses	
Moderate doses	
High doses	

Describe another example of **inhibitory conflict**, besides that described in the text. _____

_____

_____

_____

_____

_____

_____

Describe what might happen if a person who had been drinking was faced with a **high-conflict** or a **low-conflict** situation.

High-Conflict Situation	Low-Conflict Situation

List and describe the psychological effects of **alcohol**.

♦ _____

_____

♦ _____

_____

♦ _____

_____

♦ _____

_____

♦ _____

_____

Have you ever experienced a **blackout**? Describe what it was like (or what it would be like).

_____
_____
_____
_____
_____

Why are **stimulants** more likely to induce dependence than other drugs? _____
_____
_____
_____
_____
_____

Complete the following table, comparing and contrasting aspects of using **cocaine powder** versus using **crack**.

	Cocaine Powder	Crack
How administered		
Effects		
Dangers		

How does **cocaine** affect neurons to produce the psychological effects that it does? _____
_____
_____

How does **cocaine**, a drug that initially produces pleasure, ultimately lead to the loss of pleasure from other sources (e.g., food and sex)? _____
_____
_____

Caffeine and **nicotine** are common stimulants. List their effects in this table.

Caffeine	Nicotine

How do **narcotic analgesics** affect the brain, and what are the effects?

- ♦ _____
  _____
  _____
  _____

- ♦ _____
  _____
  _____
  _____

What effects does **heroin** have?

- ♦ _____

- ♦ _____

- ♦ _____

- ♦ _____

Why is it so difficult for a **heroin** addict to "kick the habit"?_____
_____
_____
_____

What effects does **LSD** have on users?

- ♦ _____

- ♦ _____

- ♦ _____

- ♦ _____

- ♦ _____

What are the effects of **marijuana** on users?

♦ _____

♦ _____

♦ _____

♦ _____

How do the effects of **marijuana** depend on the social context in which the drug is used? _____
_____
_____
_____
_____

Do you know anyone who uses one of the drugs described in the text? If so, does the drug have the effects described? _____
_____
_____
_____
_____

Coping and Social Support

Describe four benefits of a good **social support system**.

♦ _____

♦ _____

♦ _____

♦ _____

Distinguish between **perceived social support** and **enacted social support**. Which is more important in buffering against stress? _____
_____
_____
_____
_____
_____
_____

Evaluate your **social support network**. Do you feel that you have adequate social support? Why or why not? _____

_____

_____

_____

_____

_____

_____

Mind-Body Interventions

List four **mind-body interventions**:

- ♦ _____

- ♦ _____

- ♦ _____

- ♦ _____

What effects do **mind-body interventions** have? _____

_____

_____

_____

_____

_____

What is a **placebo**? Under what circumstances are placebos effective? _____

_____

_____

_____

_____

_____

_____

_____

Gender, Culture, and Coping

Describe the **positive** and **negative effects** of **multiple roles** for women:

Negative Effects	Positive Effects

How does culture influence **stress** and **coping**? _____
_____
_____
_____

Looking at Levels

How might the **nocebo effect** work on the **levels of the brain, the person, and the world,** for example when you expect to do poorly on a test? _____
_____
_____
_____
_____
_____
_____

TRY PRACTICE TEST #3 NOW!
GOOD LUCK!

After You Read . . . Thinking Back

1. What are some of the potential problems with doing research on **stress**? Can causality be asserted? Under what circumstances? _____
   _____
   _____
   _____
   _____
   _____
   _____

2. Think back to Chapter 8, in which you studied personality. Do you think there are certain personality variables that might make one more able to tolerate or **cope** with **stress**? Explain._____
   _____
   _____
   _____
   _____
   _____
   _____

3. Use your knowledge of sensation and perception to discuss how **placebos** work.
   _____
   _____
   _____
   _____
   _____
   _____

4. How would a cognitive psychologist think about stress? What would he/she say causes stress? How would he/she recommend **coping** with it? _____
   _____
   _____
   _____
   _____
   _____
   _____

5. What roles do nature and nurture play in stress? Think back to Chapter 1. How could this controversy be resolved, as it relates to stress? _____
   _____
   _____
   _____
   _____
   _____
   _____

After You Read . . . Practice Tests

PRACTICE TEST #1:
WHAT IS STRESS?

Multiple-Choice Questions

For each question, circle the letter of the best answer.

1. The body's naturally produced anti-inflammatory agents are called
    _____. (p. 375)
    a. endorphins and enkephalins
    b. dopamine and serotonin
    c. glucocorticoids
    d. epinephrine and norepinephrine

2. The second stage of Selye's three-stage stress response is _____. (p. 375)
    a. alarm
    b. exhaustion
    c. resistance
    d. coping

3. When the stress response is triggered, the hypothalamus secretes a substance that causes the
    release of _____. (p. 375)
    a. epinephrine
    b. dopamine
    c. norepinephrine
    d. glucocorticoids

4. During the primary appraisal of a situation, _____. (p. 377)
    a. cortisol is released
    b. the GAS is activated
    c. the person asks "What can I do about this?"
    d. the person asks, "Am I in danger?"

5. After the secondary appraisal comes _____. (p. 377)
    a. the tertiary appraisal
    b. coping
    c. the fight-or-flight response
    d. general adaptation

6. A perceived lack of control in the face of a stressor may lead to _____.
    (p. 377)
    a. chronic ulcers
    b. learned helplessness
    c. heart disease
    d. an anxiety disorder

7. In general, perceived control is helpful _____. (p. 377)
    a. when you can see how much worse things *could* have been
    b. in most situations
    c. in situations that are unpredictable
    d. when you are depleted of coping resources

8. When you can't decide between double-chocolate cake and strawberry mousse pie,
    because you like them both, you are experiencing an _____ conflict. (p. 378)
    a. approach-approach
    b. avoidance-approach
    c. approach-avoidance
    d. avoidance-avoidance

9. Experiencing a significant number of daily hassles has been linked to _____.
    (p. 379)
    a. psychological symptoms
    b. suppressed immune functioning
    c. physical symptoms
    d. all of the above

10. Research has not confirmed the existence of a Type A personality. However, it has indicated
    that the _____ component of the hypothesized Type A personality is
    important in predicting heart disease. (p. 379)
    a. hostility
    b. time urgency
    c. mistrustfulness
    d. competitiveness

PRACTICE TEST #2:
STRESS, DISEASE, AND HEALTH

Fill-in-the-Blank Questions

Fill in each blank with a term from the word bank.

WORD BANK	
B cells	immune
glucocorticoids	Natural killer (NK) cells
sympathetic nervous system	T cells

The _____ system functions to defend the body against infection. There are two classes

of white blood cells: _____, which mature in the bone marrow, and _____

_____, which mature in the thymus. One type of T-cell is the _____

_____, which detects and destroys damaged or altered cells before they become cancerous.

_____, which are released when the stress response is triggered, hinder the

formation of or even kill NK cells, making the body more vulnerable to infection and tumor growth.

People whose _____ responds significantly to

stress show the most change in immune system functioning. (p. 381)

Matching Questions

Match each of the following stages of sleep with the appropriate description. (pp. 384-385)

_____ 1. Stage 1   a. Sleep spindles

_____ 2. Stage 2   b. 20–50% of EEG-recorded brain activity is delta waves

_____ 3. Stage 3   c. Vivid dreaming

_____ 4. Stage 4   d. Hypnogogic sleep

_____ 5. REM sleep   e. Very deep sleep with 50% or more delta waves

Multiple-Choice Questions

For each question, circle the letter of the best answer.

1.   Stress can cause _____. (p. 382)
      a.   an increased risk of infection following injury
      b.   increased healing time
      c.   posttraumatic stress disorder
      d.   all of the above

2.   Glucocorticoids affect the immune system by _____. (p. 381)
      a.   enhancing the production of some white blood cells
      b.   hindering the formation of or killing some white blood cells
      c.   enhancing the production of some red blood cells
      d.   hindering the formation of or killing some red blood cells

3.   A stressor that increases the likelihood of heart disease is _____. (p. 383)
      a.   marriage
      b.   a major disaster
      c.   graduate school
      d.   depression

4.   Studies that investigate the relationship between stress and the immune system typically
      measure _____ as an index of immune system activity. (p. 381)
      a.   the number of circulating white blood cells
      b.   the number of circulating red blood cells
      c.   the amount of damage to white cells
      d.   both a and b

5.   The stress response increases capillary growth in order to carry more white blood cells to the
      site of an injury; however, this also _____. (p. 382)
      a.   stimulates tumor growth
      b.   causes tumor growth
      c.   increases NK activity
      d.   does all of the above

6.   You are most likely to remember dreams that occur during _____. (p. 385)
      a.   Stage 1
      b.   Stage 2
      c.   Stage 4
      d.   REM sleep

7.   Which of the following is NOT typical of REM sleep? (p. 385)
      a.   Slow heart rate
      b.   Irregular breathing
      c.   Body paralysis
      d.   Genital arousal

8.   How would an evolutionary psychologist explain humans' need for sleep? (p. 387)
      a.   It strengthens important neural connections.
      b.   It restores our bodies from the wear and tear of the day.
      c.   It keeps us in bed at night, a time when our vision is not very good.
      d.   It increases cortisol levels.

9.   After Kate has a dream in which her teeth fall out, her psychologist tells her that this means
      that she doesn't feel like she has a voice (or control) of what is happening in her life. Which
      theory of dreaming does Kate's psychologist most likely believe in? (p. 388)
      a.   Freudian theory
      b.   Evolutionary theory
      c.   Restorative theory
      d.   The activation-synthesis hypothesis

10.   Which of the following would you be LEAST likely to experience during hypnogogic sleep?
      (p. 384)
      a.   A gentle falling or floating sensation
      b.   Fear
      c.   "Seeing" flashing lights
      d.   A sudden, violent jerk

11.   One night, you go to bed really late because you are studying for your psychology exam.
      Which of the following can you expect to happen? (p. 386)
      a.   You will enter REM sleep later than usual.
      b.   You will have more deep sleep than usual.
      c.   More time will be spent in REM sleep.
      d   You will dream less than usual.

12.   Which of the following would NOT be a recommendation for someone suffering from
      insomnia? (p. 391)
      a.   Don't smoke cigarettes, eat chocolate, or drink anything containing caffeine in the
            evening.
      b.   Put a TV in your bed so it can lull you to sleep.
      c.   Keep regular sleep hours.
      d.   Consider meditation or progressive muscle relaxation.

13.   The 24-hour day _____. (p. 390)
      a.   is largely maintained through light-dark cycles (which can be either natural or
            artificial)
      b.   results from external aids, such as clocks
      c.   is not necessarily humans' "natural" rhythm
      d.   is all of the above

14. According to Karni and colleagues (1994), the best way to strengthen brain connections made during the day is to _____. (p. 388)
    a.   stay awake all night
    b.   go to sleep, but have a friend wake you up whenever you enter REM sleep
    c.   get a good night's sleep
    d.   drink alcohol before going to bed

15. A patient with brain damage that disconnects the frontal cortex from the brainstem and the limbic system, he will _____. (p. 389)
    a.   have insomnia
    b.   have vivid nightmares
    c.   stop dreaming entirely
    d.   experience sleep apnea

PRACTICE TEST #3:
STRATEGIES FOR COPING

True/False Questions

Circle TRUE or FALSE for each of the following statements.

1.   TRUE   FALSE   Venting relieves internal "pressure." (p. 396)

2.   TRUE   FALSE   Thought suppression is an effective way to diminish stress. (p. 396)

3.   TRUE   FALSE   Men are more physically aggressive than women. (p. 397)

4.   TRUE   FALSE   Males are more likely to be aggressive in response to criticisms of their intellectual ability than are females. (pp. 397-398)

5.   TRUE   FALSE   In general, people with low self-esteem are particularly likely to be aggressive. (p. 398)

6.   TRUE   FALSE   There is a relationship between age at which an individual begins drinking and the likelihood that he/she will develop an alcohol disorder. (p. 400)

7.   TRUE   FALSE   The more stressors people have in their lives, the more likely they are to use problem-focused coping strategies. (p. 395)

8.   TRUE   FALSE   Physiologically, alcohol can both depress and stimulate the nervous system. (p. 400)

9.   TRUE   FALSE   It takes about 15 minutes for alcohol to get absorbed into the blood. (p. 400)

10.   TRUE   FALSE   In low-conflict situations, people who have been drinking can typically inhibit their responses. (p. 401)

11.   TRUE   FALSE   Crack is usually inhaled through the nostrils. (p. 403)

12.   TRUE   FALSE   Stimulants such as cocaine are more likely to induce dependence than any other drug. (p. 403)

13.   TRUE   FALSE   Fifty percent of date rapes happen when men have been drinking. (p. 402)

14.   TRUE   FALSE   LSD use results in increased creativity. (p. 405)

15.   TRUE   FALSE   Heroin stimulates the CNS. (p. 404)

Matching Questions

Match each substance with its characteristics.

_____ 1.   Alcohol (p. 400)   a.   Can result in sudden death, even for occasional users

_____ 2.   Barbiturates (p. 403)   b.   Damages neurons that produce serotonin

_____ 3.   Cocaine (powder)   c.   Causes hallucinations, which sometimes recur spontaneously (p. 403)

_____ 4.   Crack (p. 403)   d.   Causes decreased awareness and increased relaxation

_____ 5.   Amphetamines   e.   Legal substance that causes alertness and insomnia
             (p. 404)

_____ 6.   MDMA ("e")   f.   In high doses, can cause effects similar to paranoid
             (p. 404)   schizophrenia

_____ 7.   Caffeine (p. 404)   g.   Causes short-term relaxation and euphoria

_____ 8.   Nicotine (p. 404)   h.   Legally prescribed to aid sleep or reduce
                                            anxiety, but lethal if combined with alcohol

_____ 9.   Heroin (p. 404)   i.   Less powerful, but more commonly used,
                                            hallucinogen

_____ 10. LSD (p. 405)   j.   Illegal substance that enhances sense of physical and
                                            mental capacity; decreases appetite

_____ 11. Marijuana (p. 405   k.   Causes relaxation, irritability, cancer, and emphysema

Multiple-Choice Questions

For each question, circle the letter of the best answer.

1.   Problem-focused coping tends to be used by people who score high on the personality
     superfactor of _____. (p. 394)
     a.   openness to experience
     b.   extraversion
     c.   conscientiousness
     d.   neuroticism

2. The tendency to interpret the intentions of others negatively is called _____ bias. (p. 397)
    a.   avoidant attribution
    b.   anger
    c.   hostile attribution
    d.   misinterpretation

3. People are more likely to use aggression as a coping mechanism if they _____. (p. 398)
    a.   have unstable but high self-esteem
    b.   have unstable but low self-esteem
    c.   are female
    d.   are easily frightened

4. Narcissists are likely to respond to a negative evaluation of their performance on a task with _____. (p. 398)
    a.   disbelief
    b.   humor
    c.   annoyance
    d.   aggression

5. If people believe that their actions can influence a stressor, they are likely to use _____; if they believe that a stressor cannot be influenced by their actions, they are more likely to use _____. (pp. 394-395)
    a.   avoidant coping strategies; nonavoidant coping strategies
    b.   nonavoidant coping strategies; avoidant coping strategies
    c.   problem-focused coping; emotion-focused coping
    d.   emotion-focused coping; problem-focused coping

6. Carla had been under tremendous stress and had gained a lot of weight. After several ineffective attempts to lose weight, she stopped dealing with it entirely and ate whatever she wanted. After that, Carla got involved in a wide variety of new activities, so that she was too busy to think about eating. Carla was first using _____ and later was using _____. (p. 394)
    a.   mental disengagement; instrumental social support
    b.   behavioral disengagement; mental disengagement
    c.   venting; thought suppression
    d.   thought suppression; venting

7. Hallucinogens are thought to influence _____. (p. 405)
    a.   serotonin
    b.   dopamine
    c.   the brainstem
    d.   the hypothalamus

8.   Placebos are likely to be more effective when _____. (p. 407)
      a.   they are in capsule, rather than pill, form
      b.   the person administering them is friendly and sympathetic
      c.   the treatment provider believes the placebo will work
      d.   all of the above are true

9.   Mind-body interventions _____. (p. 406)
      a.   work by helping a person change a stressor
      b.   work by helping a person adapt to a stressor
      c.   don't work
      d.   work by helping a person both change a stressor and adapt to it

10.   Which of the following is (are) mind-body intervention(s)? (p. 406)
      a.   Exercise
      b.   Social support
      c.   Relaxation techniques
      d.   All of the above

11.   Tolerance and withdrawal are the most important symptoms of _____.
      (p. 399)
      a.   substance dependence
      b.   substance abuse
      c.   substance addiction
      d.   substance use

12.   If someone is getting progressively less effect from her usual dose of a substance, she
      is experiencing _____. (p. 399)
      a.   withdrawal
      b.   addiction
      c.   dependency
      d.   tolerance

13.   Alcohol is called a _____ because it _____ CNS activity. (p. 400)
      a.   stimulant; increases
      b.   stimulant; decreases
      c.   depressant; increases
      d.   depressant; decreases

14.   Inhibitory conflict occurs when a person must choose between actions that are
      _____. (p. 401)
      a.   strongly desired and not strongly desired
      b.   strongly desired but repressed
      c.   socially unacceptable and personally desirable
      d.   personally desirable and physically impossible

15. Cocaine causes an experience of pleasure and euphoria by increasing the amount of available _____ and _____. (p. 403)
    a. endorphins; serotonin
    b. serotonin; epinephrine
    c. dopamine; norepinephrine
    d. dopamine; serotonin

16. Chronic heroin users experience more pain than other people when they are not using heroin because heroin _____. (p. 405)
    a. increases the intensity of pain stimulation
    b. lowers the natural pain thresholds
    c. decreases the body's supply of endorphins
    d. does all of the above

17. An indication that marijuana is not a completely benign drug is the fact that _____. (p. 405)
    a. thousands of people seek professional help each year to stop using it
    b. tolerance to THC occurs rapidly, leading to withdrawal symptoms
    c. its use leads to addiction and possible use of other drugs
    d. it is illegal

18. Which of the following is *not* a depressant? (p. 405)
    a. Heroin
    b. Valium
    c. Alcohol
    d. Barbiturates

19. Alcohol myopia is a state in which _____. (p. 401)
    a. a person who has been drinking perceives minor aspects of an experience as more important than they are.
    b. excessive intake of alcohol alters the shape of the eye, resulting in nearsightedness
    c. it becomes more difficult for a person who has been drinking to perceive objects that are farther away, particularly in low light
    d. a person who has been drinking cannot recall events that happen in the hours surrounding consumption

20. Disinhibition refers to the fact that _____. (p. 400)
    a. when they drink, some people lose their inhibitions about sex
    b. depressants activate some neurons that otherwise would not fire
    c. when they take drugs, some people become more inhibited about revealing details about themselves
    d. hallucinogens produce hallucinations

COMPREHENSIVE PRACTICE TEST

True/False Questions

Circle TRUE or FALSE for each of the following statements.

1. TRUE   FALSE   Everyone copes better with a situation they feel they can control. (p. 377)

2. TRUE   FALSE   More women than men are alcoholics. (p. 402)

3. TRUE   FALSE   Trying to suppress a thought can make you think of it more. (p. 396)

4. TRUE   FALSE   For certain problems, placebos can be an effective treatment, particularly if presented enthusiastically. (p. 407)

5. TRUE   FALSE   Women report more stress with multiple roles than do men. (p. 407)

6. TRUE   FALSE   People who are very conscientious tend to use problem-focused coping. (p. 394)

7. TRUE   FALSE   Hostile people are more likely to have heart disease than people who are not hostile. (p. 379)

8. TRUE   FALSE   Circadian rhythms are governed by part of the cerebellum. (p. 390)

9. TRUE   FALSE   Dream content is completely random. (p. 389)

10. TRUE   FALSE   Dreaming occurs only during REM sleep. (pp. 387-388)

11. TRUE   FALSE   A normal sleep-wake cycle, in the absence of light cues, is approximately 24.9 hours. (p. 390)

12. TRUE   FALSE   The most important symptom of substance dependence is disruption of work. (p. 399)

13. TRUE   FALSE   Substance dependence results from chronic substance abuse. (p. 399)

14. TRUE   FALSE   Withdrawal symptoms are the uncomfortable effects that occur when the use of a substance is discontinued. (p. 399)

15. TRUE   FALSE   The most commonly used hallucinogen is marijuana. (p. 405)

Multiple-Choice Questions

For each question, circle the letter of the best answer.

1. Walking alone in a dark alley one night, Carrie hears footsteps behind her. Her primary appraisal of the situation will lead her to _____. (p. 377)
    a. run
    b. ask herself if she should be concerned
    c. hide
    d. ask herself what she can do about the situation

2. We are less likely to be stressed about an uncontrollable situation if the situation is at least _____. (p. 377)
    a. positive
    b. predictable
    c. unexpected
    d. quick

3. In what way(s) can stress affect the growth of cancerous tumor cells? (p. 382)
    a. It can suppress the production of NK cells, which prevent the spread of tumors.
    b. It can "feed" the tumors by supplying blood through capillaries.
    c. Stress can cause both a and b.
    d. None of the above—stress has little effect on tumor growth.

4. Shirley just failed her psychology midterm and called her mother for advice. Her mother listened and reinterpreted Shirley's failure as an opportunity to pursue other majors. Shirley used a(n) _____-focused coping strategy, and her mother used a(n) _____ -focused coping strategy. (p. 394)
    a. problem; problem
    b. problem; emotion
    c. emotion; emotion
    d. emotion; problem

5. Bob is worried that his wife is cheating on him. He attempts to cope with this worry by trying to suppress it, both at home and at work. What is likely to happen to Bob? (p. 396)
    a. He will be able to suppress the thought at work, but not at home.
    b. He will be able to suppress the thought at home, but not at work.
    c. He will be able to suppress the thought at both work and home.
    d. He will actually think about his wife's possible infidelity even more.

6. Which of the following people is most likely to have an aggressive response to a bad grade? (p. 398)
    a. Zachary, who is low in narcissism
    b. Yolanda, who has negative self-esteem
    c. Xavier, who has positive self-esteem
    d. William, who is low in conscientiousness

7.	People with high levels of social support are likely to _____. (p. 406)
	a.	live longer
	b.	get sick less often
	c.	experience less depression
	d.	do all of the above

8.	Women with multiple roles (e.g., mother, employee, wife) experience all of the following EXCEPT _____. (pp. 407-408)
	a.	increased social support outside of the home
	b.	decreased feelings of self-esteem and control
	c.	increased workload
	d.	decreased psychological stress

9.	In Stage 1 sleep, which of the following would be most likely? (p. 384)
	a.	Sleepwalking
	b.	Dreaming
	c.	A feeling of falling
	d.	Muscle paralysis

10.	If you have a regular sleep cycle and are not troubled by insomnia, studying just before bed _____. (p. 388)
	a.	is a waste of study time, as you will forget everything while asleep
	b.	is a good technique, as REM sleep appears to solidify brain connections
	c.	is as good as studying at any other time
	d.	is not a good idea, as the material studied may disrupt your sleep and cause nightmares

11.	The genital arousal that occurs during REM sleep _____. (p. 385)
	a.	supports Freud's theory of dream interpretation
	b.	is unrelated to dream content
	c.	reflects a recent lack of sexual activity
	d.	supports the activation-synthesis hypothesis

12.	In most cases, people do not act out their dreams. This is because _____. (p. 385)
	a.	of muscle paralysis that occurs during REM
	b.	dreams are a mental, not physical exercise
	c.	acetylcholine released during sleep inhibits movement
	d.	of the deletion of unnecessary neural connections during dream states

13.	Sleeping pills work by _____. (p. 389)
	a.	increasing production of the hormone melatonin
	b.	decreasing production of acetylcholine, which activates the motor and visual areas of the brain
	c.	blocking production of the "wake-up" neurotransmitters, serotonin and norepinephrine
	d.	activating the suprachiasmatic nucleus (SCN), which regulates circadian rhythms

14. Which of the following is NOT a symptom of substance abuse? (p. 399)
    a. Taking more of the substance over time
    b. Using the substance leads to distress in major areas of life
    c. Using the substance occurs in dangerous situations
    d. Using the substance leads to legal problems

15. Alcohol affects the brain by _____. (p. 200)
    a. causing some neurons to fire that otherwise wouldn't
    b. depressing the nervous system
    c. triggering activation of the amygdala, which is involved in aggression
    d. doing a and b, but not c

16. Fifty percent of on-campus date rapes occur when men are under the influence of alcohol. The reason for this is probably that _____. (p. 402)
    a. the amygdala has been activated by the alcohol
    b. alcohol impairs the men's understanding of women's friendliness
    c. alcohol leads men to forget women's rejections of their advances
    d. the men experience blackouts

17. Cocaine causes a pleasurable feeling by _____. (p. 403)
    a. preventing reuptake of dopamine and norepinephrine in the synaptic cleft
    b. producing more serotonin
    c. causing spontaneous firing of sensory neurons
    d. destroying neurons that produce serotonin

18. Which of the following drugs is most likely to produce hallucinations? (p. 405)
    a. MDMA (or "e")
    b. Heroin
    c. Opiates
    d. LSD

19. Some narcotic analgesics _____. (p. 404)
    a. are derived from poppies
    b. are not addictive
    c. stimulate production of endorphins
    d. excite the central nervous system

25. Mind-body interventions have been shown to _____. (pp. 406-407)
    a. improve mood
    b. provide pain control
    c. increase lung functioning in people with asthma
    d. do all of the above

Essay Questions

Answer the following questions in the space provided.

1.   Is controllability always a good thing when it comes to dealing with stressors?

_____
_____
_____
_____
_____
_____
_____

2.   Is aggression simply a way for people with low self-esteem to feel better about themselves?_____

_____
_____
_____
_____
_____
_____
_____

3.   What aspects of social support are most important for protecting against stress?

_____
_____
_____
_____
_____
_____
_____

4.   Given that some people cope better when they perceive themselves as having control over a situation, while others cope better when they do *not* perceive control, what are the implications for working with children who have to undergo repeated painful procedures (e.g., needle sticks)? How could we assess the need (or lack thereof) for control? And once we know what type of control the child wants, how could we give it to him/her?

_____
_____
_____
_____
_____
_____
_____

5. Reports of links between stress and cancer have permeated the media. However, the majority of people do not understand the indirect ways in which stress and cancer are related. How might misperceptions of the links between stress and cancer lead an individual down the "wrong" path to health? _____

_____
_____
_____
_____
_____
_____
_____

6. Despite the serious negative consequences of alcohol and other drugs, significant numbers of people use and abuse them. Why? What is the allure? What is the solution?

_____
_____
_____
_____
_____
_____
_____

7. Why do you think that it is the *variety* of social support that is so important in protecting against getting a cold? Does it follow, then, that it is best to have a number of diverse friendships rather than a single best friend? What has been your pattern of relationships in the past, and how have they helped you cope in times of stress? _____

_____
_____
_____
_____
_____
_____

8. How stressed have you felt this year? What factors have contributed to your stress levels? How have you dealt with your feelings of stress? _____

_____
_____
_____
_____
_____
_____

9.	What are the different ways that culture may mediate the effect of stress? _____

	_____
	_____
	_____
	_____
	_____
	_____
	_____

10.	How would sleep deprivation affect the following activities of your life? Discuss.

	(a)	Performance on an exam _____

		_____
		_____
		_____

	(b)	Relationship with a roommate _____

		_____
		_____
		_____

	(c)	Ability to drive a car _____

		_____
		_____
		_____

	(d)	Physical health _____

		_____
		_____
		_____

	(e)	Appetite, weight, and body temperature _____

		_____
		_____
		_____

11.	Compare and contrast substance abuse and substance dependence._____

	_____
	_____
	_____
	_____
	_____
	_____
	_____
	_____

12.   Why should someone who has been drinking avoid possible high-conflict situations?

_____

_____

_____

_____

_____

_____

_____

_____

_____

When You Are Finished . . . Puzzle It Out

Across

2. Stimulus that disrupts equilibrium
3. Occurs after REM deprivation
4. A major depressant
5. One component of being Type A
6. Crystalline form of cocaine
10. Type of white blood cell in bone marrow
12. Brain part that registers light change
13. Most common hallucinogen
15. Repeated difficulty sleeping
16. Developed the 3-stage stress response
17. Symbolic meaning of dream
18. Behavior intended to harm another

Puzzle created with Puzzlemaker at DiscoverySchool.com.

Down

1. Plaque buildup in arteries
5. Another name for Stage 1 sleep
7. More substance needed to achieve same effect
8. Sleep stage with marked brain activity
9. First phase of the GAS
10. Loss of consciousness while drunk
11. Proposed that dreams are symbolic
14. Destroy damaged or altered cells

Chapter 11
Psychological Disorders:
More Than Everyday Problems

Before You Read . . .

Have you ever known anyone with a psychological disorder? How did you know that he or she had a disorder? In this chapter, you will learn about some of the symptoms of psychological disorders. The chapter begins with a definition of abnormality. It discusses the various explanations of the causes of abnormality (the brain, the person, and the group) and how abnormal behaviors are categorized into the major psychological disorders and personality disorders in the *Diagnostic and Statistical Manual of Mental Disorders.*

The major disorders covered in this chapter include some of the more common ones (e.g., depression, anxiety disorders, and eating disorders) and one of the more unusual and less common (e.g., schizophrenia). For each disorder, a description and discussion of causes is provided.

Chapter Objectives

After reading this chapter, you will be able to:

♦ Define *abnormality*.

♦ Explain what psychological disorders are and how they are classified and diagnosed.

♦ Define *mood disorders*, and explain what causes them.

♦ Describe the main types of anxiety disorders, including their symptoms and causes.

♦ Describe the symptoms and causes of the different types of schizophrenia.

♦ Describe the symptoms and causes of eating disorders.

♦ Explain what personality disorders are.

As You Read . . . Term Identification

Make flashcards using the following terms as you go. Use the definitions in the margins of this chapter for help. If you write the definitions in your own words, though, you will remember them better!

Agoraphobia
Anorexia nervosa
Antisocial personality disorder (ASPD)
Anxiety disorder
Attributional style
Bipolar disorder
Bulimia nervosa
Compulsion
Delusions
Diathesis-stress model
Eating disorder
Generalized anxiety disorder
Hallucinations
High expressed emotion
Manic episode
Major depressive disorder (MDD)
Mood disorder

Negative symptom
Obsession
Obsessive-compulsive disorder (OCD)
Panic attack
Panic disorder
Personality disorder
Phobia
Positive symptom
Posttraumatic stress disorder (PTSD)
Psychological disorder
Psychosis
Schizophrenia
Social causation
Social phobia
Social selection
Specific phobia

As You Read . . . Questions and Exercises

Identifying Psychological Disorders: What's Abnormal?

Defining Abnormality

Provide a definition of **abnormality**. Be sure to use the words *distress*, *disability*, and *danger*._____
_____
_____
_____
_____
_____

How can the line between **normal** and **abnormal** be drawn? What is the role of culture in drawing this line?_____

_____

_____

_____

_____

_____

Explaining Abnormality

How was abnormal behavior explained in each of the following?

In ancient Greece:
In the 17th century in New England:
In the middle of the 20th century:

What is the **biopsychosocial model**? _____

_____

_____

_____

_____

What is the **diathesis-stress model**?_____

_____

_____

_____

_____

Explain some of the things that can "go wrong" at each of the following **levels**, which may eventually lead to a psychological disorder.

Level	What Can Go Wrong?
Brain	
Person	
Group	

Describe **David Rosenhan's** study and findings. _____
_____
_____
_____
_____
_____

Categorizing Disorders: Is a Rose Still a Rose by Any Other Name?

The guide used to diagnose mental disorders in the United States is the _____
_____. It is published by the _____
_____ and is in the _____edition.

Describe what is noted on each of the five **axes** of the **DSM-IV**:

Axis	Description
I	
II	
III	
IV	
V	

Name four criticisms of the **DSM-IV**:

◆　_____

◆　_____

◆　_____

◆　_____

Looking at Levels

Do all acts of violence constitute evidence of a **psychological disorder**? Look back at your definition of a psychological disorder and consider the **levels of the brain, the person, and the group**. Use arrows to indicate how events at the different levels may interact.

The Brain	The Person	The Group

TRY PRACTICE TEST #1 NOW!
GOOD LUCK!

Axis I:
An Overview of Selected Disorders

Mood Disorders

GO SURFING ...

... to find out if you might have depression. Short depression inventories are available at the following sites:

♦ http://www.mentalhelp.net/poc/view_doc.php?id=973&type=doc&cn=Depression%20%28Unipolar%29

♦ http://www.allina.com/ahs/bhs.nsf/page/t_depression

♦ http://discoveryhealth.queendom.com/depression_abridged_access.html

♦ http://www.thewayup.com/newsletters/zung.htm

What did these surveys indicate? _____
Do you agree or disagree with the results? _____
_____

What are the "**ABC**s" that are affected by **depression**?

A: _____

B: _____

C: _____

How does **depression** affect the workplace?_____
_____
_____
_____

Have you ever been around someone who is **depressed**? What behaviors did the person engage in that either drew you in or pushed you away? How did being with the person make you feel?

_____
_____
_____
_____
_____

GO SURFING ...

... to find some of the warning signs of **suicide**. (There are lots of good sites out there.) List 10 signs here:

- ◆ _____
- ◆ _____
- ◆ _____
- ◆ _____
- ◆ _____
- ◆ _____
- ◆ _____
- ◆ _____
- ◆ _____
- ◆ _____

Anxiety Disorders

Identify each of the following **psychological disorders**.

Description	Disorder
Avoidance of places where escape may be difficult if a panic attack occurs	
Fear of public embarrassment or humiliation	
Re-experiencing of a traumatic event, avoidance of stimuli, and hypervigilance	
Frequent attacks of inexplicable autonomic arousal, accompanied by fear	
Persistent and intrusive thoughts accompanied by irrational behaviors	
A persistent and excessive fear focused on a specific object or situation	

Describe what is happening at the **level of the brain** for each of the following **disorders**:

Disorder	Level of the Brain
Panic disorder	
Phobias	
Posttraumatic stress disorder	
Obsessive-compulsive disorder	

Operant conditioning is implicated in the maintenance of several **anxiety disorders**. Describe how, for each of the following:

Disorder	Operant Conditioning Process
Phobias	
Obsessive-compulsive disorder	
Posttraumatic stress disorder	

Cognitive factors have also been implicated in a number of disorders. Describe the cognitive distortions that may precipitate or maintain the following disorders:

Disorder	Cognitive Processes
Panic disorder	
Agoraphobia	
Social phobia	
Obsessive-compulsive disorder	

GO SURFING ...

... to find out if you might have panic disorder (or another anxiety disorder). Short self-surveys are available at the following sites:
- ♦ http://www.psychcanada.com/en/panic/self_test.html
- ♦ http://www.livingwithanxiety.com/anxiety-quiz.htm
- ♦ http://www.conqueranxiety.com/anxiety_self_quiz.asp

What did these surveys indicate? _____
Do you agree or disagree with the results? _____
_____

Have you or a friend ever had a **panic attack**? If so, how would you or your friend describe it?
_____
_____
_____
_____

Summarize the causes of **panic disorder** at the **levels of the brain, the person, and the group**:

The Brain	The Person	The Group

How do events at the **different levels interact** with each other?_____
_____
_____
_____
_____

What is **social phobia** (or **social anxiety disorder**)? What are the symptoms? How prevalent is it?_____

_____

_____

_____

Do you have any **phobias**? If so …

GO SURFING …

… to find out the names of these phobias. You can see complete lists of phobias at the following sites:

♦   http://www.phobialist.com/reverse.html
♦   http://www.geocities.com/beckygretz19/weird_facts_phobias.html
♦   http://www.designedthinking.com/Fear/Phobias/Topics/topics.html

What do you have **phobias** of? What are the names of these **phobias**? _____

_____

_____

_____

_____

A common misconception is that **agoraphobia** is a fear of leaving the house. What is a more accurate definition? _____

_____

_____

_____

_____

Summarize the causes of **phobias** at the **three levels**:

The Brain	The Person	The Group

How do events at the **different levels interact** with each other?_____
_____
_____
_____
_____

GO SURFING ...

... to find out if you might have **obsessive-compulsive disorder (OCD)**. Short self-surveys are available at the following sites:

♦   http://www.ocfoundation.org/ocf1070a.htm
♦   http://www.nimh.nih.gov/publicat/ocdtrt1.htm

What did these surveys indicate? _____
Do you agree or disagree with the results? _____
_____

Summarize the causes of **OCD** at the **three levels**:

The Brain	The Person	The Group

How do events at the **different levels interact** with each other?_____
_____
_____
_____
_____

The diagnosis of **posttraumatic stress disorder (PTSD)** is made when three conditions are met:

◆ _____

◆ _____

◆ _____

Three sets of **symptoms** are persistently experienced by the person with **PTSD**:

◆ _____

◆ _____

◆ _____

Summarize the causes of **PTSD** at the **levels of the brain, the person, and the group:**

The Brain	The Person	The Group

How do events at the **different levels interact** with each other?_____
_____
_____
_____
_____

Schizophrenia

Is **schizophrenia** another name for a split personality? Explain. _____
_____
_____
_____

List some **positive** and **negative symptoms** of schizophrenia:

Positive Symptoms	Negative Symptoms

Name the four types of **schizophrenia**, based on the descriptions below:

_____ Bizarre movements or immobility
_____ Delusions of persecution and auditory hallucinations
_____ Flat or inappropriate affect; disorganized speech and behavior
_____ Doesn't meet criteria for any of the other subtypes

Summarize the causes of **schizophrenia** at the **three levels**:

The Brain	The Person	The Group

How do events at the **different levels interact** with each other?_____
_____
_____
_____
_____

Eating Disorders: You Are How You Eat?

GO SURFING ...

... to find out if you might have an eating disorder:
♦   http://www.sfsu.edu/~shs/dpm/eating.htm
♦   http://www.joannapoppink.com/quiz/bottom.html

What did these surveys indicate? _____

Do you agree or disagree with the results? _____
_____

What characteristic distinguishes **anorexia** from **bulimia**? _____

_____
_____
_____
_____

Summarize the causes of **anorexia** and **bulimia**, at the **levels of the brain, the person, and the group**:

Level of Brain		Level of Person		Level of Group	
Anorexia	Bulimia	Anorexia	Bulimia	Anorexia	Bulimia

Looking at Levels

What is the **abstinence violation effect**? At the level of the group, how might you help a friend whom you suspect has bulimia?_____
_____
_____
_____
_____
_____
_____
_____
_____

TRY PRACTICE TEST #2 NOW!
GOOD LUCK!

Axis II:
Focus on Personality Disorders

How are **Axis II disorders** different from **Axis I disorders**? _____
_____
_____
_____

List three criticisms of including **personality disorders** under Axis II (or at all) in the DSM-IV.

♦   _____
_____
_____
_____

♦   _____
_____
_____
_____
_____

♦   _____
_____
_____
_____

Look at the list of **Axis II personality disorders** found in the text. Do you know anyone who might have one of these personality disorders? Which disorder? What leads you to believe this?

♦   _____
_____
_____

♦   _____
_____
_____

♦   _____
_____
_____

List the characteristics of **antisocial personality disorder**. _____
_____
_____
_____

Explain **antisocial personality disorder** at **the levels of the brain, the person, and the group.**
Use arrows to indicate how factors at the different levels may interact.

The Brain	The Person	The Group

TRY PRACTICE TEST #3 NOW!
GOOD LUCK!

After You Read . . . Thinking Back

1.   In Chapter 4, you learned about biological preparedness. Based on this concept, are there some phobias that are likely to be more common? Some that are less? Why? _____
_____
_____
_____
_____
_____

2.   Sleep and circadian rhythms appear to play a role in several different psychological disorders. How? _____
_____
_____
_____
_____
_____

3.   In Chapter 7, you learned about different theories of emotions. How might these theories be important in studying psychological disorders? _____
_____
_____
_____
_____
_____

4.   In Chapter 10 you learned about stress and coping. How does stress influence the likelihood of having a psychological disorder? Can stress *alone* explain psychological disorders?
_____
_____
_____
_____
_____

5.   How can the idea of critical or sensitive periods, which you learned about in Chapter 9, be applied to the development of psychological disorders? _____
_____
_____
_____
_____
_____

After You Read . . . Practice Tests

PRACTICE TEST #1:
IDENTIFYING PSYCHOLOGICAL DISORDERS

True/False Questions
Circle TRUE or FALSE for each of the following statements.

1.   TRUE   FALSE   Twenty percent of Americans have a diagnosable mental illness in any given year. (p. 415)

2.   TRUE   FALSE   Delusions are mental images so vivid that they appear real. (p. 416)

3.   TRUE   FALSE   In 17th-century New England, abnormality was thought to be the work of the devil. (p. 416)

4.   TRUE   FALSE   The first edition of the DSM was published in the 1950s. (p. 419)

5.   TRUE   FALSE   There are four axes in the DSM. (p. 419)

6.   TRUE   FALSE   White American patients are more likely than African American patients to be evaluated negatively. (p. 418)

7.   TRUE   FALSE   One criticism of the DSM is that it creates psychiatric diagnoses for medical problems. (p. 419)

8.   TRUE   FALSE   There are 17 categories of disorders included in the DSM. (p. 420)

9.   TRUE   FALSE   Whether hearing voices should be considered abnormal depends on the cultural context. (p. 416)

10. TRUE   FALSE   Either a diathesis or a stress alone can explain a psychological disorder. (p. 417)

Multiple-Choice Questions

For each question, circle the letter of the best answer.

1. The inability to accurately perceive and comprehend reality, combined with a gross disorganization of behavior, is called _____. (p. 416)
    a. insanity
    b. neurosis
    c. incompetency
    d. psychosis

2. Mental images that are so vivid that they seem real, but that lack objective reality, are called _____. (p. 416)
    a. hallucinations
    b. psychoses
    c. delusions
    d. neuroses

3. The definition of a psychological disorder includes all of the following elements except _____. (p. 415)
    a. distress
    b. disability
    c. disease
    d. danger

4. According to some estimates, up to _____ percent of Americans have experienced at least one common psychological disorder in their lives. (p. 415)
    a. 36
    b. 48
    c. 57
    d. 64

5. The biopsychosocial model focuses on factors at the level of _____ as likely causes of psychological illness. (p. 416)
    a. the brain
    b. the group
    c. the person
    d. all of the above

6. Which of the following would be an example of a *diathesis*? (p. 417)
    a. An imbalance of neurotransmitter levels
    b. A natural catastrophe
    c. Relationship loss
    d. Culture

7.   Rosenhan's experiment tried to demonstrate the power of _____. (p. 418)
     a.   the diathesis
     b.   labeling
     c.   the catharsis
     d.   healing

8.   The DSM is the _____. (p. 419)
     a.   Diagnostic and Statistical Manual of Mental Disorders
     b.   Dictionary of Symptoms of Mental Disorders
     c.   Definitive Symptomotology of Mental Illness
     d.   Diary of Symptoms of Mental Illness

9.   Joel is clinically depressed. He has just been diagnosed with cancer and is having difficulty coping with his medical regimen. Joel's cancer would be noted on Axis _____ of the DSM. (p. 419)
     a.   I
     b.   II
     c.   III
     d.   IV

10. Which of the following is NOT a criticism of the DSM? (p. 419)
     a.   There are too many diagnoses.
     b.   Some of the diagnoses are about medical problems.
     c.   There is no such thing as mental illness.
     d.   Some of the diagnoses are not distinct from each other.

PRACTICE TEST #2:
AXIS I

True/False Questions
Circle TRUE or FALSE for each of the following statements.

1.   TRUE   FALSE   People who talk about suicide don't actually attempt suicide. (p. 424)

2.   TRUE   FALSE   People who attempt suicide are "crazy." (p. 424)

3.   TRUE   FALSE   Most suicidal people really want to die. (p. 424)

4.   TRUE   FALSE   People who think about suicide don't want to be helped. (p. 424)

5.   TRUE   FALSE   Discussing suicide with a person who is suicidal can be helpful. (p. 424)

6.   TRUE   FALSE   Most people who have a parent or a sibling with schizophrenia do not develop the illness themselves. (p. 437)

7.   TRUE   FALSE   Children who are at risk for schizophrenia are more reactive to stress than their peers. (p. 438)

8.   TRUE   FALSE   There is a higher incidence of problem pregnancies and birth complications for the mothers of babies who later develop schizophrenia. (p. 438)

9.   TRUE   FALSE   Schizophrenia typically has its onset during a person's twenties. (p. 436)

10.   TRUE   FALSE   Home movies of children who later develop schizophrenia reveal that they show more expressions of joy than their unaffected counterparts. (p. 438)

11.   TRUE   FALSE   People with bulimia nervosa may be overweight. (p. 441)

12.   TRUE   FALSE   Lower levels of serotonin might predispose people to bulimia nervosa. (p. 442)

13.   TRUE   FALSE   Obsessive personality traits in a family increase the risk of anorexia nervosa. (p. 442)

14.   TRUE   FALSE   Purging eliminates all the calories a person consumes. (p. 442)

15.   TRUE   FALSE   Preoccupations with food may give a person a sense of
                                    control over his or her life. (p. 442)

Fill-in-the-Blank Questions

Fill in each blank in the following paragraph with a term from the word bank.

WORD BANK	
crime	negative reinforcement
limbic system	social support
locus coerulus	type of trauma
natural disasters	

The majority of people who experience trauma do not go on to experience PTSD. The

_____ makes a difference in whether PTSD will be experienced. For example,

women are more likely to develop PTSD when their trauma resulted from _____than

from _____. A genetic predisposition to develop PTSD may be a

hypersensitivity of the _____. In addition, the _____ may be more

easily activated by mental imagery of traumatic events. At the level of the person,

_____ helps to explain why people with PTSD develop substance abuse,

because when the substance is taken, the symptoms of PTSD subside. Group factors can both

increase or decrease the likelihood that PTSD will develop, because group factors usually play an

integral role in creating the trauma; on the other hand, _____ can also

mitigate the effects of the trauma. (pp. 433-434)

Multiple-Choice Questions

For each question, circle the letter of the best answer.

1.   The most common psychological disorder is _____. (p. 424)
      a.   depression
      b.   obsessive-compulsive disorder
      c.   panic disorder
      d.   schizophrenia

2.   Most suicide attempts are motivated by the sense of _____ that is part of
      depression. (p. 424)
      a.   hopelessness
      b.   guilt
      c.   helplessness
      d.   sadness

3.   In people with bipolar disorder, the _____ is sometimes enlarged. (p. 426)
        a.   amygdala
        b.   locus coeruleus
        c.   hypothalamus
        d.   occipital lobe

4.   Marita has experienced a depressed mood for most of the day for at least 2 years, as well
        as problems with sleeping and feeling tired during the day. The most appropriate diagnosis
        for Marita would probably be _____. (p. 423)
        a.   major depressive disorder
        b.   dysthymia
        c.   bipolar disorder
        d.   mania

5.   Which of the following is NOT one of the diagnostic criteria for major depressive disorder?
        (p. 423)
        a.   Significant weight gain
        b.   Daily fatigue
        c.   Daily insomnia or hypersomnia
        d.   Depressed mood most of the day, almost daily

6.   The early phase of a manic attack is called _____. (p. 425)
        a.   hypomania
        b.   dysthymia
        c.   the prodromal phase
        d.   agitation

7.   For people with depression, unsupportive and critical relatives can increase the
        _____. (p. 427)
        a.   risk of onset
        b.   risk of relapse
        c.   length of first episode
        d.   response time to medication

8.   Which of the following is most likely to be true of a person with bipolar disorder? (p. 426)
        a.   She may have a larger amygdala than most people.
        b.   She may have a larger hippocampus than most people.
        c.   She may show an abnormal pattern of activation in the brainstem.
        d.   She may have smaller occipital lobes than most people.

9.   Which of the following neurotransmitters has been implicated in depression? (p. 426)
        a.   Substance P
        b.   Serotonin
        c.   Norepinephrine
        d.   All of the above

10. Recent increases in bipolar disorder may be attributable to _____. (p. 428)
    a.   fewer available treatment programs
    b.   the development of electric lights, which has unnaturally lengthened the day
    d.   the lengthening of the life span
    d.   more stress in childhood

11. A person who suffers attacks of intense fear or discomfort, accompanied by chest pain and difficulty breathing, would probably be diagnosed with _____. (p. 429)
    a.   generalized anxiety
    b.   depression
    c.   panic disorder
    d.   agoraphobia

12. Which of the following traumas is most likely to result in PTSD in women? (pp. 434-435)
    a.   A mugging
    b.   A plane crash
    c.   A hurricane
    d.   Being fired from work

13. Recurrent, persistent, intrusive, and uncontrollable thoughts, impulses, or images that cause anxiety are called _____. (pp. 431-432)
    a.   daily hassles
    b.   phobias
    c.   compulsions
    d.   obsessions

14. The neurotransmitter _____ probably plays a role in obsessive-compulsive disorder. (p. 432)
    a.   dopamine
    b.   GABA
    c.   acetylcholine
    d.   serotonin

15. Which of the following ways of coping would best *protect* someone from developing PTSD following a traumatic event? (p. 434)
    a.   Receiving social support
    b.   Ruminating about the event
    c.   Using relaxation techniques after the event
    d.   Using thought suppression about the event

16. Phobias involve hypersensitivity of the _____. (p. 431)
    a.   hippocampus
    b.   hypothalamus
    c.   amygdala
    d.   caudate nucleus

17. Not everyone who experiences an extremely traumatic event develops PTSD, suggesting that _____. (pp. 434-435)
  a. certain traumatic events are more likely triggers for the disorder
  b. it probably involves a genetic predisposition
  c. it is more likely to occur only in people with certain personality types
  d. all of the above

18. Positive symptoms of schizophrenia are those that _____. (p. 435)
  a. must be present for a diagnosis to be made
  b. are healthy and desirable, but not very common
  c. are present during the first half of the disorder
  d. mark the presence or excess of certain functions

19. Alogia and flat affect are _____ systems of schizophrenia. (p. 435)
  a. positive
  b. necessary
  c. negative
  d. crucial

20. Social selection is the idea that _____. (p. 439)
  a. people with mental disabilities drift to low socioeconomic classes
  b. living in urban environments triggers mental illness
  c. people who live in urban environments are biologically predisposed to mental illness
  d. people who are mentally disabled are less likely to reproduce

21. People with schizophrenia have enlarged _____. (p. 437)
  a. occipital lobes
  b. ventricles
  c. temporal lobes
  d. sulci and gyri

22. As children, people who later develop schizophrenia often have _____. (p. 438)
  a. hallucinations and delusions
  b. obsessions and compulsions
  c. positive and negative symptoms
  d. involuntary movements

23. High expressed emotion is a characteristic of families that are _____. (p. 439)
  a. critical, hostile, and overinvolved
  b. loving but underinvolved
  c. angry and withdrawn
  d. overly expressive in both positive and negative emotions

24. Fiona often twists her body into contorted positions and stands like that for hours. Fiona is probably suffering from which subtype of schizophrenia? (p. 437)
   a. Catatonic
   b. Paranoid
   c. Undifferentiated
   d. Disorganized

25. Individuals who have relatives with schizophrenia have _____ probability of developing the disorder, and the probability _____ with the degree of closeness of the relative. (p. 437)
   a. no higher; does not increase
   b. a higher; does not increase
   c. a higher; increases
   d. a varying; varies with the subtype of schizophrenia

26. In what way are people with bulimia ALWAYS different from people with anorexia? (p. 442)
   a. Anorexics are underweight; bulimics are not.
   b. Bulimics binge and purge; anorexics do not.
   c. Anorexics restrict their eating; bulimics do not.
   d. Bulimics take laxatives; anorexics do not.

27. Kinsey is always dieting and never ever eats chocolate brownies. One day, she can't resist the brownies that her mother has baked and eats a corner of one. If Kinsey experiences the abstinence violation effect when she eats the brownie, _____. (p. 444)
   a. she will feel extremely guilty for eating the brownie
   b. she will immediately stop eating the brownie and purge it from her system
   c. she will continue eating and gorge herself on brownies
   d. she will finish the one brownie and then exercise it off tomorrow

28. Which of the following is (are) NOT usually exhibited by people with eating disorders? (p. 442)
   a. Irrational beliefs
   b. Inappropriate expectations about themselves
   c. Black-and-white thinking
   d. Higher levels of serotonin

29. Which of the following individuals would be LEAST likely to have an eating disorder? (pp. 441-443)
   a. Beth, whose mother was a model
   b. John, who lives in South Africa
   c. Troy, who is a high-school wrestler
   d. Susan, whose family just immigrated from China

30.   Which of the following is NOT a possible danger of having an eating disorder? (pp. 440-442)

a.   Death
b.   Schizophrenia
c.   Amenorrhea
d.   Malnutrition

PRACTICE TEST #3:
AXIS II

True/False Questions
Circle TRUE or FALSE for each of the following statements.

1.   TRUE   FALSE   People with antisocial personality disorder are egocentric
                                   and lack charm. (p. 446)

2.   TRUE   FALSE   People with antisocial personality disorder lack conscience,
                                   empathy, and remorse. (p. 446)

3.   TRUE   FALSE   People with antisocial personality disorder have the capacity
                                   to care for how others feel. (p. 446)

4.   TRUE   FALSE   Antisocial personality disorder occurs in approximately
                                   20% of people. (p. 447)

5.   TRUE   FALSE   Antisocial personality disorder is not found in non-Western
                                   cultures. (p. 447)

Multiple-Choice Questions
For each question, circle the letter of the best answer.

1.   Someone with no guilt, conscience, or empathy for others most likely has a(n)
      _____ personality disorder. (p. 446)
      a.   avoidant
      b.   narcissistic
      c.   borderline
      d.   antisocial

2.   Research suggests that criminality _____. (p. 447)
      a.   depends on how many criminal acts someone has witnessed
      b.   is not heritable
      c.   involves heritable personality traits
      d.   involves gene Apo27

3.   Personality disorders _____. (p. 445)
      a.   are usually very obvious
      b.   may be observed only after knowing someone for a long time
      c.   are inflexible and maladaptive personality traits
      d.   b and c

4. Unlike someone with OCD, a person with obsessive-compulsive *personality* has
    _____. (p. 446)
    a. only obsessions
    b. only compulsions
    c. either obsessions or compulsions, but not both
    d. neither obsessions nor compulsions

5. Some researchers argue that personality disorders should not be included in the DSM on
    Axis II because _____. (p. 445)
    a. too few people have them
    b. they are too difficult to diagnose
    c. they are only quantatively, but not qualitatively, different from some Axis I diagnoses
    d. they are so prevalent

6. Cathy always seems to need attention to be directed toward her. Further, she is frequently
    very dramatic. Cathy probably has _____. (p. 446)
    a. narcissistic personality disorder
    b. histrionic personality disorder
    c. avoidant personality disorder
    d. paranoid personality disorder

7. Nick is uncomfortable in group settings. Whenever he sees people talking, he assumes that
    it must be about him. Nick probably has _____. (p. 446)
    a. borderline personality disorder
    b. paranoid personality disorder
    c. schizoid personality disorder
    d. schizotypal personality disorder

8. Carol rarely asks about other people and talks mostly about herself and her
    accomplishments. Carol probably has _____. (p. 446)
    a. narcissistic personality disorder
    b. histrionic personality disorder
    c. antisocial personality disorder
    d. obsessive-compulsive personality disorder

9. People with antisocial personality disorder _____. (p. 447)
    a. often had a poor attachment to their caregiver during childhood
    b. may have witnessed a lack of concern for the welfare of others by peers or parents
    c. may have an underreponsive central nervous system
    d. may have all of the above

10. Which of the following is NOT true of antisocial personality disorder? (p. 447)
    a. It occurs more often in men than women.
    b. It affects about 10% of the population.
    c. It is found in both Western and non-Western cultures.
    d. It is frequently found in male prisoners.

COMPREHENSIVE PRACTICE TEST

True/False Questions

Circle TRUE or FALSE for each of the following statements.

1.	TRUE	FALSE	Only about 10% of Americans suffer from a psychological disorder in their lifetime. (p. 415)
2.	TRUE	FALSE	African Americans are prescribed higher doses of psychotropic medication than are White Americans. (p. 418)
3.	TRUE	FALSE	More men than women have antisocial personality disorder. (p. 447)
4.	TRUE	FALSE	The most common psychological disorder is schizophrenia. (p. 424)
5.	TRUE	FALSE	Obsessive-compulsive disorder is a psychotic disorder. (p. 431)
6.	TRUE	FALSE	The DSM attempts to categorize mental disorders. (p. 419)
7.	TRUE	FALSE	Schizophrenia is another name for split personality. (p. 435)
8.	TRUE	FALSE	Some people with anorexia binge eat. (p. 441)
9.	TRUE	FALSE	People who talk about suicide won't really do it. (p. 424)
10.	TRUE	FALSE	The incidence of bipolar disorder in America appears to be decreasing. (p. 427)

Multiple-Choice Questions

For each question, circle the letter of the best answer.

1. Donte is convinced the CIA is out to get him, although in fact they are not. In this case, Donte's false belief is a(n) _____. (p. 416)
   a. hallucination
   b. diathesis
   c. delusion
   d. neurosis

2. The diathesis-stress model proposes that mental illnesses arise from
_____. (p. 417)
   a. genetic vulnerabilities
   b. biochemical imbalances
   c. environmental stressors
   d. some combination of the above

3. For the past 2 weeks, Regina has felt very fatigued. She has slept almost all the time and lost a considerable amount of weight. Not even her favorite activities, such as horseback riding, can rouse her interest. Which of the following disorders does Regina probably have?
(pp. 422-423)
   a. Major depressive disorder
   b. Chronic fatigue syndrome
   c. Anorexia
   d. Schizophrenia

4. Which of the following is NOT a criticism of the DSM? (p. 419)
   a. It includes medical problems as psychological disorders.
   b. It does not provide a discrete boundary separating abnormality from normality.
   c. It has too few disorders to adequately describe the range of mental illness.
   d. The disorders are presented as being clearly distinct from one another, even though they're not.

5. The most studied personality disorder is _____. (p. 446)
   a. depressive personality disorder
   b. dependent personality disorder
   c. antisocial personality disorder
   d. paranoid personality disorder

6. Panic attacks may arise from the hypersensitivity of cells in the _____.
(p. 429)
   a. occipital lobe
   b. locus coeruleus
   c. hypothalamus
   d. heart

7. Frank was asked to present his company's proposal to a funding board. However, Frank was *terrified* to speak in public, and consequently quit his job to avoid what he perceived would be great embarrassment. Most likely, Frank would be diagnosed with
_____. (p. 430)
   a. social phobia
   b. generalized anxiety disorder
   c. specific phobia
   d. panic disorder

8.   Which of the following is NOT a possible symptom of depression? (p. 423)
      a.   fatigue
      b.   diminished ability to concentrate
      c.   suicidality
      d.   racing thoughts

9.   As children, people who later developed schizophrenia _____.
      (p. 438)
      a.   were happier than others
      b.   exhibited fewer feelings of joy
      c.   slept more
      d.   had more irregular schedules

10.   Unsupportive and critical relatives can increase a depressed person's
      _____. (p. 439)
      a.   risk of onset
      b.   length of the first episode
      c.   risk of relapse
      d.   response time to medication

11.   If a person has OCD, other members of the family are more likely to have
      _____. (p. 432)
      a.   an anxiety disorder
      b.   OCD
      c.   some psychological disorder
      d.   schizophrenia

12.   The belief that others are out to "get" you is an example of a(n) _____ symptom of
      schizophrenia. (p. 435)
      a.   positive
      b.   disorganized
      c.   negative
      d.   undifferentiated

13.   If you have a parent with schizophrenia, the odds are that you will
      _____. (p. 437)
      a.   develop schizophrenia in your early 20s
      b.   develop schizophrenia later in life
      c.   develop schizophrenia—if you are female
      d.   not develop schizophrenia

14.   Tabitha experiences intense and pervasive fear in all different kinds of situations. Tabitha
      would probably be diagnosed with _____. (p. 428)
      a.   PTSD
      b.   panic disorder
      c.   generalized anxiety disorder
      d.   bipolar disorder

15. An increased risk of developing anorexia occurs among women who are
    _____. (p. 442)
    a. depressed
    b. anxious
    c. perfectionistic
    d. conscientious

Essay Questions

Answer the following questions in the space provided.

1. What *is* abnormality? _____
   _____
   _____
   _____
   _____
   _____
   _____

2. Why doesn't everyone who suffers a trauma develop posttraumatic stress disorder (PTSD)?
   _____
   _____
   _____
   _____
   _____
   _____

3. Why do women in the United States have higher rates of depression than men? _____
   _____
   _____
   _____
   _____
   _____
   _____

4. Why is a higher rate of schizophrenia found among lower socioeconomic classes and in
   urban areas? _____
   _____
   _____
   _____
   _____
   _____

5.   Do you think personality disorders should be included in the DSM? Why or why not?

_____
_____
_____
_____
_____
_____
_____
_____
_____

6.   Do you (or one of your friends) have any characteristics that might be considered
     "abnormal"? Do you consider yourself (or your friend) abnormal? What is the distinction
     between abnormal traits and abnormality? _____

_____
_____
_____
_____
_____

7.   Do you have a phobia? Most people do, and yet very few people seek help for these fears.
     Why? What would motivate you to seek help? If a problem doesn't bother someone, is it a
     problem at all? Can you think of disorders that don't cause personal distress?_____

_____
_____
_____
_____
_____
_____

8.   Are thoughts of suicide "abnormal"? Look back at the text's definition of *abnormality*.
     Does it make any difference whether the person wants to die because he/she is depressed
     or because he/she is terminally ill? _____

_____
_____
_____
_____
_____

9.   Do you know anyone with an eating disorder? How well does the text's description of
     abnormality fit your friend? Have you ever tried to help your friend? Why or why not?
     What did you do? How was your help received?_____

_____
_____
_____
_____
_____

10. Most of what is known about antisocial personality disorder comes from studying criminals in the prison system. What is faulty about this methodology? Is it possible that criminals represent one type of antisocial personality disorder, and that there is another type that has eluded study? _____

_____

_____

_____

_____

_____

When You Are Finished . . . Puzzle It Out

Across

6. Mental images that seem real
9. Most common mental disorder in the U.S.
10. Personality disorders coded on this axis
12. One week episode of elevated mood
14. Repetitive behaviors
16. Recurrent, persistent thoughts
17. Fear and avoidance of an object
18. Use of laxatives or vomiting
19. Predisposition to a disorder
20. Number of axes in the DSM

Down

1. Entrenched, bizarre false beliefs
2. Developed the negative triad
3. Episodes of intense fear
4. Suffered by many Vietnam veterans
5. Manual of mental disorders
7. Pattern of disregard for others
8. Disorder of a compulsive handwasher
11. Type of information in the DSM
13. "Fear of the marketplace"
15. Symptoms involving loss of functioning

Puzzle created with PuzzleMaster at DiscoverySchool.com.

Chapter 12
Treatment:
Healing Actions, Healing Words

Before You Read . . .

Have you ever been in therapy? Was it helpful? Do you know anyone who takes Prozac or another medication to treat a psychological disorder? This chapter presents an overview of the treatment of mental disorders. The first two sections cover the principles underlying the most common and most studied types of therapy: behavior, cognitive, and insight-oriented therapies (including psychodynamic and humanistic therapies). The origins of these therapies, the theories behind their use, and the specific techniques are described.

The next section presents a detailed look at psychopharmacology, with a description of the major classes of medications and their indications. You will also read about electroconvulsive therapy and transcranial magnetic stimulation in this section. Finally, this chapter explores the effectiveness of therapy and presents good information on how to pick a therapist, should you ever need one.

Chapter Objectives

After reading this chapter, you should be able to:

♦ Describe the goals and methods of behavior and cognitive therapies.

♦ Describe the focus of treatment and the techniques used in psychodynamic therapy.

♦ Explain how client-centered therapists approach treatment.

♦ Explain how medications are used to treat psychological disorders.

♦ Describe electroconvulsive therapy, as it is used today.

♦ Explain what transcranial magnetic stimulation is and how it is used in treatment.

♦ Identify other forms, or modalities, of treatment besides individual therapy.

♦ Discuss recent trends in psychotherapy that might affect the future of mental health care.

♦ List the key issues you should keep in mind when reading research studies of psychotherapy.

♦ Describe some good ways to find a therapist.

As You Read . . . Term Identification

Make flashcards using the following terms as you go. Use the definitions in the margins of this chapter for help. If you write the definitions in your own words, though, you will remember them better!

Antipsychotic medication
Behavior modification
Behavior therapy
Benzodiazepine
Bibliotherapy
Client-centered therapy
Cognitive distortion
Cognitive restructuring
Cognitive therapy
Dream analysis
Electroconvulsive therapy (ECT)
Exposure
Family therapy
Free association
Group therapy
Incongruence
Individual therapy
Insight-oriented therapy
Interpretation
Modality
Monoamine oxidase inhibitor (MAOI)
Outcome research
Progressive muscle relaxation
Psychoanalysis
Psychodynamic therapy
Psychoeducation
Psychopharmacology
Psychotherapy integration
Resistance
Selective serotonin reuptake inhibitor (SSRI)
Self-help group
Self-monitoring techniques
Serotonin/norepinephrine reuptake inhibitor
        (SNRI)
Stimulus control
St. John's wort
Systematic desensitization
Systems therapy
Tardive dyskinesia

Technical eclecticism
Token economy
Transference
Tricyclic antidepressant (TCA)

As You Read . . . Questions and Exercises

Therapies Focusing on Mental Processes and Behavior

Behavior Therapy

What are the **ABCs** of **behavior therapy**?

A = _____

B = _____

C = _____

GO SURFING ...

... to one of the following sites, which contain the instructions for **progressive muscle relaxation**.
♦   http://ourworld.compuserve.com/homepages/har/les1.htm
♦   http://www.guidetopsychology.com/pmr.htm

Ask a friend to read the instructions for **progressive muscle relaxation** aloud to you. Practice this technique several times over the next week. Does it make you more relaxed? _____
_____

Explain how **exposure with response prevention** can be used to treat a client's checking compulsions (e.g., checking that the oven is turned off multiple times before leaving the house).
_____
_____
_____
_____
_____
_____

Name a **behavior** that you would like to **modify**: _____
_____

How could you use **operant conditioning techniques** to **modify** this **behavior?** _____

_____

_____

_____

Do you have any problematic behaviors that might benefit from **self-monitoring techniques**? If so, what are they? What information could **self-monitoring techniques** provide you with?

_____

_____

_____

Identify each of the following **behavioral techniques**:

Description	Technique
Relaxation in the presence of a feared object or situation	
Making a binge eater eat, but not letting her purge	
Relaxing from head to toe	
Preventing a person with anorexia from exercising alone	
Rewarding a child for staying on task by giving her stickers that can later be traded for pencils, etc.	

On what grounds did **cognitive psychologists** criticize **behavior therapy?** _____

_____

_____

_____

GO SURFING ...

... to find out how **behavior therapy** is used with children who have attention deficit hyperactivity disorder. (There are lots of good sites out there!)

Explain the approach. _____

_____

_____

_____
_____
_____
_____
_____
_____
_____
_____

Cognitive Therapy: It's the Thought That Counts

According to cognitive therapists, psychological disorders arise from _____
_____ .

According to **Albert Ellis**, there are three processes that interfere with healthy functioning. Define each, and provide an example from your life.

Process	Definition	Personal Example
Self-downing		
Hostility and rage		
Low frustration tolerance		

Compare and contrast **Albert Ellis's** and **Aaron Beck's** theories of **cognitive therapy**.

Similarities	Differences

Below are five common **cognitive distortions**. For each, give a definition and a personal example.

Distortion	Definition	Personal Example
Dichotomous thinking		
Mental filter		
Mind reading		
Catastophic exaggeration		
Control beliefs		

Using the alphabetic sequence **ABCDEF**, fill in the following blanks to describe how **RET** works:

Distressing feelings arise because an **A**_____, along with a person's
B_____, lead to **C**_____. The therapist
must help the client to **D**_____ the beliefs, which will lead to an
E_____ and **F**_____ by the client.

What is **cognitive restructuring**? Can you identify thoughts that you would like to restructure?

_____
_____
_____
_____

Why is **psychoeducation** an important part of **cognitive therapy**? _____

_____

_____

_____

_____

What does the **cognitive** part of **CBT** entail? _____

_____

_____

_____

What does the **behavioral** part of **CBT** entail? _____

_____

_____

_____

Suppose that you wanted to develop a training program to help aggressive children develop better social skills. How could you use **cognitive-behavioral therapy** to do this? Name the **cognitive** and the **behavioral** components that you might include in your treatment.

◆　　**Cognitive:** _____

_____

_____

_____

_____

_____

_____

_____

_____

◆　　**Behavioral:** _____

_____

_____

_____

_____

_____

_____

_____

Psychodynamic Therapy: Origins in Psychoanalysis

Freud said that there are three parts to personality: the **id**, the **ego**, and the **superego**. How can this structure of personality create psychological disorders? _____
_____
_____
_____
_____

How did Freud say that **psychoanalysis** could resolve these disorders? _____
_____
_____
_____
_____

What techniques did Freud use during **psychoanalysis**?

♦ _____

♦ _____

♦ _____

How is **psychoanalysis** different from contemporary **psychodynamic therapy**?_____
_____
_____
_____
_____

What factors led to these differences?

♦ _____
_____

♦ _____
_____

How is **transference** helpful? How can it be harmful? _____
_____
_____
_____
_____
_____
_____

Humanistic Therapy: Client-Centered Therapy

How does humanistic therapy differ from psychodynamic therapy?_____

_____

_____

_____

_____

_____

How do **client-centered** and other **humanistic therapists** approach treatment? What techniques would do they use? _____

_____

_____

_____

_____

_____

Which type of **therapist** would you prefer to see: a psychodynamic therapist or a humanistic therapist? Why? _____

_____

_____

_____

_____

GO SURFING ...

... and make up a problem to ask "Eliza," an artificial intelligence program that was initially designed to simulate a client-centered therapist. There are various Eliza programs on the Web, including at:

♦   http://www-ai.ijs.si/eliza/eliza.html
♦   http://www.manifestation.com/neurotoys/eliza.php3
♦   http://www.wilprint.com/eliza.html
♦   http://www.uwp.edu/academic/psychology/demos/elizaj/eliza.htm

In what ways, if any, is Eliza like a **client-centered therapist**? In what ways is the program unlike such a therapist? _____

_____

_____

_____

Looking at Levels

Parents often use **token economies** to modify the **behavior** of their children. Explain how such programs may work to decrease aggression in a child, at **the levels of the brain, the person, and the group**. Draw arrows to indicate how events at the different levels might interact.

The Brain	The Person	The Group

Are there moral and ethical issues concerning the use of token economies? Discuss. _____
_____
_____
_____
_____

TRY PRACTICE TEST #1 NOW!
GOOD LUCK!

Therapies Focusing on
Brain and Body

Psychopharmacology

Complete the following table, providing the names of specific **drugs** under each classification, the type(s) of disorders typically treated with those drugs, and the side effects.

Classification	Specific Drugs	Disorders Treated	Side Effects
Antipsychotics (atypical)			
Antipsychotics (traditional)			
Benzodiazepines			
Mood stabilizers			
Monoamine oxidase inhibitors (MAOIs)			
Selective serotonin reuptake inhibitors (SSRIs)			
Serotonin/norepinephrine reuptake inhibitors (SNRIs)			
Tricyclics			

What is **lithium** used to treat? What are the side effects? _____
_____
_____

Is **St. John's wort** effective for treating depression? Discuss. _____
_____
_____

Electroconvulsive Therapy (ECT)

What is **electroconvulsive therapy (ECT)**? Why was it developed? _____
_____
_____
_____
_____

For whom is **ECT** now considered appropriate? How is it administered? What are the potential side effects? _____
_____
_____
_____
_____
_____

Would you ever have **ECT** performed on you? Why or why not? _____
_____
_____
_____
_____

Transcranial Magnetic Stimulation (TMS)

What is **transcranial magnetic stimulation (TMS)**? _____
_____
_____
_____
_____

For whom is **TMS** appropriate? _____
_____
_____
_____

How is **TMS** different from **ECT**? _____
_____
_____
_____

Does **TMS** have any advantages over **ECT**? What are they? _____
_____
_____

Looking at Levels

How might a placebo work at the **levels of the brain, the person, and the group** to effect changes that resemble those of an antidepressant? Draw arrows to indicate how events at the different levels might interact.

The Brain	The Person	The Group

TRY PRACTICE TEST #2 NOW!
GOOD LUCK!

Which Therapy Works Best?

Modalities: When Two or More Isn't a Crowd

What can **group therapy** offer that individual therapy cannot? _____
_____
_____
_____
_____

What is the fundamental assumption of **systems therapy**? _____
_____
_____
_____
_____

Describe how reframing can be used in **family therapy**: _____
_____
_____
_____
_____

Have you ever been involved in **group therapy**? If so, what type? What techniques were used? Did you feel it was helpful? If so, how? _____

_____

_____

_____

_____

Innovations in Psychotherapy

What is **psychotherapy integration**? _____

_____

_____

_____

_____

What is **technical eclecticism**? _____

_____

_____

_____

_____

What is the difference between **psychotherapy integration** and **technical eclecticism**? _____

_____

_____

_____

What are the benefits of using either of these **integrative approaches**? _____

_____

_____

_____

What factors are common to all **theoretical orientations**? _____

_____

_____

_____

_____

How has the trend toward using **therapy protocols** affected the practice of **psychotherapy**?

_____

_____

_____

_____

Issues in Psychotherapy Research

What is **outcome research**? _____
_____
_____
_____

What are the questions that should be asked when designing and **evaluating** studies of **psychotherapy**? Why is each of these questions important?

◆ _____
  _____
  _____
  _____

◆ _____
  _____
  _____
  _____

◆ _____
  _____
  _____
  _____

◆ _____
  _____
  _____
  _____

◆ _____
  _____
  _____
  _____

◆ _____
  _____
  _____
  _____

◆ _____
  _____
  _____
  _____

What are the disadvantages of taking **medication** compared to participating in **therapy**?

♦ _____

♦ _____

♦ _____

♦ _____

♦ _____

For what two disorders is **medication** clearly the preferred form of treatment? Why?

♦ _____
_____

♦ _____
_____

What type of therapy would probably be the most **effective** for treating each of the following?

♦ Depression: _____

♦ Obsessive-compulsive disorder: _____

♦ Panic disorder: _____

♦ Agoraphobia: _____

♦ Specific phobias: _____

♦ Social phobia: _____

♦ Posttraumatic stress disorder: _____

How to Pick a Psychotherapist

What steps should you take to find a psychotherapist?

♦ _____

♦ _____

♦ _____

♦ _____

♦ _____

Looking at Levels

Explain how factors at **the levels of the brain, the person, and the** group affect the success of **treatment for OCD**. Draw arrows to indicate how factors at the different levels may interact.

The Brain	The Person	The Group

TRY PRACTICE TEST #3 NOW!
GOOD LUCK!

After You Read . . . Thinking Back

1. In Chapter 1, you learned how psychological studies are conducted. The effectiveness of psychological treatment is especially difficult to study. Why is this? _____

    _____
    _____
    _____
    _____
    _____
    _____

2. In Chapter 2, you learned about neural functioning. How does Prozac (or any of the other SSRIs) work at the neural level? _____

    _____
    _____
    _____
    _____
    _____
    _____

3. In Chapter 10, you learned about dreaming. Does Freud's technique of dream analysis make sense, given current knowledge about dreaming? Why or why not? _____

    _____
    _____
    _____
    _____
    _____
    _____

4. What are the principles of cognitive psychology (as discussed in Chapter 1)? How are these applied in cognitive therapy? _____

    _____
    _____
    _____
    _____
    _____

5. Given what you learned about repressed memories in Chapter 5, how successful do you think psychoanalytic techniques are likely to be? Explain. _____

    _____
    _____
    _____
    _____
    _____

After You Read . . . Practice Tests

PRACTICE TEST #1:
THERAPIES FOCUSING ON MENTAL PROCESSES AND BEHAVIOR

True/False Questions
Circle TRUE or FALSE for each of the following statements.

1. TRUE   FALSE   RET was developed by Aaron Beck. (p. 458)

2. TRUE   FALSE   Self-monitoring techniques are important because they help to identify the triggers of problematic behaviors. (p. 458)

3. TRUE   FALSE   RET says that people develop illogical thoughts because of what happened to them during their childhoods. (p. 458)

4. TRUE   FALSE   Beck viewed cognitive distortions as hypotheses to be tested. (p. 459)

5. TRUE   FALSE   RET is successful in treating psychotic disorders. (p. 460)

6. TRUE   FALSE   In cognitive therapy, patients often record their dysfunctional thoughts daily. (p. 460)

7. TRUE   FALSE   Cognitive and behavioral techniques are often integrated in practice. (p. 455)

8. TRUE   FALSE   Exposure with response prevention is a common cognitive distortion. (p. 456)

9. TRUE   FALSE   The only effective treatment for OCD is medication. (p. 456)

10. TRUE   FALSE   The D in the RET alphabetical sequence ABCDEF stands for "dispute." (p. 460)

11. TRUE   FALSE   Humanistic therapists distinguish between a client's behavior and the person. (p. 465)

12. TRUE   FALSE   Rogers viewed people's distressing symptoms as caused by unconscious conflicts. (p. 464)

13. TRUE   FALSE   Client-centered therapists are sometimes confrontational with clients. (p. 465)

14. TRUE   FALSE   Client-centered therapists help clients to see that only bad people do bad things. (p. 465)

15.   TRUE   FALSE   Humanistic therapies are especially effective in treating schizophrenia. (p. 465)

Fill-in-the-Blank Questions
Fill in each blank in the following paragraph with a term from the word bank.

WORD BANK	
defense mechanisms	interpretation
dreams	resistance
free association	transference
hypnosis	

Freud started out using _____, but eventually developed

_____ as his method of getting patients to talk about whatever

was on their minds. He particularly wanted them to talk about their _____,

as he considered these to be the "royal road to the unconscious." Psychodynamic

therapists also use _____ to understand the unconscious meanings of

patients' words and behaviors. Through this process, patients become aware of their

_____, which are designed to minimize the anxiety that arises

from unconscious but negative thoughts and feelings. At some point during the therapy

process, patients may experience _____ (for example,

by coming in late to sessions) and _____ (which allows them

to "correct" earlier relationships by interacting with the therapist as if he/she were a

person from the past). (pp. 461-464)

Multiple-Choice Questions
For each question, circle the letter of the best answer.

1.   Which of the following techniques is NOT based on classical conditioning principles? (p. 456)
   a.   Systematic desensitization
   b.   Progressive muscle relaxation
   c.   Behavior modification
   d.   Exposure

2.   Stimulus control is a technique used by _____. (p. 456)
        a.   psychoanalysts
        b.   Gestalt therapists
        c.   client-centered therapists
        d.   behavior therapists

3.   Ellis developed a treatment called _____. (p. 458)
        a.   client-centered therapy
        b.   insight-oriented therapy
        c.   rational-emotive therapy
        d.   free association

4.   Donita is afraid that she will not be admitted to nursing school and that she will end up on
        welfare, like her mother. In fact, Donita's GPA is 3.4, making admittance very likely. Which
        cognitive distortion is Donita using? (p. 459)
        a.   Mind reading
        b.   Control beliefs
        c.   Dichotomous thinking
        d.   Catastrophic exaggeration

5.   Daphne is seeing a psychologist to treat her depression. Her psychologist asks her to keep a
        written record of her automatic negative thoughts. In this case, Daphne's psychologist is
        most likely following _____'s theory and is using the technique of
        _____. (p. 460)
        a.   Ellis; systematic desensitization
        b.   Freud; psychoanalysis
        c.   Beck; cognitive restructuring
        d.   Ellis; psychoeducation

6.   Cognitive therapy also makes extensive use of _____. (p. 460)
        a.   family therapy
        b.   psychoanalysis
        c.   insight therapy
        d.   psychoeducation

7.   In the case of OCD, the goal of exposure with response prevention would be to
        _____. (p. 456)
        a.   get the client to habituate to the anxiety caused by the stimulus
        b.   reduce the client's cognitive distortions
        c.   change the client's obsessive thoughts
        d.   educate the client about the cause of the high anxiety

8.   Which of the following is NOT one of the processes that Ellis says interferes with healthy
        functioning? (p. 458)
        a.   Thinking that you know what others are thinking of you
        b.   Being critical of oneself for performing poorly or being rejected
        c.   Being unkind to or critical of others for performing poorly

        d.   Blaming everyone and everything for undesireable conditions

9.   In behavior therapy, ABC stands for _____. (p. 455)
        a.   affect, behavior, cognition
        b.   antecedents, behavior, consequences
        c.   antecedents, belief, control
        d.   attitude, behavior, consequences

10.   How do RET and Beck's cognitive therapy differ? (p. 459)
        a.   RET focuses on behavior, whereas Beck's therapy focuses on thoughts.
        b.   RET focuses on cognition, whereas Beck's therapy focuses on behavior.
        c.   In RET, therapists persuade the client that beliefs are irrational, whereas in Beck's
                therapy, this is learned through interactions with the world.
        d.   In RET, clients learn that their beliefs are irrational through their interactions with
                the world, whereas in Beck's therapy, clients are persuaded of this by the therapist.

11.   The original insight-oriented therapy is _____. (p. 461)
        a.   Gestalt therapy
        b.   psychoanalysis
        c.   client-centered therapy
        d.   integrative psychotherapy

12.   The goal of psychoanalysis is _____. (p. 461)
        a.   changing one's overall reward structure
        b.   understanding one's unconscious motivations
        c.   developing healthier interpersonal relationships
        d.   changing the way one thinks about life's stressors

13.   People rarely undertake psychoanalysis today because it _____. (p. 462)
        a.   doesn't provide enough understanding about the cause of their problems
        b.   can lead to painful realizations
        c.   can negatively transform personality
        d.   is costly and time-consuming

14.   Which of the following is a FALSE statement about how current psychodynamic therapies
        are different from traditional psychoanalysis? (p. 462)
        a.   Past relationships are seen as less important in current therapies.
        b.   The relationship with the therapist is less important in current therapies.
        c.   The emphasis on sexual and aggressive drives is downplayed in current therapies
        d.   Current psychodynamic therapy takes longer and is more costly than psychoanalysis.

15.   When patients come to relate to their therapists as they did to people who were important in
        their lives, _____ is said to have taken place. (p. 464)
        a.   transference
        b.   insight
        c.   countertransference
        d.   interpretation

16.   Rogers developed _____ therapy. (p. 464)
    a.   short-term psychodynamic
    b.   patient-centered
    c.   Gestalt
    d.   client-centered

17.   Rogers defined *incongruence* as a mismatch between _____. (p. 464)
    a.   what others think you should be and what you are
    b.   what you used to be and what you are now
    c.   what you are and what you want to be
    d.   how you behave and how you think

18.   Viktor begins to cancel his appointments with his therapist, citing work conflicts. Viktor is most likely experiencing _____. (p. 463)
    a.   transference
    b.   hostility
    c.   resistance
    d.   interpretation

19.   The key technique of the client-centered therapist is to _____. (p. 465)
    a.   help the client uncover unconscious motivations
    b.   provide unconditional positive regard
    c.   help to change irrational thought patterns
    d.   reward the client for progress toward his or her goals

20.   The clients most likely to benefit from insight therapies _____. (p. 465)
    a.   have affective disorders
    b.   are older
    c.   have the time and money to spend on extensive therapy
    d.   are relatively healthy, articulate people

PRACTICE TEST #2:
THERAPIES FOCUSING ON BRAIN AND BODY

True/False Questions
Circle TRUE or FALSE for each of the following statements.

1. TRUE   FALSE   Electroconvulsive therapy (ECT) is an effective treatment for schizophrenia. (p. 470)

2. TRUE   FALSE   ECT is helpful in treating severe depression. (p. 470)

3. TRUE   FALSE   We don't know why ECT works. (p. 470)

4. TRUE   FALSE   ECT is administered under anesthesia. (p. 470)

5. TRUE   FALSE   Usually, only one session of ECT is necessary to treat depression. (p. 470)

Multiple-Choice Questions
For each question, circle the letter of the best answer.

1. The atypical antipsychotic medications are effective at decreasing _____. (p. 468)
    a.   hallucinations
    b.   delusions of grandeur
    c.   cognitive distortions
    d.   all of the above

2. Selective serotonin reuptake inhibitors are used to treat _____. (p. 469)
    a.   the positive symptoms of schizophrenia
    b.   the negative symptoms of schizophrenia
    c.   depression
    d.   antisocial personality disorder

3. Prozac is a(n) _____. (p. 469)
    a.   MAOI
    b.   benzodiazepine
    c.   SSRI
    d.   atypical neuroleptic

4.   Risperdal is used to treat _____. (p. 468)
      a.   schizophrenia
      b.   bipolar disorder
      c.   depression
      d.   anxiety

5.   Which of the following medications would be most likely to be used to treat someone with
      obsessive-compulsive disorder? (p. 469)
      a.   Benzodiazepines
      b.   Lithium
      c.   Antipsychotic medications
      d.   SSRIs

6.   Which of the following statements about electroconvulsive therapy (ECT) is FALSE?
      (p. 470)
      a.   It is once again being used to treat mental illness.
      b.   It is only used in state-run hospitals.
      c.   It is sometimes used to treat severe depression.
      d.   It is the treatment of choice for schizophrenia if medication does not work.

7.   A side effect of ECT is _____. (p. 470)
      a.   memory loss
      b.   high blood pressure
      c.   dry mouth
      d.   tardive dyskinesia

8.   Although it is still experimental, transcranial magnetic stimulation (TMS) shows early signs
      of being an effective treatment for _____. (p. 470)
      a.   psychotic depression
      b.   generalized anxiety disorder
      c.   nonpsychotic depression
      d.   obsessive-compulsive disorder

9.   An advantage of TMS over ECT is that TMS _____. (p. 470)
      a.   results in fewer side effects
      b.   can be administered without anesthesia
      c.   does not require hospitalization
      d.   does all of the above

10.   Long-term use of antipsychotic medications can cause tardive dyskinesia, which is
      _____. (p. 468)
      a.   an irreversible movement disorder of the facial muscles
      b.   uncontrollable drooling and shouting
      c.   shuffling movements of feet
      d.   blunted affect and unresponsiveness

PRACTICE TEST #3:
WHICH THERAPY WORKS BEST?

Fill-in-the-Blank Questions

Fill in each blank in the following paragraph with a term from the word bank.

WORD BANK	
Alcoholics Anonymous	support
bibliotherapy	twelve
Higher Power	weekly

Self-help groups are sometimes called _____ groups and do not usually

have a clinically-trained leader. _____ was the first self-help

program and is based on _____ steps of recovery. Most such programs view a

belief in a(n) _____ as crucial to recovery, and it appears

that individuals who attend at least _____ gain the most benefit. The

use of books and tapes for therapeutic purposes is called _____. (p. 474)

Multiple-Choice Questions

For each question, circle the letter of the best answer.

1.   The most common theoretical orientation among family therapists is _____
        therapy. (p. 473)
        a.   behavioral
        b.   psychodynamic
        c.   communication
        d.   systems

2.   Research has found that it is important for clients to _____ to obtain benefits
        from 12-step groups such as Alcoholics Anonymous. (p. 474)
        a.   attend sessions on a weekly basis
        b.   believe in a Higher Power, such as God
        c.   own up to their responsibilities
        d.   bond with the other individuals in the group

3.   When a therapist integrates specific techniques without regard for an overarching theory, the
      therapist is said to be using _____. (p. 475)
      a.   integrative modality therapy
      b.   practical eclecticism
      c.   psychotherapy integration
      d.   technical eclecticism

4.   Therapy protocols are _____. (p. 475)
      a.   ethical guidelines for therapists
      b.   guidelines for setting up one's office and establishing fees
      c.   detailed session-by-session manuals of how therapy should proceed
      d.   descriptions of particular types of clients and the types of therapy they should
            receive

5.   The *dodo bird verdict* of psychotherapy seemed to suggest that _____.
      (p. 476)
      a.   no psychotherapy is effective
      b.   the forms of psychotherapy studied were not effective
      c.   the forms of psychotherapy studied were equally effective
      d.   medication is not effective

6.   What type of therapy is most likely to be recommended for someone with OCD?
      (pp. 476-477)
      a.   Psychodynamic
      b.   Cognitive
      c.   Behavioral
      d.   Client-centered

7.   Medication can directly assist people with schizophrenia by _____. (p. 479)
      a.   decreasing psychotic symptoms
      b.   providing the opportunity to learn new relationship skills
      c.   helping them realize the need to take medication
      d.   doing all of the above

8.   It is especially difficult to evaluate the effectiveness of _____ therapy.
      (p. 477)
      a.   behavioral
      b.   psychodynamic
      c.   cognitive-behavioral
      d.   cognitive

9.   A drawback of using medication instead of therapy to treat depression and anxiety is that
      _____. (p. 478)
      a.   medication is simply less effective, both in the short-term and the long-term
      b.   when medication is discontinued, the relapse rate is high
      c.   clients become addicted to the medications used to treat anxiety and depression
      d.   irreversible side effects such as tardive dyskinesia can cause life-long distress

10.   Which of the following is NOT a piece of advice to use when picking a psychotherapist?
      (p. 480)
      a.   Pick someone who makes you uncomfortable, as this means that he or she is probing
            deeply for information.
      b.   Contact several psychotherapists.
      c.   Ask your insurance company for providers who it will cover.
      d.   Ask for referrals from friends and family members.

COMPREHENSIVE PRACTICE TEST

True/False Questions

Circle TRUE or FALSE for each of the following statements.

1.   TRUE   FALSE   Dream analysis is a crucial technique for cognitive therapists. (p. 462)

2.   TRUE   FALSE   A client-centered therapist points out clients' faults during therapy. (p. 465)

3.   TRUE   FALSE   For most anxiety disorders, MAOIs are the medication prescribed. (p. 468)

4.   TRUE   FALSE   ECT is effective in treating severe depression. (p. 670)

5.   TRUE   FALSE   Many insurance companies will pay for only a certain number of psychotherapy sessions. (p. 475)

Multiple-Choice Questions

For each question, circle the letter of the best answer.

1.   Freud believed that psychoanalysis could _____. (p. 462)
   a.   help people understand unconscious motives
   b.   modify cognitions
   c.   lead to self-actualization
   d.   be practiced by anyone

2.   During psychoanalysis, Susan said, "I think I hate—I mean ate—something bad." The analyst pointed out to Susan that her slip of the tongue (saying "hate" instead of "ate") was significant and suggested some underlying unconscious conflict. The analyst was using the technique of _____. (p. 463)
   a.   interpretation
   b.   transference
   c.   blocking
   d.   incongruence

3.   Research comparing how effective different forms of treatment are for symptoms of a particular disorder is called _____ research. (p. 476)
   a.   systems
   b.   outcome
   c.   efficacy
   d.   psychotherapeutic

4. Which of the following techniques is NOT based on learning theory? (p. 456)
   a. Behavior modification
   b. Progressive muscle relaxation
   c. Psychoeducation
   d. Exposure

5. The C in the ABCs of behavior therapy stands for _____. (p. 455)
   a. control
   b. consequences
   c. caring
   d. cognition

6. Systematic desensitization is based on principles of _____. (p. 456)
   a. social learning
   b. psychoanalysis
   c. operant conditioning
   d. classical conditioning

7. Julie has an overwhelming compulsion to clap her hands every time she walks through a door. Her therapist treats her by having her walk back and forth through a doorway while keeping her hands at her sides, thus preventing her from clapping them. Most likely, Julie's therapist is a(n) _____ therapist and is using the technique of _____. (p. 456)
   a. behavior; exposure with response prevention
   b. behavior; systematic desensitization
   c. cognitive; behavioral restructuring
   d. insight-oriented; interpretation

8. Which of the following is NOT a process that interferes with healthy functioning, according to Ellis? (p. 458)
   a. Incongruence
   b. Hostility and rage
   c. Self-downing
   d. Low tolerance for frustration

9. Which of the following types of therapists would be most likely to say, "Tell me about your dreams." (p. 462)
   a. Client-centered
   b. Cognitive
   c. Psychodynamic
   d. Behavioral

10. Cognitive therapists make use of psychoeducation, which is _____.
(p. 460)
   a. having clients try to psychoanalyze themselves
   b. attending continuing education conferences
   c. educating clients about therapy and research pertaining to their disorders
   d. providing education opportunities to clients who are in psychiatric hospitals

11. The MAOIs are not widely prescribed for depression because _____.
(pp. 468-469)
   a. they are generally effective only with atypical depression involving increased appetite and hypersomnia
   b. they interact with certain foods to cause fatally high blood pressure
   c. they can cause tardive dyskinesia and take several months to start working
   d. of both a and b

12. Since the 1980s, the use of ECT has been _____. (p. 470)
   a. more frequent
   b. banned in the United States
   c. less frequent
   d. banned in Europe

13. Olivia has recently been diagnosed with OCD. Her psychiatrist is most likely to treat Olivia with _____. (p. 469)
   a. SSRIs
   b. St. John's wort
   c. MAOIs
   d. lithium

14. Rachelle and Mark have recently married, thus blending their two families. When their children begin fighting, Rachelle and Mark are likely to seek treatment from a therapist specializing in _____. (p. 473)
   a. cognitive therapy
   b. systems therapy
   c. psychoanalysis
   d. behavior therapy

15. For which disorders has medication been shown to be clearly superior to psychotherapy?
(p. 478)
   a. Depression and anxiety
   b. Social and simple phobias
   c. Bulimia and anorexia
   d. Schizophrenia and bipolar disorder

Essay Questions

Answer each of the following questions in the space provided.

1.   How is psychodynamic therapy different from psychoanalysis? _____
_____
_____
_____
_____
_____
_____

2.   How does the humanistic approach to therapy differ from the psychodynamic approach?
_____
_____
_____
_____
_____
_____

3.   How are Beck's and Ellis' versions of cognitive therapy similar and different? _____
_____
_____
_____
_____
_____
_____

4.   Why might a systems therapist refuse to see only one individual in a family? _____
_____
_____
_____
_____
_____
_____

5.   Do you think that dreams are a path to the unconscious? Why or why not? Go back and
read the section on dreams in Chapter 10. What are the alternative explanations for the
function of dreams? _____
_____
_____
_____
_____
_____

6. Do all parents express conditions of worth to their children? In what ways? Do you think that such conditions are potentially damaging and may lead a child to need therapy when older? Is unconditional positive regard appropriate for all types of clients? How about clients with antisocial personality disorder? _____

_____

_____

_____

_____

_____

_____

7. Why does electroconvulsive therapy continue to offend some people, despite its relative effectiveness? How would you feel if a friend or family member were to have ECT?

_____

_____

_____

_____

_____

_____

8. The text mentions that there is currently no objective measure of insight. Why do you think it is difficult to measure insight? If you were to develop such a measure, what types of questions would you include? _____

_____

_____

_____

_____

_____

_____

9. To know whether therapy has worked, why not just ask the client or the therapist? What types of biases might each have? _____

_____

_____

_____

_____

_____

_____

10. In general, which is more effective in treating psychological disorders—medication or therapy? _____

_____

_____

_____

_____

_____

_____

When You Are Finished . . . Puzzle It Out

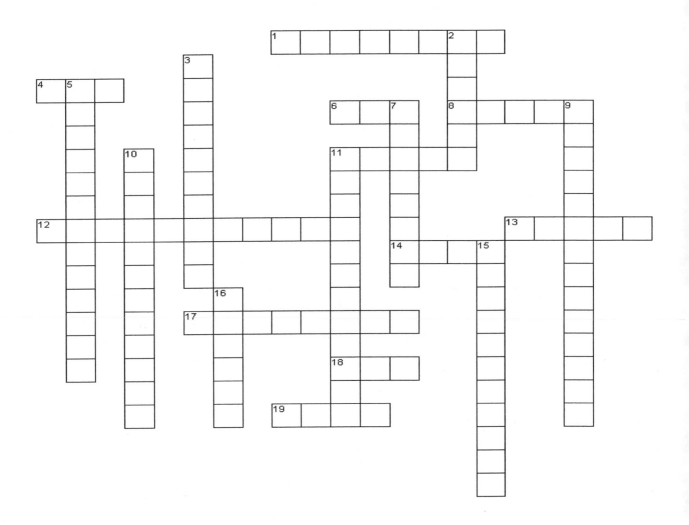

Across
1. Habituation-based therapeutic technique
4. Good therapy for depression
6. Controlled brain seizure as treatment
8. Developed RET
11. First antidepressant medication
12. Herbal therapy for depression
13. Developed psychoanalysis
14. Example: Elavil
17. Form of therapy
18. Experimental magnetic therapy
19. Prozac is an example of this

Puzzle created with PuzzleMaster at DiscoverySchool.com.

Chapter 13
Social Psychology: Meeting of the Minds

Before You Read . . .

Think of all the different ways that you interact with people everyday—perhaps with a romantic partner, in groups like classes and clubs, in the workplace, in public. How do you interact socially? How do you think about these interactions?

This chapter presents an overview of social psychology—the study of how we think about people (social cognition) and how we interact with people (social behavior). Can we predict behaviors from attitudes, or is it the other way around? What happens when our attitudes and behaviors are inconsistent? Sometimes our attitudes are negative; we may stereotype people and feel prejudiced. Our attitudes arise partly from the attributions we make about our own fate and that of others.

The section on social behavior discusses liking and loving relationships, the social organization of groups, and group behavior. Conformity, compliance, and obedience are discussed, as is decision making in groups. Finally, the chapter covers prosocial behavior and altruism, including the characteristics of people who help, the people they *choose* to help, and the circumstances under which they engage in helping behavior.

Chapter Objectives

After reading this chapter, you should be able to:

♦   Define *social psychology*, *social behavior*, and *social cognition*, and explain why they are important.

♦   Describe attitudes, and explain how they are formed.

♦   Define *persuasion*, and explain why persuasion attempts work or don't work.

♦   Define *stereotypes*, and explain how they are formed and how they can lead to prejudice.

♦   Discuss the reasons for prejudice and describe how prejudice can be reduced.

♦   Define *attributions* and identify the various types of attributions and attributional biases.

♦   Identify and briefly describe the factors that affect interpersonal attractions.

♦   Describe the different kinds of love, and explain Sternberg's triangular model of love.

♦   Define *norms*, *roles*, and *status* and explain the effects of being in a group on an individual's behavior.

- Define and differentiate between *conformity* and *compliance*, identify factors that affect them, and describe techniques that influence compliance.

- Describe Milgram's studies on obedience.

- Describe the factors involved in group behavior and decision making, including social loafing and social facilitation.

- Describe the factors that affect prosocial behavior and bystander intervention.

As You Read . . . Term Identification

Make flashcards using the following terms as you go. Use the definitions in the margins of this chapter for help. If you write the definitions in your own words, though, you will remember them better!

Altruism
Attitude
Attribution
Attributional bias
Belief in a just world
Bystander effect
Cognitive dissonance
Compassionate love
Compliance
Conformity
Deindividuation
Diffusion of responsibility
Door-in-the-face technique
External attribution
Foot-in-the-door technique
Fundamental attribution error
Group
Group polarization
Groupthink

Ingroup
Internal attribution
Lowball technique
Mere exposure effect
Norm
Obedience
Outgroup
Passionate love
Persuasion
Prejudice
Prosocial behavior
Recategorization
Self-serving bias
Social cognition
Social cognitive neuroscience
Social facilitation
Social loafing
Social psychology
Stereotype
Triangular model of love

As You Read . . . Questions and Exercises

Social Cognition: Thinking About People

Attitudes and Behavior: Feeling and Doing

Name and describe the three components of **attitudes**.

◆ _____
   _____

◆ _____
   _____

◆ _____
   _____

Can you think of a time when **attitudes** affected what information you processed about a specific event? (For example, think about an experience for which you and someone else have very different memories.) Describe the situation. _____
_____
_____
_____

Attitudes are more likely to affect behavior when they are . . .

◆ _____

◆ _____

◆ _____

◆ _____

◆ _____

Think of an example from your life of a situation when your behavior affected your **attitude** about something. Why might this have occurred? _____

_____

_____

_____

_____

_____

What is **cognitive dissonance**? _____

_____

_____

Describe the conclusions of Festinger and Carlsmith about **cognitive dissonance**.

♦ _____

_____

_____

_____

♦ _____

_____

_____

_____

What are two different ways by which we try to decrease **cognitive dissonance**?

♦ _____

_____

_____

♦ _____

_____

_____

What factors will increase the likelihood of **persuading** someone?

♦ _____

♦ _____

♦ _____

♦ _____

♦ _____

♦ _____

What do **social cognitive neuroscientists** do? _____

_____

_____

_____

_____

Stereotypes: Seen One, Seen 'Em All

Why do we **stereotype** people? _____

_____

_____

What errors do we make when **stereotyping** people? _____

_____

_____

_____

_____

_____

What is the relationship between **stereotyping** and **prejudice**? _____

_____

_____

_____

_____

_____

GO SURFING ...

... at http://www.understandingprejudice.org/demos/ and take the following tests:
- ♦ The Baseline Survey
- ♦ The Slide Tour of Prejudice
- ♦ Ambivalent Sexism Questionnaire
- ♦ Slavery and the U.S. Presidents
- ♦ What's Your Native IQ?
- ♦ Test Yourself for Hidden Biases
- ♦ The Baseline Survey, to see if your thinking has changed

Describe the results of the tests here. _____

_____

_____

_____

_____

_____

Prejudice can stem from emotions in the following two ways. Give an example of each from your own life.

◆   **The presence of negative feelings:** _____

_____

_____

◆   **An absence of positive feelings:** _____

_____

_____

Think of a group of which you are a member. Do group members (e.g., the **ingroup**) think of themselves favorably? Do they think of others (e.g., the **outgroup**) less favorably? Explain.

_____

_____

_____

Explain how each of the following processes may contribute to the development and maintenance of **prejudice**:

Process	Explanation
Scarce resources	
Competition	
Social categorization and ingroup bias	
Social learning theory	

Describe a **jigsaw classroom**. _____

_____

_____

_____

Have you ever participated in a **jigsaw classroom**? If so, how effective was it in reducing **prejudice**? In conveying material? If not, do you think you would like to take part in a **jigsaw classroom**? Why or why not? _____

_____

_____

_____

Attributions: Making Sense of Events

In the table below, indicate the types of statements you might make as internal or external attributions in the given situations.

Situation	Type of Attribution	
	Internal	External
You ace a test.		
You fail a test.		

GO SURFING ...

... at http://discoveryhealth.queendom.com/lc_short_access.html and take the **Locus of Control and Attributional Style Test**.

What kind of **attributional style** do you have? Explain _____

_____

_____

_____

_____

_____

What comment might a person make about the following situations, using the **fundamental attribution bias**?

Situation	Comment
A woman is raped.	
A waitress forgets an order.	
A homeless person asks for money.	
A man confesses to a crime.	

According to the **self-serving bias**, what type of attributions (internal or external) do you make in each of the following situations?

Situation	Type of Attribution
You get a good grade on an exam, despite the fact that you didn't study very hard.	
Your roommate gets a good grade on an exam, despite the fact that he didn't study very hard.	
You get a bad grade on an exam, despite the fact that you studied very hard.	
Your roommate gets a bad grade on an exam, despite the fact that he studied very hard.	

How does **belief in a just world** lead to blaming the victim? _____
_____
_____
_____

Looking at Levels

How do factors at **the levels of the brain, the person, and the group** interact to explain how you feel about people who are **victims of acquaintance rape** following a long night of drinking? Draw arrows to indicate how the events at the different levels might interact.

The Brain	The Person	The Group

TRY PRACTICE TEST #1 NOW!
GOOD LUCK!

Social Behavior: Interacting with People

Relationships: Having a Date, Having a Partner

In light of the **repeated contact hypothesis**, what is likely to happen among men and women who live in the same dormitory? _____
_____
_____
_____
_____

What are the three factors that influence us to **like** someone else?

◆ _____

◆ _____

◆ _____

What features are considered **attractive** in men, worldwide?

- ♦ _____

- ♦ _____

- ♦ _____

- ♦ _____

What features are considered **attractive** in women, worldwide?

- ♦ _____

- ♦ _____

- ♦ _____

What are the three components of **consummate love**? Briefly explain each.

- ♦ _____
  _____

- ♦ _____
  _____

- ♦ _____
  _____

Think of the last romantic relationship you were in. Was the relationship high or low on each of the three **components**?

- ♦ _____

- ♦ _____

- ♦ _____

Complete the following table about attachment types.

Attachment Type	Description	Percentage of Americans With This Type
Secure		
Avoidant		
Anxious-ambivalent		

GO SURFING ...

... at http://p034.psch.uic.edu/cgi-bin/crq.pl and take the **Attachment Style Questionnaire**.

According to this questionnaire, what type of **attachment** do you have now? _____
_____
_____

Do you agree or disagree with these results? Why? _____
_____
_____

Describe one study that supports the **evolutionary theory** of mate selection and one study that fails to support it.

Supports Evolutionary Theory	Does Not Support Evolutionary Theory

Social Organization: Group Rules

What four characteristics define a **group**?

♦ _____

♦ _____

♦ _____

♦ _____

What is **deindividuation**? Does it explain violence by individuals in anonymous crowds? Why or why not? _____
_____
_____
_____
_____
_____
_____
_____
_____

What are some of the **norms** at your school? _____
_____
_____
_____

Yielding to Others: Going Along With the Group

Under what circumstances would someone be more or less likely to **conform** to a group standard or opinion?

Circumstances That Increase Conformity	Circumstances That Decrease Conformity

Conformity is a change in behavior brought about by _____, whereas **compliance** is a change in behavior brought about by _____.

What are the six principles underlying effective **compliance** techniques?

- ♦ _____

- ♦ _____

- ♦ _____

- ♦ _____

- ♦ _____

- ♦ _____

Which of the above principles underlies each of the following **compliance** techniques?

- ♦ Foot-in-the-door: _____

- ♦ Lowball technique: _____

- ♦ Door-in-the-face: _____

Identify which compliance technique is described by each scenario:

Compliance Scenario	Technique
Your roommate asks you to drive her home – three states away! You say "no," but then agree to drive her to the airport – it's only an hour away.	
Your roommate asks you if she can borrow your notes from last week when she was sick. You agree and then find yourself giving her your notes every week!	
You agree to buy a car for $15,000 (telling yourself you'll spend no more than that), but then end up driving away with a $20,000 car because you wanted the "extras" that didn't come with the $15,000 price tag.	

In **Milgram's study**, what percentage of people obeyed instructions to give the highest level of shock under the following conditions?

Condition	Percentage
Milgram's original study	
College student gives the order.	
Two authority figures disagree with one another.	
"Teacher" holds electrode to "learner's" skin.	
Commands are given over the phone.	

Performance in Groups: Working Together

How does the **heterogeneity** of a group affect group communication? _____

_____

_____

_____

How can the negative effects of **heterogeneity** be reduced?

◆ _____

◆ _____

◆ _____

◆ _____

What is **group polarization**? _____

_____

_____

When is **groupthink** more likely to occur?

- ◆ _____

- ◆ _____

- ◆ _____

- ◆ _____

Describe a situation in which you or someone else engaged in **social loafing**. _____
_____
_____
_____

Have you worked on a group project? Which of the **group processes** in this chapter have you observed? Was social loafing or social facilitation present? Did your group have to come to some decision about something? How was the decision made? _____
_____
_____
_____
_____
_____
_____

Helping Behavior: Helping Others

What are the characteristics of a person likely to offer **help**? Of a person likely to receive help?

Characteristics of a "Helper"	Characteristics of a "Helpee"

According to Darley and Latane, what factors are likely to increase **bystander intervention**? What factors are likely to decrease bystander intervention?

Factors Increasing Bystander Intervention	Factors Decreasing Bystander Intervention

What do you think motivates others to be helpful? If an **altruistic** act is defined as one for which you don't expect anything in return—not even a sense of feeling good—is there really any such thing as a truly altruistic act? _____

_____

_____

_____

_____

_____

_____

Looking at Levels

Are the factors that influence cult behavior similar to the factors that influence the behavior of students who rush a fraternity? Explain, at **the levels of the brain, the person, and the group**, how a fraternity can exert so much power over inductees. Draw arrows to indicate how events at the different levels may interact.

The Brain	The Person	The Group

TRY PRACTICE TEST #2 NOW!
GOOD LUCK!

After You Read . . . Thinking Back

1. In Chapter 1, you learned about the ethics of psychological research. Would Milgram's study be allowed today? Why or why not? _____
    _____
    _____
    _____
    _____
    _____
    _____
    _____
    _____

2. In Chapter 7, you learned that cognition can affect emotion. In Chapter 5, you learned that emotion can affect cognition (e.g., memory). How are both of those themes reflected in this chapter? _____
    _____
    _____
    _____
    _____
    _____
    _____
    _____
    _____
    _____

3. In Chapter 9, you learned about the tasks of adulthood. Which tasks would be met by having a partner?_____
    _____
    _____
    _____
    _____

4. Why are the tasks of adulthood important? _____
    _____
    _____
    _____
    _____

5. How are stereotypes similar to and different from prototypes, which you learned about in Chapter 6? _____
    _____
    _____
    _____
    _____
    _____
    _____
    _____

After You Read . . . Practice Tests

PRACTICE TEST #1: SOCIAL COGNITION

True/False Questions
Circle TRUE or FALSE for each statement.

1. TRUE   FALSE   Slow talkers are more effective as persuaders than fast talkers. (p. 493)

2. TRUE   FALSE   When you pay close attention to the content of an argument, you are being affected by the peripheral route to persuasion. (p. 493)

3. TRUE   FALSE   Persuasion is more effective when strong emotions are aroused. (p. 493)

4. TRUE   FALSE   A person who is perceived as honest is more persuasive. (p. 493)

5. TRUE   FALSE   Sometimes just being exposed to someone can improve your attitude toward him or her. (p. 493)

Multiple-Choice Questions
For each question, circle the letter of the best answer.

1. Which of the following is NOT a component of an attitude? (p. 489)
    a. Affective
    b. Behavioral
    c. Instinctual
    d. Cognitive

2. Attitudes are more likely to affect behavior when the attitudes are _____. (p. 490)
    a. strong
    b. directly relevant to the behavior
    c. relatively stable
    d. all of the above

3. When an attitude and a behavior, or two attitudes, are inconsistent with one another, the resulting feeling is called _____. (p. 491)
    a.   intrapsychic conflict
    b.   attitudinal conflict
    c.   cognitive dissonance
    d.   persuasive dissonance

4. Which of the following is an example of peripheral persuasion? (p. 493)
    a.   You have a long phone conversation with a representative of a long-distance telephone company and then switch phone companies.
    b.   A soda company pays a TV network to have their soda featured on a hit sit-com, and soda sales then jump.
    c.   You read a pop-up window on your computer carefully before closing it.
    d.   You examine candidates' positions on all issues before deciding how you will vote.

5. When we experience a conflict between a stereotype and actual behavior that is too significant to simply ignore, we tend to _____. (p. 495)
    a.   change the stereotype
    b.   ignore the person
    c.   create a new subtype within the stereotype
    d.   switch the person to another stereotyped group

6. Unconscious prejudice arises from _____. (p. 495)
    a.   the presence of negative feelings
    b.   the absence of positive feelings
    c.   ambivalent feelings
    d.   both a and b

7. Which of the following would NOT decrease prejudice? (p. 498)
    a.   A competition for resources
    b.   Increased contact between the different groups
    c.   Recategorization
    d.   Working toward a shared goal

8. When your friend is late meeting you for the movies, you say to yourself, "Katie is just a chronically late person – I should have known," thus making a(n) _____ attribution. (p. 500)
    a.   internal
    b.   situational
    c.   external
    d.   ingroup

9.   The strong inclination to attribute someone's behavior to internal causes is called the
      _____. (p. 500)
      a.   fundamental attribution error
      b.   ingroup bias
      c.   self-serving bias
      d.   actor-observer effect

10.   After finding out that a fellow student was raped, Ryan blames her, saying that she shouldn't
      have been out at a party that late anyway. Ryan is probably _____. (p. 500)
      a.   using the self-serving bias
      b.   trying to maintain his belief in a just world
      c.   using an ingroup bias
      d.   using a theory of causal attribution

PRACTICE TEST #2:
SOCIAL BEHAVIOR

Multiple-Choice Questions

For each question, circle the letter of the best answer.

1. Repeated contact with a person typically leads to _____. (p. 503)
    a. decreased liking for that person
    b. no change in feelings for that person
    c. increased liking for that person
    d. feelings of love for that person

2. People tend to rate as "attractive" those facial features that are _____. (p. 504)
    a. masculine
    b. average
    c. unusual
    d. asymmetrical

3. According to Sternberg, only _____ love has passion, intimacy, and commitment. (p. 505)
    a. compassionate
    b. agape
    c. consummate
    d. reciprocal

4. People who are uncomfortable with intimacy and closeness are said to have a(n) _____ attachment style. (p. 505)
    a. secure
    b. anxious
    c. avoidant
    d. ambivalent

5. Car salespeople are notorious for using the _____ technique to get people to buy more car than they had bargained for. (p. 511)
    a. Foot-in-the-door
    b. Door-in-the-face
    c. Lowball
    d. Kick-from-behind

6. Buss has argued that women prefer men who _____. (p. 506)
    a. are attractive
    b. are faithful
    c. have good earning potential
    d. have a good "pedigree"

7.   Which of the following is NOT a defining characteristic of a group? (p. 507)
         a.   Regular interaction among members
         b.   Emotional connection
         c.   Physical proximity
         d.   Interdependence

8.   In Milgram's original experiment, _____ of the participants shocked the
         confederate with the highest voltage. (p. 513)
         a.   15%
         b.   45%
         c.   65%
         d.   95%

9.   In Emilio's freshman seminar class, all class members signed a "declaration of expectations"
         that they would attend classes prepared. Since then, nobody has missed a class. Thus, class
         attendance became part of the _____. (p. 508)
         a.   group stereotype
         b.   ingroup style
         c.   group's attributions
         d.   group norm

10.   In Asch's original conformity experiment, overall, _____ of the participants conformed
         with the obviously wrong majority. (p. 509)
         a.   one fifth
         b.   one third
         c.   one fourth
         d.   one half

11.   Which of the following statements about conformity is FALSE? (p. 510)
         a.   Rates of conformity have remained constant over the past several decades.
         b.   Rates of conformity are higher in collectivist cultures.
         c.   Men and women conform at the same rates.
         d.   Conformity is higher in very cohesive groups.

12.   A change in behavior brought about through a direct request is called
         _____. (p. 510)
         a.   conformity
         b.   compliance
         c.   norm readjustment
         d.   agreement

13.   Making a ridiculously large request, followed up by a more reasonable smaller request, is
         called the _____ technique. (p. 511)
         a.   foot-in-the-door
         b.   door-in-the-face
         c.   lowball
         d.   big-and-then-little

14. Milgram's experiment used something like the _____ technique to get people to obey. (p. 513)
    a. foot-in-the-door
    b. forced compliance
    c. door-in-the-face
    d. reciprocity

15. A group will reach a better decision when _____. (p. 514)
    a. there is a correct solution
    b. there is a leader
    c. the members of the group like each other
    d. the members of the group are heterogeneous

16. In group polarization, the attitudes of the group members _____. (p. 514)
    a. become more moderate
    b. move in the opposite of the original direction
    c. become more heterogeneous
    d. become more extreme, in the same direction as their initial opinions

17. Later studies using Milgram's obedience technique indicated that _____.
    (p. 513)
    a. women were equally as likely as men to shock someone
    b. people from other countries, such as Jordan and Germany, were equally as likely as men to shock someone
    c. women were less likely than men to shock someone
    d. both a and b are true

18. When consensus becomes more important than the critical analysis of different individual opinions, _____ has occurred. (p. 514)
    a. group polarization
    b. groupthink
    c. social loafing
    d. social compensation

19. Social facilitation is more likely to occur _____. (p. 515)
    a. among homogeneous group members.
    b. among heterogeneous group members
    c. for difficult tasks
    d. for well-learned tasks

20. Which of the following would INCREASE the likelihood that a person would help someone in need? (p. 518)
    a. If the person helping were alone
    b. If the person helping were in a group
    c. If the person needing help were dissimilar to the helper
    d. If the person helping expects to experience negative consequences for helping

COMPREHENSIVE PRACTICE TEST

True/False Questions

Circle TRUE or FALSE for each of the following statements.

1.   TRUE   FALSE   When people experience cognitive dissonance, they often have heightened arousal. (p. 491)

2.   TRUE   FALSE   A good way to decrease prejudice is to engage in competitive games with the stereotyped group. (p. 498)

3.   TRUE   FALSE   The old adage "opposites attract" has been supported by empirical research. (p. 504)

4.   TRUE   FALSE   The majority of Americans live their lives so as to avoid closeness and interdependence. (p. 505)

5.   TRUE   FALSE   Milgram found that 65% of his subjects would obey his orders and administer the maximum possible shock to another person. (p. 513)

6.   TRUE   FALSE   Men and women are equally likely to conform. (p. 510)

7.   TRUE   FALSE   Heterogeneity in groups can have both positive and negative effects. (p. 515)

8.   TRUE   FALSE   As the number of bystanders increases, the likelihood of helping decreases. (p. 517)

9.   TRUE   FALSE   People may be more likely to blame a rape victim if they have a strong belief in a just world. (p. 501)

10.   TRUE   FALSE   People who are uncomfortable with intimacy and closeness are said to have an anxious-ambivalent attachment style. (p. 505)

Multiple-Choice Questions

For each question, circle the letter of the best answer.

1.   Attitudes are more likely to affect behavior when they are _____. (p. 490)
    a.   easily recovered from memory
    b.   unconscious
    c.   implicit
    d.   cognitive

2.	Which of the following do we do to minimize cognitive dissonance? (p. 492)
	a.	We change our attitudes.
	b.	We change our behaviors.
	c.	We trivialize the inconsistency between the two attitudes (or attitude and behavior).
	d.	We do any of the above.

3.	Persuasion is *least* likely to be successful when _____. (p. 493)
	a.	the person doing the persuading seems honest
	b.	the person doing the persuading is attractive
	c.	the person doing the persuading talks slowly
	d.	strong emotions are aroused in the attempt at persuasion

4.	There has been on ongoing tension between the professors and the administration at Local University. Social psychologists would probably recommend that _____. (p. 498)
	a.	the groups ignore each other
	b.	the groups compete on some activity
	c.	contact between the groups should be increased
	d.	the groups trade places for a day

5.	According to the self-serving bias, we tend to attribute our successes to _____ _____ causes and our failures to _____ causes. (p. 501)
	a.	internal; internal
	b.	external; external
	c.	internal; external
	d.	external; internal

6.	According to the belief in a just world, _____. (p. 501)
	a.	chance plays a major role in what happens to people
	b.	a divine being intercedes on the behalf of all people
	c.	people deserve what they get, and get what they deserve
	d.	our own successes are due to good fortune

7.	According to evolutionary theory, men look for women who _____. (p. 506)
	a.	are independent and self-supporting
	b.	are dependent upon men for support
	c.	are older than they are
	d.	appear "fertile" because they have well-proportioned bodies and symmetrical features

8. Judy and Neal have been married for 40 years. When asked to describe their relationship, they say that they are best friends and lovers. It is their goal to be married as long as they both live. They set aside time each week to work on their relationship. Which of the following terms best describes the type of love they share? (p. 505)
   a. Passionate
   b. Intimate
   c. Committed
   d. Consummate love

9. In which of the following situations would someone be *less* likely to conform? (p. 509)
   a. In a situation in which the task is difficult or ambiguous
   b. In a situation in which a group member openly disagrees with the consensus
   c. In a cohesive group
   d. In a group in which the members are both male and female

10. In the past, Brianna has always been against the idea of home schooling. Much to her chagrin, she is assigned to write a paper on the benefits of home schooling. After completing the assignment, Brianna is likely to _____. (p. 493)
    a. feel even more strongly against homeschooling
    b. not experience any change in her attitude
    c. be unsure about her feelings
    d. be more supportive of homeschooling

11. Which of the following is an example of an internal attribution? (p. 500)
    a. "I am not good at math."
    b. "The teacher made the test too hard."
    c. "My roommates were too noisy for me to study last night."
    d. "The classroom was too dark for me to see the test well."

12. In general, the more heterogenous a group is, _____. (p. 515)
    a. the less effectively it communicates
    b. the more likely there is to be group conflict
    c. the more innovative and flexible the group may be
    d. all of the above

13. Students in large lecture halls sometimes pass notes to one another during class, apparently (mistakenly) thinking that their individual behavior will not be noticed in this group setting. This is an example of _____. (p. 507)
    a. deindividuation
    b. groupthink
    c. social loafing
    d. social compensation

14.	According to Darley and Latane, bystander intervention occurs when: _____. (p. 517)
	a.	an emergency is noticed by the bystander
	b.	the bystander assumes some responsibility to intervene
	c.	the bystander is motivated to help
	d.	all of the above occur

15.	The jigsaw technique is sometimes used to _____. (p. 498)
	a.	reduce conformity
	b.	train children about the dangers of obedience
	c.	decrease prejudice
	d.	persuade individuals

Essay Questions
Answer each question in the space provided.

1.	If you knew that a woman was opposed to abortion, could you predict that she would never have one? _____

	_____
	_____
	_____
	_____
	_____
	_____
	_____
	_____
	_____
	_____
	_____

2.	If you want to persuade someone that your point of view is correct, what should you do?

	_____
	_____
	_____
	_____
	_____
	_____
	_____
	_____
	_____
	_____
	_____
	_____

3. If you were designing a program to combat homophobia (a negative attitude toward homosexual individuals—a type of prejudice), what elements would you include?

_____
_____
_____
_____
_____
_____
_____
_____
_____
_____

4. How can the various attributional biases affect how a jury views a woman who has been raped? _____

_____
_____
_____
_____
_____
_____
_____
_____

5. Using social psychology principles of group behavior, explain how a fraternity can convince pledges to do things they would probably not do on their own (e.g., drink too much or eat live goldfish). _____

_____
_____
_____
_____
_____

After You Are Done . . . Puzzle It Out

Across

4. Belief about people in category
5. Conducted famous obedience studies
9. Most common attachment style
10. Rules that govern group members
12. Difference between two conflicting attitudes
13. One's own group
14. Behavior change due to a request
17. Attribution that cause is self
19. Intimacy, passion and _____
20. Attempts to change attitudes

Down

1. Loss of sense of self
2. Kitty _____
3. Behavior that benefits others
6. Liking something familiar
7. Compliance with an order
8. Behavior change due to group norms
11. Proposed triangular model of love
15. Negative attitude toward out-group members
16. Motivation to help another person
18. Explanation for cause of event

Puzzle created with Puzzlemaker at DiscoverySchool.com.

Answer Keys

Chapter 1: What Kind of Psychologist Are You?

If you chose the same letter for most of all of the items, you may be inclined to be that kind of psychologist:

a = psychodynamic   d = humanism
b = behaviorism   e = evolutionary psychology
c = cognitive psychology

Chapter 1: Practice Test #1

True/False Questions
1.   True
2.   True
3.   False
4.   False
5.   True

Multiple-Choice Questions
1.   a
2.   d
3.   d
4.   b
5.   c
6.   a
7.   b
8.   d
9.   a
10. b

Chapter 1: Practice Test #2

Fill-in-the-Blank Questions
Psychology
Philosophy
Science
Physiology
Structuralism
Introspection
Gestalt
Psychodynamic
Unconscious drives
Functionalism

Evolutionary
Behaviorism
Behavior
Mental processes
Cognitive
Computer
Information processing
Brain scans
Cognitive neuroscience
Brain

Matching Questions

1. e
2. c
3. g
4. a
5. d
6. h
7. b
8. f

Matching Questions

1. g
2. d
3. k
4. a
5. o
6. m
7. f
8. n
9. c
10. i
11. b
12. q
13. p
14. e
15. l
16. h
17. j

Multiple-Choice Questions

1. b
2. a
3. a
4. b
5. b
6. a

7. d
8. b
9. d
10. a
11. c
12. d
13. d
14. d
15. b

Chapter 1: Practice Test #3

True/False Questions

1. False
2. True
3. True
4. True
5. False
6. False
7. True
8. False
9. True
10. True

Matching Questions

1. b
2. f
3. d
4. a
5. e
6. c

Matching Questions

1. b
2. d
3. a
4. e
5. c

Multiple-Choice Questions

1. c
2. b
3. a
4. c
5. a
6. b
7. b

8. b
9. a
10. a
11. b
12. a
13. a
14. b
15. d
16. d
17. a
18. d
19. b
20. b
21. b
22. d
23. a
24. c
25. c
26. c
27. b
28. b
29. d
30. a

Chapter 1: Comprehensive Practice Test

True/False Questions
1. False
2. False
3. True
4. False
5. False
6. True
7. True
8. True
9. False
10. False

Matching Questions
1. i
2. h
3. a
4. c
5. e
6. g
7. d

8. b
9. f

Matching Questions
1. c
2. e
3. f
4. g
5. a
6. d
7. b

Identification Questions
1. Negative
2. Negative
3. Positive
4. Positive
5. Negative

Identification Questions
1. IV = amount of water; DV = occurrence of kidney stones
2. IV = species (rats or mice); DV = size
3. IV = whether or not girls are gymnasts; DV = likelihood of anorexia
4. IV = completion of study guides; DV = grades
5. IV = presence of books; DV = whether or not children like to read

Multiple-Choice Questions
1. c
2. d
3. b
4. a
5. b
6. b
7. a
8. b
9. b
10. d
11. d
12. b
13. d
14. a
15. d
16. b
17. b
18. c
19. a
20. a

21. c
22. b
23. a
24. c
25. d
26. b
27. a
28. c
29. b
30. d
31. d
32. a
33. c
34. c
35. c

Chapter 1: Puzzle It Out

Across
2. debriefing
5. Wundt
7. unconscious
9. reliability
11. sample
13. variable
16. population
17. effect
18. Freud
19. case study

Down
1. psychology
3. Gestalt
4. survey
6. theory
8. data
9. response bias
10. Skinner
12. behavior
14. James
15. Rogers

Chapter 2: Practice Test #1

Fill-in-the-Blank Questions
synapse
neurotransmitters
neuromodulators
glial
excitatory
inhibitory
reuptake

Matching Questions
1. c
2. e
3. f
4. a

5.   d
6.   b

Multiple-Choice Questions

1.   d
2.   a
3.   a
4.   b
5.   a
6.   b
7.   c
8.   c
9.   a
10.   c

Chapter 2: Practice Test #2

Matching Questions

1.   f
2.   a
3.   i
4.   j
5.   b
6.   h
7.   c
8.   e
9.   d
10.   k
11.   g

Matching Questions

1.   e
2.   a
3.   h
4.   g
5.   c
6.   b
7.   i
8.   f
9.   d

Matching Questions

1.   c
2.   a
3.   d
4.   b

Multiple-Choice Questions

1. b
2. a
3. b
4. a
5. c
6. a
7. b
8. a
9. d
10. b

Chapter 2: Practice Test #3

Fill-in-the-Blank Questions

neuroimaging techniques
computer-assisted tomography (CT)
magnetic resonance imaging (MRI)
positron emission tomography (PET)
functional magnetic resonance imaging (fMRI)

Multiple-Choice Questions

1. b
2. a
3. a
4. c
5. d
6. b
7. d
8. b
9. c
10. a

Chapter 2: Practice Test #4

True/False Questions

1. True
2. True
3. False
4. False
5. True
6. True

Multiple-Choice Questions
1.   c
2.   b
3.   c
4.   a
5.   c
6.   c
7.   b
8.   c
9.   a
10.   a

Chapter 2: Comprehensive Practice Test

True/False Questions
1.   False
2.   True
3.   False
4.   False
5.   True

Multiple-Choice Questions
1.   d
2.   a
3.   a
4.   b
5.   a
6.   c
7.   d
8.   b
9.   a
10.   b
11.   b
12.   c
13.   c
14.   d
15.   c

Chapter 2: Puzzle It Out

Across

3.	amygdala
5.	PET
7.	CNS
8.	lobes
12.	heritability
14.	myelin
15.	neuron
16.	gyri
18.	plasticity
19.	synapse

Down

1.	glial cells
2.	negative
4.	genotype
6.	dendrite
8.	lesion
9.	thalamus
10.	pruning
11.	hippocampus
13.	SSRI
17.	reflex

Chapter 3: Practice Test #1

Matching Questions

1. a
2. c
3. d
4. b

Multiple-Choice Questions

1. c
2. d
3. d
4. b
5. d
6. d
7. c
8. c
9. d
10. b

Chapter 3: Practice Test #2

Multiple-Choice Questions

1. b
2. c
3. b
4. d
5. b
6. c
7. c
8. d
9. a

10.   a
11.   b
12.   b
13.   d
14.   d
15.   a

Chapter 3: Practice Test #3

True/False Questions

1.   False
2.   True
3.   True
4.   False
5.   False
6.   True
7.   True
8.   True
9.   True
10.   True

Matching Questions

1.   c
2.   d
3.   b
4.   a

Multiple-Choice Questions

1.   c
2.   a
3.   a
4.   c
5.   c
6.   b
7.   a
8.   b
9.   b
10.   d

Chapter 3: Comprehensive Practice Test

True/False Questions

1. True
2. True
3. True
4. True
5. False
6. False
7. True
8. True
9. True
10. False

Identification Questions

Top-down
Bottom-up
Top-down
Bottom-up

Multiple-Choice Questions

1. a
2. b
3. a
4. d
5. b
6. c
7. a
8. d
9. a
10. c
11. b
12. a
13. c
14. a
15. a

Chapter 3: Puzzle It Out

Across

3. pupil
4. astigmatism
6. blind spot
11. threshold
14. pop-out
17. endorphins
19. taste buds
20. rods

Down

1. fovea
2. bias
5. ganglion cells
7. phermones
8. attention
9. frequency
10. kinesthetic
12. figure
13. green
15. top-down
16. afterimage
18. loudness

Chapter 4: Practice Test #1

Matching Questions

1. b
2. e
3. g
4. h
5. j
6. a
7. f
8. c
9. i
10. d

Multiple-Choice Questions

1. b
2. d
3. c
4. d
5. a
6. d
7. d
8. c
9. c
10. b
11. b
12. b
13. b
14. a
15. a

Chapter 4: Practice Test #2

Fill-in-the-Blank Questions
discrimination
hippocampus
acetylcholine
nucleus accumbens
dopamine

Multiple-Choice Questions
1. b
2. d
3. c
4. a
5. c
6. c
7. a
8. a
9. b
10. c

Chapter 4: Practice Test #3

True/False Questions
1. False
2. True
3. False
4. True
5. True

Multiple-Choice Questions
1. a
2. b
3. d
4. b
5. b
6. b
7. a
8. c
9. a
10. d

Chapter 4: Comprehensive Practice Test

True/False Questions

1. True
2. False
3. True
4. True
5. False
6. True
7. False
8. True
9. False
10. True

Multiple-Choice Questions

1. A
2. B
3. D
4. B
5. B
6. B
7. C
8. B
9. A
10. A
11. D
12. C
13. B
14. A
15. C
16. B
17. A
18. B
19. C
20. D

Chapter 4: Puzzle It Out

<table>
<tr><td colspan="2">Across</td><td colspan="2">Down</td></tr>
<tr><td>3.</td><td>insight</td><td>1.</td><td>partial</td></tr>
<tr><td>5.</td><td>Pavlov</td><td>2.</td><td>phobia</td></tr>
<tr><td>7.</td><td>CR</td><td>4.</td><td>Thorndike</td></tr>
<tr><td>9.</td><td>positive</td><td>6.</td><td>latent</td></tr>
<tr><td>10.</td><td>acquisition</td><td>8.</td><td>reinforcer</td></tr>
<tr><td>13.</td><td>primary</td><td>11.</td><td>CER</td></tr>
<tr><td>15.</td><td>Sultan</td><td>12.</td><td>token</td></tr>
<tr><td>16.</td><td>Skinner</td><td>13.</td><td>placebo</td></tr>
<tr><td>17.</td><td>Albert</td><td>14.</td><td>maps</td></tr>
<tr><td>18.</td><td>interval</td><td>16.</td><td>shaping</td></tr>
</table>

Chapter 5: Practice Test #1

True/False Questions
1.   True
2.   True
3.   True
4.   False
5.   True
6.   True
7.   True
8.   False
9.   False
10.   True

Multiple-Choice Questions
1.   b
2.   c
3.   a
4.   d
5.   c
6.   a
7.   b
8.   d
9.   b
10.   c

Chapter 5: Practice Test #2

Multiple-Choice Questions
1.   b
2.   a
3.   d
4.   c
5.   c
6.   b
7.   c
8.   b
9.   a
10.   c
11.   a
12.   d
13.   c
14.   b
15.   c

Chapter 5: Practice Test #3

True/False Questions
1.   True
2.   False
3.   True
4.   True
5.   True
6.   True
7.   True
8.   False
9.   False
10.   True

Multiple-Choice Questions
1.   d
2.   a
3.   d
4.   c
5.   c
6.   c
7.   b
8.   b
9.   b
10.   b
11.   b
12.   c

13.	d
14.	a
15.	c

Chapter 5: Comprehensive Practice Test

True/False Questions

1.	True
2.	False
3.	True
4.	True
5.	True
6.	True
7.	True
8.	True
9.	True
10.	False

Multiple-Choice Questions

1.	b
2.	a
3.	c
4.	d
5.	a
6.	c
7.	a
8.	b
9.	d
10.	c
11.	a
12.	b
13.	c
14.	c
15.	d
16.	a
17.	b
18.	a
19.	c
20.	b

Chapter 5: Puzzle It Out

Across

4.   chunk
7.   method of loci
8.   retrograde
9.   flashbulb
12. recognition
14. codes
15. dynamic
17. infantile
18. Ebbinghaus

Down

1.   primacy effect
2.   explicit
3.   semantic
5.   elaborative
6.   decay
7.   mnemonics
8.   rehearsal
10. incidental
11. cues
13. iconic
16. habits

Chapter 6: Practice Test #1

True/False Questions

1.   True
2.   True
3.   True
4.   True
5.   True

Multiple-Choice Questions

1.   b
2.   d
3.   c
4.   a
5.   d
6.   a
7.   c
8.   b
9.   d
10. b

Chapter 6: Practice Test #2

True/False Questions

1.   False
2.   False
3.   True
4.   False
5.   True

Fill-in-the-Blank Questions

representation
strategies
algorithm
hueristic
analogy

Multiple-Choice Questions

1. b
2. c
3. c
4. c
5. a
6. d
7. b
8. c
9. c
10. c
11. b
12. b
13. d
14. d
15. a
16. b
17. b
18. c
19. d
20. b

Chapter 6: Practice Test #3

Matching Questions

1. c
2. d
3. e
4. f
5. b
6. a

Multiple-Choice Questions

1. c
2. c
3. d
4. a
5. d
6. a
7. d

8.	b
9.	a
10.	d
11.	d
12.	a
13.	d
14.	c
15.	d

Chapter 6: Practice Test #4

True/False Questions
1.	False
2.	True
3.	False
4.	True
5.	True
6.	True
7.	True
8.	False
9.	True
10.	False

Multiple-Choice Questions
1.	d
2.	a
3.	c
4.	b
5.	a
6.	b
7.	b
8.	c
9.	b
10.	b

Chapter 6: Comprehensive Practice Test

True/False Questions
1.	False
2.	False
3.	False
4.	True
5.	False
6.	True
7.	False
8.	True

9. False
10. False

Multiple-Choice Questions

1. b
2. b
3. c
4. d
5. c
6. c
7. d
8. b
9. b
10. a
11. d
12. b
13. a
14. b
15. b
16. c
17. d
18. c
19. d
20. a

Chapter 6: Puzzle It Out

Across

1. phonemes
4. Down syndrome
5. prodigy
8. test bias
12. microenvironment
16. heuristic
18. Binet
20. images

Down

2. Spearman
3. morpheme
6. Gardner
7. creativity
9. mental set
10. prototype
11. gifted
13. IQ
14. EI
15. schemas
17. WAIS
19. norming

Chapter 7: Practice Test #1

True/False Questions

1. True
2. False
3. False
4. True
5. True
6. True
7. False
8. True
9. False
10. False

Multiple-Choice Questions

1. a
2. d
3. a
4. c
5. d
6. c
7. b
8. b
9. a
10. d

Chapter 7: Practice Test #2

Multiple-Choice Questions

1. d
2. a
3. c
4. a
5. c
6. a
7. c
8. a
9. d
10. b
11. b
12. c
13. b
14. b
15. a

Chapter 7: Practice Test #3

True/False Questions

1. False
2. False
3. False
4. False
5. True
6. False
7. False
8. True
9. True
10. False
11. True
12. False
13. True
14. True
15. False

Multiple-Choice Questions

1. a
2. c
3. b
4. c
5. c
6. c
7. c
8. b
9. d
10. c
11. d
12. a
13. b
14. a
15. c

Chapter 7: Comprehensive Practice Test

True/False Questions

1. True
2. True
3. True
4. False
5. False
6. True
7. False
8. False
9. False
10. True

Multiple-Choice Questions

1. a
2. c
3. d
4. b
5. a
6. b
7. c
8. a
9. c
10. b
11. a
12. a
13. d
14. d
15. c
16. a
17. b
18. b
19. a
20. c

Chapter 7: Puzzle It Out

Across
4.   bisexual
5.   polygraph
6.   want
8.   androgens
11. homeostasis
16. self-actualization
18. obesity
19. Ekman
20. need

Down
1.   approach
2.   drive
3.   display rules
7.   Maslow
9.   insulin
10. estrogens
12. set point
13. incentive
14. LeDoux
15. six
17. fear

Chapter 8: Practice Test #1

Multiple-Choice Questions
1.   b
2.   c
3.   b
4.   a
5.   b
6.   c
7.   b
8.   a
9.   a
10. a
11. a
12. d
13. b
14. c
15. d
16. b
17. d
18. a
19. c
20. c

Chapter 8: Practice Test #2

Multiple-Choice Questions
1.   d
2.   d
3.   a
4.   d

5. b
6. c
7. c
8. d
9. d
10. c
11. b
12. a
13. c
14. a
15. d
16. d
17. a
18. d
19. a
20. d

Chapter 8: Practice Test #3

Multiple-Choice Questions

1. a
2. d
3. b
4. a
5. a
6. b
7. c
8. c
9. d
10. b
11. d
12. d
13. a
14. d
15. d
16. b
17. b
18. d
19. b
20. c

Chapter 8: Practice Test #4

True/False Questions

1. False
2. False
3. True

4. False
5. False
6. False
7. True
8. True
9. False
10. False

Multiple-Choice Questions
1. b
2. a
3. c
4. d
5. a
6. c
7. d
8. a
9. a
10. c

Chapter 8: Comprehensive Practice Test

True/False Questions
1. True
2. False
3. False
4. True
5. True
6. False
7. False
8. False
9. True
10. False

Multiple-Choice Questions
1. b
2. d
3. b
4. c
5. a
6. d
7. c
8. a
9. b
10. c
11. c
12. a

13.	b
14.	c
15.	a
16.	d
17.	b
18.	a
19.	b
20.	a

Chapter 8: Puzzle It Out

Across
1.	Rorschach
3.	projective
5.	Rogers
6.	Maslow
8.	Cattell
9.	first-borns
11.	collectivist
13.	phallic
15.	locus of control
16.	traits
18.	sensation seeking
19.	five

Down
2.	acquiescent
4.	neuroticism
7.	heritability
10.	NEO-PI
12.	id
14.	Harris
17.	superfactors
20.	Eysenck

Chapter 9: Practice Test #1

Fill-in-the-Blank Questions
egg
sperm
gametes
female
male
trimesters
zygote
embryo
fetus

True/False Questions
1.	True
2.	True
3.	False
4.	True
5.	False

Multiple-Choice Questions
1.   a
2.   c
3.   a
4.   a
5.   d
6.   a
7.   c
8.   d
9.   c
10.   d

Chapter 9: Practice Test #2

True/False Questions
1.   False
2.   True
3.   False
4.   True
5.   False

Fill-in-the-Blank Questions
schemas
assimilation
accommodation

Fill-in-the-Blank Questions
self-concept
cognitive
two
three
social relations
formal operational period

Multiple-Choice Questions
1.   b
2.   a
3.   d
4.   a
5.   b
6.   b
7.   d
8.   a
9.   b
10.   b

Chapter 9: Practice Test #3

Multiple-Choice Questions
1.   a
2.   c
3.   c
4.   a
5.   b
6.   d
7.   c
8.   d
9.   a
10. a

Chapter 9: Practice Test #4

Multiple-Choice Questions
1.   d
2.   b
3.   a
4.   d
5.   b
6.   d
7.   a
8.   d
9.   d
10. c

Chapter 9: Comprehensive Practice Test

True/False Questions
1.   True
2.   False
3.   True
4.   True
5.   False
6.   True
7.   True
8.   False
9.   False
10. True

Multiple-Choice Questions
1.   c
2.   a
3.   d

4.	d
5.	b
6.	b
7.	b
8.	b
9.	d
10.	c
11.	a
12.	a
13.	c
14.	c
15.	c

Chapter 9: Puzzle It Out

Across

5.	attachment
10.	adolescence
12.	visual cliff
13.	grammar
15.	Vygotsky
16.	SIDS
18.	Bowlby
19.	genes
20.	teratogen

Down

1.	Kohlberg
2.	preoperational
3.	fetus
4.	girls
6.	habituation
7.	reflex
8.	four
9.	CDS
11.	schema
14.	zygote
17.	Moro reflex

Chapter 10: Practice Test #1

Multiple-Choice Questions

1.	c
2.	c
3.	d
4.	d
5.	b
6.	b
7.	b
8.	a
9.	d
10.	a

Chapter 10: Practice Test #2

Fill-in-the-Blank Questions
immune
B cells
T cells
natural killer cell
glucocorticoids
sympathetic nervous system

Matching Questions
1.   d
2.   a
3.   b
4.   e
5.   c

Multiple-Choice Questions
1.   d
2.   b
3.   d
4.   a
5.   a
6.   d
7.   a
8.   c
9.   a
10.   b
11.   c
12.   b
13.   d
14.   c
15.   c

Chapter 10: Practice Test #3

True/False Questions
1.   False
2.   False
3.   True
4.   True
5.   False
6.   True
7.   False
8.   True
9.   False

10.   True
11.   False
12.   True
13.   True
14.   False
15.   False

Matching Questions

1.   d
2.   h
3.   j
4.   a
5.   f
6.   b
7.   e
8.   k
9.   g
10.   c
11.   i

Multiple-Choice Questions

1.   c
2.   c
3.   a
4.   d
5.   c
6.   b
7.   a
8.   d
9.   b
10.   d
11.   a
12.   d
13.   d
14.   a
15.   c
16.   c
17.   a
18.   a
19.   a
20.   b

Chapter 10: Comprehensive Practice Test

True/False Questions

1.   False
2.   False

3.   True
4.   True
5.   True
6.   True
7.   True
8.   False
9.   True
10. False
11. True
12. False
13. True
14. True
15. True

Multiple-Choice Questions

1.   b
2.   b
3.   c
4.   d
5.   d
6.   c
7.   d
8.   b
9.   c
10. b
11. b
12. a
13. c
14. a
15. d
16. b
17. a
18. d
19. a
20. d

Chapter 10: Puzzle It Out

Across

2.   stressor
3.   rebound
4.   alcohol
5.   hostility
6.   crack
10.   B cells
12.   SCN
13.   marijuana
15.   insomnia
16.   Selye
17.   latent
18.   aggression

Down

1.   atherosclerosis
5.   hypnogogic
7.   tolerance
8.   REM
9.   alarm
10.   blackout
11.   Freud
14.   NK cells

Chapter 11: Practice Test #1

True/False Questions

1.   True
2.   False
3.   True
4.   True
5.   False
6.   False
7.   True
8.   True
9.   True
10.   False

Multiple-Choice Questions

1.   d
2.   a
3.   c
4.   b
5.   d
6.   a
7.   b
8.   a
9.   c
10.   c

Chapter 11: Practice Test #2

True/False Questions

1.   False
2.   False
3.   False
4.   True
5.   True
6.   True
7.   True
8.   True
9.   True
10. False
11. True
12. True
13. True
14. False
15. True

Fill-in-the-Blank Questions

type of trauma
crime
natural disasters
locus coeruleus
limbic system
negative reinforcement
social support

Multiple-Choice Questions

1.   a
2.   a
3.   a
4.   a
5.   a
6.   c
7.   b
8.   a
9.   d
10. b
11. c
12. a
13. d
14. d
15. a
16. c
17. d
18. d

19.   c
20.   a
21.   b
22.   d
23.   a
24.   a
25.   c
26.   a
27.   c
28.   d
29.   b
30.   b

Chapter 11: Practice Test #3

True/False Questions
1.   False
2.   True
3.   False
4.   False
5.   False

Multiple-Choice Questions
1.   d
2.   c
3.   d
4.   d
5.   c
6.   b
7.   b
8.   a
9.   d
10.   b

Chapter 11: Comprehensive Practice Test

True/False Questions

1. False
2. True
3. True
4. False
5. False
6. True
7. False
8. True
9. False
10. False

Multiple-Choice Questions

1. c
2. d
3. a
4. c
5. c
6. b
7. a
8. d
9. b
10. c
11. a
12. a
13. d
14. c
15. c

Chapter 11: Puzzle It Out

Across
6. hallucinations
9. MDD
10. two
12. manic
14. compulsions
16. obsessions
17. phobia
18. purging
19. diathesis
20. five

Down
1. delusions
2. Beck
3. panic attacks
4. PTSD
5. DSM
7. ASPD
8. OCD
11. axis
13. agoraphobia
15. negative

Chapter 12: Practice Test #1

True/False Questions
1. False
2. True
3. False
4. True
5. False
6. True
7. True
8. False
9. False
10. True
11. True
12. False
13. False
14. False
15. False

Fill-in-the-Blank Questions
hypnosis
free association
dreams
interpretation
defense mechanisms
resistance
transference

Multiple-Choice Questions

1. c
2. d
3. c
4. d
5. c
6. d
7. a
8. c
9. b
10. c
11. b
12. b
13. d
14. d
15. a
16. d
17. c
18. c
19. b
20. d

Chapter 12: Practice Test #2

True/False Questions

1. True
2. True
3. True
4. True
5. False

Multiple-Choice Questions

1. a
2. c
3. c
4. a
5. d
6. b
7. a
8. c
9. d
10. a

Chapter 12: Practice Test #3

Fill-in-the-Blank Questions
support
Alcoholics Anonymous
twelve
Higher Power
weekly
bibliotherapy

Multiple-Choice Questions
1. d
2. a
3. d
4. c
5. c
6. c
7. d
8. b
9. b
10. a

Chapter 12: Comprehensive Practice Test

True/False Questions
1. False
2. False
3. False
4. True
5. True

Multiple-Choice Questions
1. a
2. a
3. b
4. c
5. b
6. d
7. a
8. a
9. c
10. c
11. b
12. a
13. a

14. b
15. d

Chapter 12: Puzzle It Out

Across
1. exposure
4. CBT
6. ECT
8. Ellis
11. MAOIs
12. St. John's wort
13. Freud
14. TCAs
17. modality
18. TMS
19. SSRI

Down
1. Rogers
3. resistance
5. bibliotherapy
7. thoughts
9. self-help groups
10. incongruence
11. mental filter
15. self-downing
16. tokens

Chapter 13: Practice Test #1

True/False Questions
1. False
2. False
3. True
4. True
5. True

Multiple-Choice Questions
1. c
2. d
3. c
4. b
5. c
6. d
7. a
8. a
9. a
10. b

Chapter 13: Practice Test #2

Multiple-Choice Questions
1. c
2. b
3. c
4. c
5. c
6. c
7. c
8. c
9. d
10. b
11. a
12. b
13. b
14. a
15. a
16. d
17. d
18. b
19. d
20. a

Chapter 13: Comprehensive Practice Test

True/False Questions
1. True
2. False
3. False
4. False
5. True
6. True
7. True
8. True
9. True
10. False

Multiple-Choice Questions

1. a
2. d
3. c
4. c
5. c
6. c
7. d
8. d
9. b
10. d
11. a
12. a
13. a
14. d
15. c

Chapter 13: Puzzle It Out

Across

4. stereotype
5. Milgram
9. secure
10. norms
12. dissonance
13. in-group
14. compliance
17. internal
19. commitment
20. persuasion

Down

1. deindividuation
2. Genovese
3. prosocial
6. mere exposure effect
7. obedience
8. conformity
11. Sternberg
15. prejudice
16. altruism
18. attribution

NOTES